I0528415

Matthean Christology:
The Mission of Christ and the Meaning of the Cross

The following book was written as a thesis and submitted in fulfilment of the requirements for the degree Philosophiae Doctor in Theology and New Testament at the North-West University under the supervision of Prof. Dr. Francois P. Viljoen.

Wesley C. McCarter

Parson's Porch Books

Matthean Christology: The Mission of Christ and the Meaning of the Cross
ISBN: Softcover 978-1-960326-84-3
Copyright © 2024 by Wesley C. McCarter

All rights reserved. No part of this book may be reproduced or transmitted in any form or by any means, electronic or mechanical, including photocopying, recording, or by any information storage and retrieval system, without permission in writing from the publisher.

Parson's Porch Books is an imprint of Parson's Porch *&* Company (PP*&*C) in Cleveland, Tennessee. PP*&*C is a self-funded charity which earns money by publishing books of noted authors, representing all genres. Its face and voice is **David Russell Tullock** who you can contact at: dtullock@parsonsporch.com.

Parson's Porch *&* Company *turns books into bread & milk* by sharing its profits with the poor.

www.parsonsporch.com

Dedication

Bridget, my wife, has been a constant support and lifelong soulmate.

Aubrie and Ellen, my beautiful daughters, are my great joys in life.

Jimmy and Kathy, my parents, have always pointed me to God.

Joseph, my brother, is one of the few who have spurred me on.

My mentor and friend, Dr. David Woolard, has shown me genuine scholarship.

My academic mentor and friend, the late Dr. Frank Scurry, pushed me on.

My research promoter, Prof. Dr. Francois Viljoen, is a true scholarly guide.

The Lord has blessed me.

Abstract

This book aims to demonstrate that the Matthean Gospel makes a unique contribution to New Testament theology with regards to the mission of Christ and the meaning of the cross by forming a macro inclusio. The study is an exercise in biblical theology which aims to address Matthew's unique Christological perspective. The assertion, therefore, is that Matthew provides a sufficient and distinctive explanation of the mission of Jesus Christ that links his death to the forgiveness of sins. This is demonstrated especially by an inclusio at the beginning and end of the Gospel account, Matt 1:21 and 26:28. Although there has been a renewed interest in biblical theology in recent years, Matthew's theology has still not received as much attention as some other areas of New Testament studies. Moreover, although some aspects of Matthean Christology have been explored, the mission of Christ and the meaning of his death on the cross according to Matthew and the doctrine of the forgiveness of sins in his Gospel account have not been given sufficient consideration. As a result of this deficit in Matthean studies, the two-part thesis of this research project is that (1) Matthew's Gospel account offers a unique explanation of the mission and the cross of Jesus Christ, and, together with that focus, (2) the doctrine of the forgiveness of sins is one of the major themes in the Gospel of Matthew. In accord with the thesis, standards are given for determining the passages most relevant. After determining the relevant passages, these passages are then analyzed individually. Current scholarship on the subject is also examined to determine the Matthean understanding of the cross of Christ and the forgiveness of sins. Apart from the other canonical Gospel accounts, this book seeks to demonstrate that Matthew has a distinct perspective on Jesus' mission, the meaning of the cross, and the important Christian concept of the forgiveness of sins.

Key Words

Matthew, Christology, inclusio, save, sins, forgiveness, cross, blood, covenant, I have come, gospel, purpose, theology, biblical theology

Table Of Contents: Overview

Contents

Chapter One: Introduction

1.1 Background and Problem Statement

1.1.1 Background

Prominent New Testament scholars from across the world and spanning a range of theological traditions have propelled Matthean studies immensely in the last several decades. New Testament scholars such as Robert Gundry (1995), Ulrich Luz (1995), Jack Kingsbury (1988 and 1991), and RT France (2004) have published major books on Matthean theology which have furthered scholarship in the First Gospel in the last forty years possibly more than several generations before.

Numerous articles (e.g., Carter, 1998, 2001; Gibbs, 2008; Repschinski, 2006; Nel, 2015; et al.) and commentaries (e.g., Carson, 2010; Morris, 1992; France, 2007; Gundry, 1994; Davies and Allison, 1988-1997; et al.) have also been published on the Gospel of Matthew by various scholars on a wide variety of themes. The periodicals speak to the purpose of Jesus' coming (Carter, 1998), a Christology of salvation from sin (Repschinski, 2006), the theme of Christian forgiveness in Matthew's Gospel (Nel, 2015), and more. The commentaries on Matthew offer annotations on the entirety of the Gospel while the present book intends to focus on an individual theme not fully addressed in any of the major commentaries. These works all have their places and have contributed to Matthean studies. The commentaries mentioned above are all excellent examples of rigorous scholarship, and there are countless others. Each of these works give necessary advancement to the subject but leave room for more investigation, again, especially on a specific motif. There is still space within the field for special studies on Matthean themes. The work at hand seeks to do just that by exploring the theme of forgiveness of sins in Matthew's Gospel by way of investigating what may prove to be a macro inclusio in Matt 1:21 and 26:28. To the researcher's knowledge, no such study has ever been conducted on this particular theme via an inclusio and its connections throughout the text.

Although there has been a great variety of Matthean studies in recent times, Matthean theology is nevertheless surpassed by the abundance of attention and studies on the other Gospels as well as Pauline studies (Ham, 2000:56). As Leon Morris has written about the relationship of the four Gospels in scholarship, "[T]his [Matthean] Gospel has suffered in modern discussions in comparison with the others. . . . [I]n modern times Matthew has often been slighted" (Morris, 1992:1). Moreover, not only has the First Gospel been, to some extent, slighted in Gospels studies (Carson and Moo, 2005:159), but theological studies on the atonement have been inclined to focus on the

Pauline corpus, for example, much more than they have Matthew's Gospel.[1] There are several biblical theological scholars who are at work to bring attention to Matthew's Gospel. For example, according to Andreas Köstenberger, editor of the respectable *Biblical Theology of the New Testament Series*, a volume on Matthean Theology is in the works for publication by the distinguished Matthean scholar Michael Wilkins.[2]

This study also seeks to draw attention back to Matthean studies by focusing on Matthew's Christology as it may be demonstrated by a macro inclusio concerning Christ's mission and the meaning of his cross. The research project at hand will be an exercise in biblical theology which focuses on the connected themes of the mission of Christ and the meaning of the cross. Skeptical writers typically dismiss this theme of forgiveness of sins,[3] critical writers often explain it away,[4] and evangelicals tend to neglect it.[5] These approaches will be addressed throughout the chapters of the book.

Several voluminous studies on major Matthean themes have been completed. For example, on Discipleship (Wilkins, 2015); on Empire (Carter, 2001); and on Torah (Viljoen, 2018). However, no such book-length research has been presented on the relation of the forgiveness of sins and the cross of Christ in Matthew's Gospel.

There are several available journal articles which have been published in recent years on various Matthean themes. The article by Repschinski (2006) may be a helpful document for the current study. The same is true of Carter's article (1998) as well as Gibbs' (2008). These publications are three examples of only a few that speak directly to the subject at hand. Several others will be reviewed in chapter two of the book. Repschinski has supplied a well-written and discerning yet brief article in the *Catholic Biblical Quarterly* on the theme of

---

[1] Somewhat anecdotal but revealing was a simple perusal of the bibliography in William Lane Craig's (2020) recent book, *Atonement and the Death of Christ: An Exegetical, Historical, and Philosophical Exploration*. This is one of the most up-to-date major publications on the atonement and is written by a competent scholar. When comparing the number of sources on the subject between the canonical Gospels and the epistles of Paul, the overwhelming number of works are on the latter, which, of course, dwarfs any attention given to Matthew.

[2] Andreas Köstenberger. https://www.biblicalfoundations.org/current-issues-in-new-testament-studies-biblical-theology. Internet. Accessed May 28, 2021.

[3] For example, (Ehrman, 2014, 2016; Crossan, 1991; Borg, 2007).

[4] For example, (Lüdemann, 1996, 1999, 2001; Miller, 2017).

[5] Again, the lack of material on the theology of Matthew and, to give a more precise example, the doctrine of the atonement in Matthew's Gospel, in particular, demonstrate the neglect of the subject in New Testament studies.

the forgiveness of sins in Matthew. Arguing that going back to the beginning of the Gospel will help to bring clarity to Matthew's Christology, Repschinski concentrates his article on Matt 1:21. He acknowledges that this is a small study, but it may prove to be a helpful document in the current research. Carter, a well-known and respected scholar in the field of Matthean studies, has also published an article for the *Catholic Biblical Quarterly* on the subject of the "I have come" statements by Jesus in the First Gospel. This article is helpful to the current research because it demonstrates and elaborates upon the mission of Christ as Matthew understands it. He takes a progressive approach arguing that Jesus' mission aims to effect political ramifications. The last journal mentioned here is that of Gibbs in the *Concordia Theological Quarterly*. The article highlights a few specific passages in the Gospel of Matthew and discusses the theme of atonement in the selections. The author highlights that the Gospel account is about Jesus' work of salvation.

A thesis titled, "Inclusio in the Hebrew Bible: A Historical-Developmental Approach" was written by Anthony Chapman (2013). The thesis was accepted by Dr. Shamir Yona at Ben Gurion University of the Negev. In the thesis, Chapman reviews the history of scholarship on the literary feature of inclusio. He also proposes criteria for discerning the presence of an inclusio. This thesis is somewhat unique in the field. Although it is focused on the Hebrew Scriptures, the work will likely prove to be helpful in the production of the current research project because of its unique contribution on inclusio.

Furthermore, a basic component of the Church's gospel proclamation throughout the centuries has been the forgiveness of sins by the sacrificial and atoning death of Jesus Christ. The current work aims to support the historic claim by demonstrating that the Matthean Gospel upholds that truth with its own distinctive content and design. Matthew is believed to have a robust theological understanding of Christ's mission and the meaning of the cross that is put on display with the literary feature of inclusio (Matt 1:21 and 26:28) and is highlighted as an important theme throughout the Gospel.

This study aims to meaningfully contribute towards the field of New Testament studies, and Matthean studies in particular, which is currently incomplete in this specific area. There is room for more research projects to be undertaken and completed within the Gospel of Matthew. The topic proposed for this study is an analysis of key Matthean texts with regards to the mission of Christ, the meaning of the death of Christ on the cross, and the divine forgiveness of sins.

The initially proposed key texts are as follows:

Matthean Text	Summary	Explanation
Matt 1:21	Jesus: He will save his people from their sins	This is part of the large inclusio which will be demonstrated in chapter 3 of the book. This is an explicit statement, unique to Matthew, which connects his mission to the forgiveness of sins.
Matt 9:2, 5-7, 12-13	The Son of Man has power on earth to forgive sins	This is a forgiveness passage which will be expounded in chapter 4 of the book. Jesus states clearly and emphatically his authority to forgive the sins of mankind.
Matt 16:21-25; 17:22-23; 20:17-19; 26:1-2, 12	Jesus predicts his suffering and death by crucifixion	These are mission passages related to the cross which will be expounded in chapter 5 of the book. Jesus states explicitly his impending death.
Matt 18:11	The Son of Man has come to save that which was lost	This is a mission passage related to the cross which will be expounded in chapter 5 of the book.
Matt 20:27-28	The Son of Man [has come] to give his life as a ransom for many	This is a mission passage related to the cross which will be expounded in chapter 5 of the book.
Matt 26:28	Christ's blood shed for many for the forgiveness of sins	This is part of the macro inclusio which will be demonstrated in chapter 3 of the proposed book. This is an explicit statement, unique to Matthew, which connects his mission to the forgiveness of sins.
Matt 26:24, 31, 54, 56	Fulfillment of Scripture	Related to the cross which will be expounded in chapter 5 of the book.
Mat 27:46	My God, My God, why have You forsaken Me	This is a mission passage related to the cross which will be expounded in chapter 5 of the book.
Matt 27:50-54	Immediate events at time of Christ's death	This is a mission passage related to the cross which will be expounded in chapter 5 of the book.

The book aims to demonstrate that Matthew, among many more themes which are expounded by other writers, maintains the forgiveness of sins as a key component of Jesus' mission, and it is achieved by his death by crucifixion.

1.1.2 Preliminary Literature Review

The researcher aims to conduct a more thorough review of the relevant literature in Chapter Two. In that chapter, some of the most pertinent peer-reviewed journal articles are to be synopsized. Moreover, some of the most cited commentaries will be considered. In this preliminary literature review section of the introduction, a few of the most germane articles and commentaries are reviewed. One will note that each of the publications recognized below are relevant to the research but leave a gap in the field, that is, none of the works below, or any others to the researcher's knowledge, carry out a full length study of the macro inclusio of Matt 1:21 and 26:28 demonstrating what an inclusio is, how this inclusio meets the definition, what it means in relation to the mission of Christ and the meaning of the cross, and how the inclusio is supported and echoed throughout the Gospel of Matthew. The researcher proposes that the inclusio of Matt 1:21 and 26:28 is central to Matthew's Christology, especially in his mission to save his people from their sins by his atoning death on the cross, and, while several scholars have acknowledged the connections, no publication to date has argued and defended the aforementioned macro inclusio and explicated its significance to Matthean Christology in relation to his mission and cross. An initial bibliography has been included at the end of the first chapter in order to identify the sources used in the initial and the ongoing stages of the research project.

Daniel Antwi (1991) has authored an article titled, "Did Jesus Consider His Death to be an Atoning Sacrifice?" In the first place, the connection between the temple cult and the notion of the forgiveness of sins is made. After this connection is formed, the point of Jesus' conscious recognition of his own death as an act of atonement which replaces the cultic institution is argued. Antwi briefly reviews some of the most germane passages on the forgiveness of sins in the Synoptic Gospels. There is some interaction with the Gospel of Matthew specifically, but the article is not focused upon it.

A helpful work was composed by Warren Carter (1998). In "Jesus' 'I have come' Statements in Matthew's Gospel," the author proposes seven passages utilizing the verb ἦλθον, "I have come" or "I came" which he says convey Jesus' own declarations about his mission (Carter, 1998:44). By the end of the article, the scholar draws direct lines of connection between the texts of Matt 1:21; 20:28; and 26:28 (Carter, 1998:62). While Carter neither designates the connection as an inclusio nor elaborates much upon it, he does identify the links between the passages and says that they help the reader to interpret Jesus' mission.

"'For He will Save His People from their Sins' (Matthew 1:21): A Christology for Christian Jews" by Boris Repschinski (2006) is one of the more pertinent items for the current research. However, the article focuses on the question of Matthew's audience. Was it a Jewish community or not? Repschinski says it was Jewish (2006:249). Salvation primarily concerns Israel, but Matthew does broaden salvation out to the Gentiles at the end with the Great Commission. Where I agree and want to link from this article is Repschinski's argument that one needs to read Matthew's Gospel from the beginning to the end, and not the other way around. Matthew 1:21 has echoes throughout the entirety of the Gospel account. Overall, the article is brief, and so there is much to build upon and expand.

The volume on Matthew in the Teach the Text Commentary series was contributed by Brown (2015). The commentary is helpful as it covers most of the verses in the text and emphasizes application in preaching and teaching. The author acknowledges the direct connection between Matt 1:21 and 26:28 but without any elaboration (Brown, 2015:18).

Quarles' (2022) commentary in the Evangelical Biblical Theology Commentary series is, to date, one of the most recent, large publications on the Gospel of Matthew. Seems to do an excellent job keeping the Old Testament background for the Gospel on the minds of the readers.[6] Jesus is made the main character rather than the reader in this commentary (Quarles, 2022:107). In a series focusing on biblical theology, this commentary speaks to Christological interests in the First Gospel. Christological titles (Quarles, 2022:46-71) as well as Christological descriptions (Quarles, 2022:72-78) are discussed. The work, like many others, has its strengths and weaknesses. One of the weaknesses is that a commentary cannot cover in detail every theme. The large inclusio highlighting the theme of forgiveness is not detailed in this commentary.

Dividing the Matthean Gospel into several sections and units, Wilson's (2022) volume in the Eerdmans Critical Commentary series is another recent addition to the field of Matthean studies. Wilson seems to view the Gospel as a document intending to teach first century Jews who had been isolated from their previous community and who had formed a new community of Christians. The commentator works to reconstruct the first century community and setting. The mission of Christ is mentioned without a detailed study of it. The Emmanuel theme and its, supposed, corresponding inclusio are highlighted. The inclusio of Matt 1:21 and 26:28 concerning the salvation from sins through Christ's forgiveness is mentioned in brief but with no detailed review or explanation of it (Wilson, 2022:124-126). The author asserts that the two bookends of the Gospel (Matt 1:21, 26:28) "creates a thematic frame around the entire story of Jesus" (Wilson, 2022:125). However, the commentator does not make an attempt to prove an inclusio, much less to explain the literary device and its use by Matthew.

1.1.3 Problem Statement

The problem to be addressed is the lack of comprehensive research in Matthew's Gospel account on the theme of the human problem of sin and the divine solution of forgiveness of sin by Christ's sacrifice on the cross as

---

[6] For example, see the discussion of Psalm 22 and Isaiah 53 (Quarles, 2022:499) or the references to Zechariah (Quarles, 2022:671-672).

revealed by a literary device. The feature may be called a macro inclusio as seen in the brackets of Matt 1:21 and 26:28. The research project seeks to discover Matthew's theology of Christ's mission and the meaning of his cross from the distinctive perspective of the literary.

Therefore, the book aims to make a unique and useful contribution to bridge the gap between literary studies and biblical studies, offering a fresh perspective on familiar theological themes. The literary strategy of the biblical author, if put on full display in the project, may provide an interesting and stimulating contribution to the academic guild and beyond because the macro inclusio has not yet been fully explored. The proposal is that Matthew's Gospel account offers a rich and unique explanation of the mission of Christ and the meaning of the cross, and this elucidation of the work of Christ is much needed in the contemporary church and global society. This will need to be shown in the forthcoming chapters of the current book.

1.2 Research Questions

The main research question is: Does the Matthean Gospel make a unique contribution to New Testament theology with regards to the mission of Christ and the meaning of the cross by forming a large inclusio with references to "sins" at the beginning and end of his Gospel account?

While allowing for fluidity in the study, the initial perspective is that the research may focus on the following additional questions which flow out of the main research question:

1) What is the approach taken by skeptical authors, critical scholars, and evangelical writers to the subject of the mission of Christ and the meaning of the cross, and is there a discernible standard in these contemporary publications by which to discern the relevant texts in the Matthean Gospel for the explanation of the mission and cross of Christ?

2) How should an inclusio be defined?

3) Are passages related to sin and passages related to the cross of Christ linked in Matthew's Gospel to provide an explanation of Christ's mission and the meaning of the cross?

4) Is the forgiveness of sins one of the primary Matthean themes?

5) What relevance does Matthew's Christology, especially with regards to the mission of Christ and the meaning of the cross, have for the contemporary church and the broader society?

1.3 Aim and Objectives

1.3.1 Aim

The aim of this research project is to examine passages in Matthew's Gospel, in the context of the whole book, along with recent scholarship, to determine whether the Gospel makes a unique contribution to New Testament theology with regards to the mission of Christ and the meaning of the cross by way of a specific literary device.

1.3.2 Objectives

Primary Objective:

The primary objective is to analyze the text of the Gospel of Matthew and current Matthean scholarship to determine if the First Gospel makes a unique contribution to New Testament theology with regards to the mission of Christ and the meaning of the cross by forming a macro inclusio with references to "sins" at the beginning and end of his Gospel account.

Accompanying Objectives:

1) Analyze recent Matthean scholarship to determine the approach taken by skeptical authors, critical scholars, and evangelical writers to the subject of the mission of Christ and the meaning of the cross and to determine the criteria by which to discern the texts relevant to the Matthean explanation of Christ's mission and cross.

2) Analyze the text of the Gospel of Matthew and current Matthean scholarship as well as broader biblical studies to determine an accurate definition of inclusio.

3) Analyze the text of the Gospel of Matthew to determine if the passages related to sin and passages related to the cross of Christ are linked to provide an explanation of Christ's mission and the meaning of the cross.

4) Analyze the text of the Gospel of Matthew to determine if the forgiveness of sins is one of the primary Matthean themes.

5) Provide original and substantiated conclusions on Matthean Christology with regards to the mission of Christ and the meaning of the cross that will potentially be of benefit to the academic guild, the contemporary church, and the broader society.

1.4 Central Theoretical Argument

The central theoretical argument of this research project is that the Matthean Gospel makes a unique contribution to New Testament theology with regards to the mission of Christ and the meaning of the cross by forming a macro inclusio with references to "sins" at the beginning and end of his Gospel account, Matt 1:21 and 26:28.

1.5 Motivation for Research Project

The writer was born into and matured in an evangelical Christian tradition that emphasizes the New Testament, especially as it applies to the contemporary Christian believer. The focus on New Testament Christianity motivated the researcher to pursue New Testament Studies on the college and then graduate levels. The Gospel of Matthew has held a special place in the researcher's mind and ministry since his time in college taking two particular classes with a professor who would become his academic and ministerial mentor. The courses were in the area of Gospels studies, and one focused on the Sermon on the Mount in Matthew. In that college course, expert hermeneutical skills and the benefits thereof were put on full display. This captivated the writer in such a way as to inspire him to go on to graduate and doctoral studies in the area of biblical studies, to preach and teach the Gospel of Matthew and the other Christian Scriptures as a minister in local churches, and eventually to hold a professorship in a seminary where classes on the Gospel of Matthew, among several other subjects, have been taught.

The current work allows the opportunity for the researcher to focus and improve his research and writing skills and to do so in an area of his capability but also on a topic of his affection. After delivering expository sermons covering every verse of the Gospel of Matthew and lecturing on the Gospel in academic settings in recent years, the writer realized that he could potentially make a contribution to Matthean studies with this current project. The following chapters are an attempt to do just that.

1.6 Research Methodology

In his classic work, *No Place for Truth*, David Wells speaks of his theological approach in these words: "I do so on the assumption that theology is a knowledge that belongs first and foremost to the people of God and that the proper and primary audience for theology is therefore the Church, not the learned guild. Whatever this guild might contribute to the life and construction of theology is to be gratefully received, but the university fraternity is not its primary auditor. I say this because theology is not simply a philosophical reflection about the nature of things but is rather the cogent articulation of the knowledge of God. Its substance is not drawn from mere human reflection, no matter how brilliant, but from the biblical Word by which is nurtured and disciplined. And its purpose is not primarily to participate in the conversation of the learned but to nurture the people of God. That is its nature and that is its purpose. It is here in the Church that the circle of knowing—the kind of knowing that has Christ as its object and his service as its end—is to be found. It is here, then, that the audience for theology is to be found. And so it is the community of faith that the theologian addresses fundamentally, because it is only by faith that the knowledge of God is first arrived at and only by faith that it is sustained" (Wells, 1993:6). This statement is emphatically embraced and upheld by the current researcher, and it helps to set the broad methodological framework for the research project. To speak to the alternative, Wells goes on to assert of theologians of late, "They, too, began not with divine revelation but with human experience, not with God's interpretation of life but with the interpretation that in our self-asserted freedom we have devised for ourselves" (Wells, 1993:66). The intention of this research is to work from a biblical theological perspective to deduce what was the original biblical author's theology and not to write from mere human experience.

Responding to the complaint that the historical-critical method of interpretation is often connected to the presuppositions of the Enlightenment, Hagner and Young remark, "Practicing the HCM from within the church, and without adhering to Enlightenment presuppositions, can lead to results that are positive for faith, as the authors of this chapter have experienced in their own work. To mention only some of our significant presuppositions, we assume that God has worked decisively in history through his son Jesus Christ; that the cross was the focal point of that event; that the cross not only effected a change in the human condition before God but also conveyed a radical message about the nature of God himself; and that the inclusion of four Gospels within the NT canon implies that there is value not only in the historical witness of the evangelists to this event but also in their distinctive interpretations of it for faith. This is the context out of which the authors of this chapter apply the HCM to the Gospels, and in so doing we have found our faith strengthened rather than destroyed" (Powell, 2009:19). The current researcher is sympathetic to this position. Furthermore, the researcher sympathizes with the position of the Faculty of Theology of the North-West University in stating that the Bible is the Word of God and is, thus, uniquely inspired by the Holy Spirit.[7] The researcher considers the Bible to be the sole rule of faith and practice for Christian people and Christian Churches. Therefore, the research will be conducted in keeping with this historic Christian perspective. While this research project will not focus on a particular theological tradition or denomination, it will be worked out within a broadly Reformed, Evangelical tradition.

Now that the broad methodological framework has been set forth, the process may be better defined. As an exercise in biblical theology, the research will seek to determine how Matthew articulated his own theology and how to then best present that theology to the contemporary reader. An outstanding

---

[7] This perspective by the NWU Faculty of Theology is made clear on several pages of the University website and several available documents. For example, on the homepage for the M&D programs, the website states, "We practice theology from the conviction that the Bible is the authoritative Word of God. . . ." (NWU Website. http://theology.nwu.ac.za/node/21117. Internet. Accessed July 25, 2019).

biblical theologian, James Hamilton, is quick to acknowledge that "there is more than one way to do biblical theology" (Hamilton, 2010:43). While Hamilton's work focused on a "central theme" approach for the entirety of the Scriptures, this work will focus more on a classic, book-by-book approach.[8] Within that "classic approach," the current work will seek to learn what is the message that the original author, the apostle Matthew, intended to convey in his own day, especially as it relates to the mission of Christ and the meaning of the cross (Quarles, 2013:5-9; Jipp, 2024:18). In order to accomplish this goal, the biblical theologian must be descriptive, historical, and inductive. The research aims to be descriptive of the major theological features throughout the Gospel account. It aims to be historical by considering the biblical doctrine in its original setting. Finally, it aims to be inductive by being sensitive to the terminology and conceptual categories of the biblical writers (Köstenberger, 2012). To say more about the task, one does well to follow the counsel of Hamilton and Schreiner when they write: "Biblical theology seeks to understand the Bible in its own terms. . . . One of the key tasks of biblical theology is to trace the connections between themes and show the relationships between them" (Hamilton, 2010:45). Thus, the goal is to rightly deduce what is most important in the theological thinking of the biblical author and then to demonstrate that message and the connections between the primary themes (Schreiner, 2001:15).

Schematic Representation of the Classic Biblical Theological Approach:

Steps	Type	Explanation
Step 1	Descriptive	The research aims to be descriptive of the major theological features throughout the Gospel account.
Step 2	Historical	The research aims to be historical by considering the biblical doctrine in its original setting.
Step 3	Inductive	The research aims to be inductive by being sensitive to the terminology and conceptual categories of the biblical writers

The biblical theological method should help the researcher to analyze the Gospel of Matthew in such a way as to determine the criteria by which to discern what texts are relevant to the Matthean understanding of salvation from and forgiveness of sins through the death of Jesus Christ on the cross.

---

[8] This approach is outlined by Köstenberger (2012).

Once the key texts have been ascertained, they will then be exegetically examined from a classic grammatical-historical approach, in their own contexts as well as the wider context of the Gospel of Matthew, and the most recent scholarly interpretations of those passages will also be studied.[9] This approach falls under the umbrella of the historical-critical method. This method, according to Hagner and Young, "has been practiced for centuries by a vast array of interpreters, most of whom incorporated into their practice nuances and perspectives of their own" (Powell, 2009:11).

The classic, grammatical-historical approach to exegesis aims to do the following: (1) Read the text of the Gospel of Matthew in its entirety. The text, as it stands today, is the distinctive item of consideration for the current research. (2) Ascertain main ideas by observing repeated words, phrases, and themes in the text. (3) Separate out passages containing words, phrases, and themes that are relevant to Matthew's distinctive perspective of the mission of Christ and the meaning of the cross. (4) Analyze the structure of the passages that have been selected. (5) Analyze key vocabulary using respected lexicons such as those by Bauer, Danker, Arndt, and Gingrich (2000); Brown (1986); and Louw and Nida (1988). (6) Analyze grammar using respected commentaries and other recent publications. (7) Ascertain and analyze literary and rhetorical features using recent publications on the subject(s). (8) Establish and analyze any Old Testament background using personal research of the text, respected commentaries and other publications. (9) Research the historical and cultural background using respected publications on the subject(s). (10) Consider the broader biblical and theological contexts. (11) Detail the exegetical interpretation of the passage. (12) Provide application for the contemporary church and the society at large.[10]

Schematic Representation of the Classic Grammatical-Historical Approach:

---

[9] The classic grammatical-historical approach dates to pre-Reformation times but certainly came to prominence in the writings of Reformers such as Martin Luther and John Calvin. The Reformed Movement and much of Evangelical Protestantism has followed by predominantly implementing the grammatical-historical method of biblical interpretation. This method seeks to understand the biblical *author's original meaning* in order to fully realize and appreciate the biblical text and apply it today. The grammatical-historical exegetical method is described straightforwardly in a handbook such as (Fee, 2002). Another methodological textbook by (Tate, 2006) is useful and has a section on discovering and interpreting in an intercalation, which will be particularly helpful to this research project.
[10] Adapted from (Fee, 2002).

Steps	Type	Explanation
Step 1	Read	Read the text of the Gospel of Matthew in its entirety. The text, as it stands today, is the distinctive item of consideration for the current research.
Step 2	Main Idea(s)	Ascertain main ideas by observing repeated words, phrases, and themes in the text.
Step 3	Isolate	Separate out passages containing words, phrases, and themes that are relevant to Matthew's distinctive perspective of the mission of Christ and the meaning of the cross.
Step 4	Structure	Analyze the structure of the passages that have been selected.
Step 5	Vocabulary	Analyze key vocabulary using respected lexicons such as those by Bauer, Danker, Arndt, and Gingrich (2000); Brown (1986); and Louw and Nida (1988).
Step 6	Grammar	Analyze grammar using respected commentaries and other recent publications.
Step 7	Literature	Ascertain and analyze literary and rhetorical features using recent publications on the subject(s).
Step 8	Background Part 1	Establish and analyze any Old Testament background using personal research of the text, respected commentaries, and other publications.
Step 9	Background Part 2	Research the historical and cultural background using respected publications on the subject(s).
Step 10	Context	Consider the broader biblical and theological contexts.
Step 11	Interpretation	Detail the exegetical interpretation of the passage.
Step 12	Application	Provide application for the contemporary church and the society at large.

Broadly recapitulated, the following methods will be used to answer the various research questions:

1) The text of The Gospel According to Matthew will be carefully analyzed using accepted theological and hermeneutical principles.[11] Criteria will

---

[11] Again, following the classic, book-by-book biblical theological approach as outlined by Köstenberger (2012) and the classic, grammatical-historical exegetical approach as outlined by Fee (2002). The principles will be exemplified in the body of the research itself. The principles are also typified in scholars such as (Morris, 1992)

be established and put forth by which passages may be included or excluded from the catalog of key texts concerning the subject at hand.

2) Matthean scholarship, especially those publications focusing on Matthean Christology, will be researched, compared, and contrasted. The most recent scholarship, with some historically significant contributions included, will be the focus of the research so that the study may build upon the body of knowledge already published as well as push to the limits of the knowledge on the subject.

3) Scholarship concerning recent and relevant interpretive theory, both theological and non-theological, will be consulted.

1.7 Concept Clarification

The words, "Matthean Christology" in the title refer to the category in which the research is assigned. This study is an exercise in biblical theology, meaning that it is a study of what Matthew expresses. Moreover, it is Christological in the sense that it explores Matthew's understanding of Christ's purpose and accomplishments. Regarding the subtitle of the research project, "The mission of Christ and the meaning of the cross," the statement indicates that the ambition of the research is to center on these two important themes in order to determine if they are in concert with one another.

1.8 Sources for the Proposed Research Project

Certainly, many sources will need to be added to the bibliography and consulted during the research from a broad spectrum of viewpoints. The intention is to investigate current scholarship on the subject. The investigator *loosely* defined "current scholarship" as those books, articles, papers, and dissertations that have been published in the last forty years. Therefore, the initial bibliography includes, predominately, major works that have been published from 1980 to the present. However, historically significant publications will also be included.

Throughout the book the Bible is quoted frequently. The biblical quotations are either the writer's own translations or drawn from the *New King James Version*, first published fully in 1982 by Thomas Nelson.

1.9 Overview of Chapters

The outcome of the research is intended to be a new, book-length contribution to the fields of New Testament and Matthean studies.

---

and (Carson, 2010). Also see an excellent definition for the selected exegetical method by (Treier and Elwell, 2017).

Whereas the outline and structure of the research may change during its development, the proposed structure of the book is as follows:

Chapter 1.Introduction and methodology
Chapter 2.Literature review of recent Matthean scholarship
Chapter 3.The inclusio with references to "sins" at the beginning and end of
Matthew's Gospel, Matt 1:21 and 26:28
Chapter 4.The forgiveness of sins in Matthew's Gospel
Chapter 5.Sin and the cross in Matthew's Gospel
Chapter 6.Full and final construction of the argument that the Matthean
Gospel presents a unique contribution to New Testament theology with regards to the mission of Christ and the meaning of the cross
Chapter 7.Conclusion and application of the study to the contemporary
church and the broader society

1.10 Schematic Representation of the Research Project

Research Questions	Aim and Objectives	Research Methods
Does the Matthean Gospel make a unique contribution to New Testament theology with regards to the mission of Christ and the meaning of the cross by forming a large inclusio with references to "sins" at the beginning and end of his Gospel account?	The aim of this research project is to examine passages in Matthew's Gospel, in the context of the whole book, along with recent scholarship, to determine whether the Gospel makes a unique contribution to New Testament theology with regards to the mission of Christ and the meaning of the cross.	The text of The Gospel According to Matthew will be carefully analyzed using accepted hermeneutical principles (see above). Recent Matthean scholarship will be researched.
1) What is the approach taken by skeptical authors, critical scholars, and evangelical writers to the subject of the mission of Christ and the meaning of the cross, and is there a discernible standard in these contemporary publications by which to discern the relevant texts in	1) Analyze recent Matthean scholarship to determine the approach taken by skeptical authors, critical scholars, and evangelical writers to the subject of the mission of Christ and the meaning of the cross and to determine the criteria by which to discern the texts relevant to	Matthean scholarship, especially those publications focusing on Matthean Christology, will be researched, compared, and contrasted. The most recent scholarship, with some historically significant contributions

the Matthean Gospel for the explanation of the mission and cross of Christ?	the Matthean explanation of Christ's mission and cross.	included, will be the focus of the research.
2) How should an inclusio be defined?	2) Analyze the text of the Gospel of Matthew and current Matthean scholarship as well as broader biblical studies to determine an accurate definition of inclusio.	The text of Matthew will be carefully analyzed using accepted hermeneutical principles (see above). Scholarship concerning recent and relevant interpretive theory, both theological and non-theological, will be consulted.
3) Are passages related to sin and passages related to the cross of Christ linked in Matthew's Gospel to provide an explanation of Christ's mission and the meaning of the cross?	3) Analyze the text of the Gospel of Matthew to determine if the passages related to sin and passages related to the cross of Christ are linked to provide an explanation of Christ's mission and the meaning of the cross.	The text of Matthew will be carefully analyzed using accepted hermeneutical principles (see above). Recent Matthean scholarship will be researched.
4) Is the forgiveness of sins one of the primary Matthean themes?	4) Analyze the text of the Gospel of Matthew to determine if the forgiveness of sins is one of the primary Matthean themes.	The text of Matthew will be carefully analyzed using accepted hermeneutical principles (see above). Recent Matthean scholarship will be researched.
5) What relevance does Matthew's Christology, especially with regards to the mission of Christ and the meaning of the cross, have for the contemporary church and the broader society?	5) Provide original and substantiated conclusions on Matthean Christology with regards to the mission of Christ and the meaning of the cross that will potentially be of benefit to the academic guild, the contemporary church, and the broader society.	The text of Matthew will be carefully analyzed using accepted hermeneutical principles (see above). Recent Matthean scholarship will be researched.

Chapter 2: Literature Review of Recent Matthean Scholarship

In this chapter, some of the most pertinent peer-reviewed journal articles will be considered. This literature review does not intend to be exhaustive but to sample some of the most relevant periodicals to the current research project. In this way, then, commentaries and other books will be excluded from the literature review.[12] The journal articles reviewed here will be taken in chronological order according to the dates of publication.

2.1. Synopsis of Articles on Relevant Matthean Themes

Daniel Antwi (1991), Professor of New Testament Studies at Trinity College in Ghana, has authored an article titled, "Did Jesus Consider His Death to be an Atoning Sacrifice?" In the first place, the connection between the temple cult and the notion of the forgiveness of sins is made. After this connection is formed, the point of Jesus' conscious recognition of his own death as an act of atonement which replaces the cultic institution is argued. Antwi briefly reviews some of the most germane passages on the forgiveness of sins in the Synoptic Gospels. There is some interaction with the Gospel of Matthew specifically, but the article is not focused upon it. All of the Gospels are considered. As the essay concludes, the author believes that he has demonstrated that the view Jesus takes toward the religious establishment and mechanisms of first century Judaism "reveals the startling truth that by performing acts of forgiveness of sins without the cultic apparatus, Jesus was redefining the role of the court as an institution for atonement. It can just be said that the roots of New Testament soteriological interpretation of the death of Jesus can be traced back to Jesus himself" (Antwi, 1991:28).

A helpful work was composed by Warren Carter (1998), formerly professor at Saint Paul School of Theology. In "Jesus' 'I have come' Statements in Matthew's Gospel," the author proposes seven passages utilizing the verb ἦλθον, "I have come" or "I came" which he says convey Jesus' own declarations about his mission (Carter, 1998:44). Carter claims that these seven passages would have been identified as a distinctive group of passages by the audience because of shared stylistic features (Carter, 1998:45). These passages within the main body of the Matthean Gospel and Carter's study of them may prove to be useful as this project reviews the flow of the text within the proposed inclusio at the beginning and end of the Gospel. This article is helpful to the current research because it demonstrates and elaborates upon the

---

[12] For a useful, albeit brief, summary of more modern published major commentaries, see (Carson and Moo, 2005:159-162).

mission of Christ as Matthew understands it. By the end of the article, the scholar draws direct lines of connection between the texts of Matt 1:21; 20:28; and 26:28. He writes, "the audience understands this seventh saying [Matt 20:28] to mean that Jesus performs his divinely commissioned purpose of saving from sins not only in his deeds and words *but also in his death*. This understanding will be confirmed in 26:28" which utilizes the keyword "sins" from 1:21 (Carter, 1998:62).[13] While Carter neither designates the connection as an inclusio nor elaborates much upon it, he does identify the links between the passages and says that they help the reader to interpret Jesus' mission.

Clay Ham (2000), formerly of Dallas Christian College, authored, "The Last Supper in Matthew" which, among several items related to the Last Supper, explores the phrase, "Poured out for many for the forgiveness of sins" in Matt 26:28. The phrase does not appear in the parallel passages concerning the Last Supper and, thus, deserves attention in Matthean studies.[14] The article contrasts the four accounts and then focuses on the Old Testament background for the phrase.[15] Another helpful item from this article is the endeavor to answer the question: "how does the Last Supper passage serve in a climactic way for themes important to the book as a whole?" (Ham, 2000:66). The answer is, in part, "at the meal Jesus explains the significance of his death in relation to the covenant which brings forgiveness of sins" (Ham, 2000:69). The supposition that the Lord's Last Supper serves as a climax for several Matthean themes seems to be correct and in agreement with the current book. In summary, the author goes on to write, "Matthew's account makes explicit promise of the forgiveness of sins as part of the covenant established by Jesus' death. . . . [The actions of Jesus in the Last Supper] sum up the mystery of Jesus Christ: his salvific mission and his redemptive death" (Ham, 2000:69). These details are in line with the presumptions of this research project and will be explored further in subsequent chapters. The article by Ham will likely have a good deal of relevance, for example, in chapters four and five.

"'For He will Save His People from their Sins' (Matthew 1:21): A Christology for Christian Jews" by Boris Repschinski (2006) from the University of Innsbruck is one of the more pertinent items for the current thesis. The article focuses on the question of Matthew's audience. Was it a Jewish community or not? Repschinski says it was Jewish (2006:249). Salvation primarily concerns Israel, but Matthew does broaden salvation out to the

---

[13] Emphasis mine in italics.

[14] Matt 26: 26-29; Mark 14:22-25; Luke 22:15-20; and 1 Cor 11:23-25. "The accounts show a variety of similar features" (Ham, 2000:56). However, Matthew supplies the unique phrase.

[15] Particularly, Isa 53:11-12 and Jer 31:31-34 but potentially overtones from Exod 24:8 and Zech 9:11.

Gentiles at the end with the Great Commission. Where I agree and want to link from this article is Repschinski's argument that one needs to read Matthew's Gospel from the beginning to the end, and not the other way around. Arguing that going back to the beginning of the Gospel will help to bring clarity to Matthew's Christology, Repschinski concentrates his article on Matt 1:21. This verse, the author claims, has echoes throughout the entirety of the Gospel account. Overall, the article is brief, and so there is much to build upon and expand. The author provides numerous ideas to explore. He focuses on salvation just as much as he does sins.

Where this publication will deviate from Repschinski's work is on the subject of the identity of the community. His work focuses on the community more than the current research intends to do. Where does Matthew's community fit in the discussion? While attempting to discern the original audience may prove to be helpful in some regards, there seems to be too much speculation to be of any ultimate value. The text as it has been received will be the basis of this work. Repschinski does highlight the connection between Matt 1:21 and 26:28 in passing and also notes that these passages are unique to Matthew, he does not expound upon the connection (2006: 257, 261, 263). This book attempts to do exactly that, expound upon that particular connection.

Jeffrey Gibbs (2008), Emeritus Professor of Exegetical Theology at Concordia Seminary, St. Louis, Missouri, in "The Son of God and the Father's Wrath: Atonement and Salvation in Matthew's Gospel" from the Concordia Theological Quarterly outlines the idea of atonement throughout Matthew, especially the narrative sections. Gibbs begins with what he refers to as an obvious point: "[T]his is what the Gospel of Matthew is about: Jesus who will save" (2008:211). He concludes his article on the same point, forming his own sort of inclusio. What Gibbs wants to convey is the idea that the Son of God came to die to avert the Father's wrath, but his mission was much more than just his death (2008:225). The Son of God lived, ministered, healed, and he rose from the dead in power.

"Saved by Obedience: Matthew 1:21 in Light of Jesus Teaching on the Torah" is a piece published by Thomas Blanton (2013) in the Journal for Biblical Literature. Blanton seeks to build upon the work of Carter (1998) and Repschinski (2006) by more adequately defining the nature of the "sin" from which Jesus is depicted as saving his people (Blanton, 2013:393). Sin is seen in the context of the Torah. The ideas put forward in this article challenge the standard interpretation of Matt 1:21 with the various passages throughout Matthew that touch on the same themes. Based on this article, if Blanton was asked if an inclusio with Matt 26:28 is actual, he would likely still claim that it is insufficient to fully explain Matt 1:21. Of course, this does not discredit the notion that there is an actual macro inclusio in Matthew, but it would soften the significance of it if Blanton's thesis is true.

Marius Nel (2015), Professor in the Faculty of Theology of Stellenbosch University, published a relevant article titled, "The Motive of Forgiveness in the Gospel According to Matthew." The conclusion delivers a solid summary of the point of his article (Nel, 2015:8). Like Repschinski (2006) and others, Nel devotes much space to reconstructing the background of the book and of the Matthean community. He brings out the practicality of forgiveness and discusses how Christ's disciples are to live in forgiveness in light of Jesus' teaching and the forgiveness that Jesus gives. Most relevant to the study at hand is the fact that Nel identifies Matt 1:21 and 26:28 as an inclusio. However, he does not attempt to elucidate, clarify, or defend that notion. Somewhat striking is the notion that a writer can acknowledge a large inclusio without detailing the implications of it. Possibly, Nel believes that the categorization of Matt 1:21 and 26:28 as an inclusio is already widely accepted in scholarship. Beyond this point, Nel's article outlines the agents of forgiveness in the First Gospel: God the Father is an exemplar to be imitated as a forgiver, and he also commands his followers to forgive others; Jesus is depicted as the only true mediator of God's forgiveness which defines his life and mission consummating with his death on the cross; and lastly, the disciples are God's ongoing agents of the ministry of forgiveness (Nel, 2015:5-8). Christ's disciples, including the Matthean community, are now "a family of brothers (and sisters) who have experienced God's forgiveness and who should therefore also forgive those who transgress against them" (Nel, 2015:8). Throughout the article and reiterated in the conclusion, the author stresses that Matthew's Gospel should not be read as static or standardized but as a "dynamic story" (Nel, 2015:8).

One of the more recent publications of note is the one presented in The Catholic Biblical Quarterly entitled, "An Embedded Chiastic Order in Matthew?" and was authored by Christopher Decaen (2021) of Thomas Aquinas College. In this publication, Decaen argues for a large chiastic structure which reveals the main motif of "God with us." While one may grant that this is an important pattern in Matthew's Gospel, one does not have to assert that this is the only theme or even the primary one.[16] What is helpful from this article is the exploration of literary structures. Several of the aspects put forward by Decaen concerning chiasms are also ideas the present research will attempt to present and defend of the similar literary device of inclusio. To give just three examples, Decaen argues that, "macro structures were not uncommon among the NT writers;" the literary device "must somehow affect the reader (or listener) so as to move him or her toward the intended understanding of the figures, themes, or purposes of the story;" and he asserts that "a chiasm is both a literary and a *rhetorical* device" (Decaen, 2021:58). These are all details that the present researcher finds to be true of inclusio and intends to develop and demonstrate in the following pages.

---

[16] See more in chapter three on this point.

"Jesus and the Forgiveness of Sins: An Aspect of His Prophetic Mission" was released by Tobias Hägerland (2012) of Lund University in Sweden. This is a book length, scholarly treatment on the subject of the forgiveness of sins as a major part of the mission of Christ. The work does not focus on Matthew's Gospel alone but explores the whole canonical Gospels tradition. Considering the first century, Jewish context as well as early Christianity, Hägerland reflects upon Jesus' ministry as prophet and healer. The ministry of the forgiveness of sins is presented as permeating Jesus' ministry as he teaches and performs good deeds but also as he commissions his own disciples. The researcher seeks to demonstrate that the theme of forgiveness of sins is original to the historical Jesus. However, he roots this ministry of forgiveness merely in the prophetic tradition (Hägerland, 2012:214).

2.2. Synopsis of Carson and Moo's Introduction on Matthew

Reviewing some of the more relevant periodicals has been the primary focus of this chapter, but a few comments may be made on Carson and Moo's "An Introduction to the New Testament" (2005:134-168). A respectable introduction, Carson and Moo have done a masterful job introducing their readers to the various New Testament documents. Their chapter on Matthew is no exception. In each chapter, they end their discussion on the given New Testament book with a section on the contribution of said book to the whole corpus of 27 books. This section highlights the most important and unique ideas from the book. On Matthew, Carson and Moo link its place closely to the other Synoptic Gospels before overviewing six key contributions. These items may be reviewed before giving comment as to what is missing from the list.

First, Carson and Moo bring out the importance of the large blocks of discourse from Jesus in Matthew's Gospel account. The Gospel of John also has lengthy discourses, but some of Matthew's are unique (for example, the Sermon on the Mount). Second, the Matthean account of Jesus' virginal conception complements Luke and the other Gospels. Matthew also provides other unique birth narratives. Third, Jesus' life and ministry—his mission—is distinctively connected to the Old Testament in the First Gospel. Fourth, linking to the previous point, Matthew focuses on Jesus' "fulfilment" of the law. This point resonates throughout his book. Fifth, Matthew's work makes a significant contribution to the foundation of the early church as one that was transitioning from the old covenant to the new. Lastly, number six on Carson and Moo's list, is their summary that Matthew has unique "shadings" and "colorings." Much of what Matthew has to convey is not unique among the Gospels, but it is nuances in special ways by the author of the First Gospel.

The same authors also note five major themes (Carson and Moo, 2005:158). These include one, that Jesus is the promised Messiah; two, that many Jews failed to realize Jesus' identity; three, the kingdom of God has dawned; four, Jesus' messianic reign continues in the life and work of the church; and lastly, this messianic reign is the foretaste of the kingdom's consummation at Christ's return.

One may quickly realize, considering the title and main purpose of the current research project, that what is conspicuously absent from these lists of Matthean themes and contributions to the New Testament supplied by Carson and Moo is anything concerning the atonement of Christ, that is, the meaning of the cross (other than the third theme, to a minor degree). One might add, moreover, that, besides the third and fourth points on "fulfilment" in the contributions, the authors do not state that Matthew's Gospel has much to contribute concerning the mission of Christ.

The current research project does not argue that Matthew's contribution on the mission of Christ and the meaning of the cross necessarily surpasses or supersedes the themes and contributions listed by Carson and Moo. A more modest proposition is put forward in this work. The argument in the following chapters is that Matthew does in fact provide a unique explanation for the mission of Christ and the meaning of the cross. To borrow Carson and Moo's words (2005:164), "there are shadings" and "colorings" on the person and work of Jesus Christ that are unique to the Matthean Gospel. This piece of writing may provide commentary on another important theme in Matthew that can be added alongside those previously listed.

2.3. Synopsis of Chapman's Thesis on Inclusio

Anthony Chapman (2013) has set forth a thesis titled, "Inclusio in the Hebrew Bible: A Historical-Developmental Approach." The thesis was accepted by Dr. Shamir Yona at Ben Gurion University of the Negev. Chapman reviews the history of scholarship on the literary feature of inclusio in his research including classical and Christian views, rabbinical understandings, and the assessments of both earlier and modern biblical scholarship. He also proposes criteria for discerning the presence of an inclusio, proposing a sliding scale of stronger to weaker uses. While Chapman's research is focused on the Hebrew Scriptures, the thesis will likely prove to be helpful in the production of the current research project because of its unique contribution on the topic of inclusio in the Scriptures. Chapman's work is concentrated, detailed, and systematic on inclusio and makes for a well-developed treatment of the subject. He provides a history of scholarship on the issue, various definitions of the literary device along with his own definition, criteria for evaluating potential inclusios, and several examples of both shorter and longer sections. Some of these items will be covered in chapter three of the current work in relation to the Gospel of Matthew.

2.4. Synopsis of Matthean Commentaries

While commentaries have not been the focus of this literature review, naming some of the more important volumes for this research project may be helpful. Not only has D. A. Carson co-authored one of the best New Testament introductions, but he has also written one of the most respected major commentaries on Matthew's Gospel for The Expositor's Bible Commentary series (Carson, 2010). No serious reader of the Gospel of Matthew will overlook Carson's work. The commentary on Matt 1:21 makes references to historical background and Old Testament usage and ideas, but there is no reference to a macro inclusio with Matt 26:28. The commentator only makes reference in passing at Matt 26:28 to an "important connection" with Matt 1:21 (Carson, 603). There is no assertion of an inclusio, much less an explanation of it. The commentator makes much about the background of Isaiah 53.

Grant Osborne completed the volume for the Zondervan Exegetical Commentary on the New Testament series (Osborne, 2010). This commentary does not provide much by way of unique commentary, yet the book does a superb job of summarizing the main points of the Gospel. The commentary at Matt 1:21 does make reference to Matt 26:28 among many other references. However, there is no affirmation of an inclusio. Again, the scholar makes reference to Isaiah 53 as important background. At Matt 26:28 there is no connection made back to Matt 1:21 at all.

Craig Keener published a commentary with Eerdmans titled, "The Gospel of Matthew: A Socio-Rhetorical Commentary" (Keener, 2009). Keener is not quite as well-rounded as Carson, but his volume includes the best commentary on the historical and cultural backgrounds, in the researcher's opinion. No connections are made between Matt 1:21 and 26:28. However, the commentator affirms that Matthew is teaching the reader that Jesus is the one who saves his people by the cross (Keener, 97). The scholar maintains that Matt 26:28 "likely tells us much about Jesus' view of his mission" and that the likely connection to Isaiah 52-53 "tells us a great deal about how Jesus viewed his own death" (Keener, 630–631).

R. T. France contributed the highly-respected volume on Matthew to the New International Commentary on the New Testament series (France, 2007). The commentator thinks that the reader is invited "to reflect on the nature of the Messiah mission" through the interpretations given to the two names in Matt 1: 21 (France, 53). Not much is made of the inclusio, but the commentator certainly uses Matt 20:28 and 26:28 to interpret what is said in Matt 1:21. France comments, "His mission will culminate in his death 'as a ransom for many' (20:28), 'for the forgiveness of sins' (26:28)" (France, 54). In the commentary on Matt 26:28, the scholar, like many others, acknowledges the likely background as Isaiah 53. He states that this phrase "also recalls to the reader the original statement of Jesus' mission in 1:21" (France, 994). He goes on to comment, "The result is the most comprehensive statement in Matthew's gospel of the redemptive purpose and achievement of Jesus' death" (France, 994).

The two volumes titled, "The Christbook" and "The Churchbook" by Dale Bruner are exemplary commentaries (Bruner, 2004). The scholar acknowledges that in Matt 1:21 it is not said how Jesus will save his people from their sins and that there is no explicit allusion to the cross (Bruner, 28). However, the author tells the reader to read the interpretation of this verse from the context of the whole gospel. He uses Matt 26:28 as an interpretive help for Matt 1:21. In the latter passage, the commentator refers back to the earlier verse and says, "The blood brings forgiveness" (Bruner, 967). Yet, no formal affirmations are made of a macro inclusio in the Gospel of Matthew.

The Concordia Commentary series' volume on Matthew was authored by Jeffrey Gibbs (Gibbs, 2006-2018). On Matt 1:21, the scholar comments, "From this point in the narrative, the very name 'Jesus' will evoke the purpose for which this Jesus has come: the purpose of God saving his people from sin—from their own sins. How and to what extent will Jesus save? Clearly, by his ransom-death (20:28) and his outpoured blood (26:28)" (Gibbs, 107). No formal acknowledgment is made of an inclusio, but the connections are apparent to the author.

What seems to be the gold standard of research and commentary on the Gospel of Matthew is the three-volume set in the International Critical Commentary series by W. D. Davies and D. C. Allison titled, "A Critical and Exegetical Commentary on the Gospel According to Saint Matthew" (1988-1997). The commentators do not use the language of inclusio but certainly tie a close connection between Matt 1:21 and 26:28. The scholars state that the cross is already in view even at this early stage in references made to Matt 26:28. "Thus the entire gospel is to be read in the light of its end," write the authors (Davies and Allison, 1988:210). There are many other commentaries to consult that provide significant contributions to Matthean studies, but those listed here are some of the most notable.

2.5. Synopsis of Books on Matthean Themes

Once more, the literature review has focused on the most germane periodicals for the current research. However, like the list of helpful commentaries above, one might also list important books for the study. These include single volumes on the theology of Matthew. Patrick Schreiner has released, "Matthew, Disciple and Scribe: The First Gospel and Its Portrait of Jesus" (Schreiner, 2019). Charles Quarters has published, "A Theology of Matthew: Jesus Revealed as Deliverer, King, and Incarnate Creator" (Quarles, 2013). Stephen Westerholm has written, "Understanding Matthew: The Early Christian Worldview of the First Gospel" (Westerholm, 2006). Longtime Matthean scholar Ulrich Luz has a volume with Cambridge titled, "The

Theology of the Gospel of Matthew" (1993). Jack Kingsbury's two different works are also still very helpful, "Matthew as Story" (1988) and "Matthew: Structure, Christology, Kingdom" (1975). The abovementioned volumes on Matthean theology are only a share of the resources available on the Gospel of Matthew, and, yet, these volumes represent some of the works most germane to the present study.

As stated previously, the preceding literature review is not intended to be exhaustive but to sample some of the most relevant peer-reviewed articles for the current research project. Progress has certainly been made in Matthean studies in the last few decades, but there is room to make more advancement. In the following chapters, the goal is to make another contribution to the discussion.

Chapter 3: The Inclusio with References to "Sins" at The Beginning and End of Matthew's Gospel, Matt 1:21 And 26:28

The Gospel of Matthew enjoyed a central position in the life and education of the Christian Church in the early centuries of her history.[17] This was by no accident. The Gospel placed first in the New Testament is lengthy, well-developed, and effective. While Matthew had a treasured standing in early centuries, Matthean studies as a field of inquiry has fluctuated over recent decades, but a slow and steady development has continued.[18]

The following chapter will explore one of the literary and rhetorical features sewn into the fabric of the Matthean Gospel. This chapter constitutes the heart of the current research project. The central theoretical argument of this research project is that the Matthean Gospel makes a unique contribution to New Testament theology with regards to the mission of Christ and the meaning of the cross by forming a large inclusio with references to "sins" at the beginning and end of his Gospel account, Matt 1:21 and 26:28. The chapter will gradually construct the argument, developing it section by section, and building to a fully and clearly presented case for the above-stated thesis.

At the outset, the different terms for the literary device known as "inclusio" will be catalogued from various sources. From there, the assorted definitions of inclusio may be stated and discussed. After this work has been accomplished, the researcher will provide his own definition of the literary feature which will be used in the continuing analysis.

The use of inclusio in biblical literature will be exhibited, first in the Old Testament Literature, especially in the Psalms, and then in the New Testament Literature, including the Gospels as well as the epistles. This outline of the chapter allows the argument to progressively narrow to focus on the

---

[17] "As the opening book of the New Testament, the early church gave Matthew's gospel deep respect for centuries. It came from the pen of an apostle and reflected an intimate acquaintance with the Jewish customs of Jesus" (Burge, Cohick, and Green, 2009:166).

[18] Those providing a useful survey of the history of Matthean studies but also contemporary study include, but are not limited to, Graham Stanton, ed., 1983, The Interpretation of Matthew; Ulrich Luz, 2007, Matthew in History: Interpretation, Influence, and Effects; Donald Senior, 1996, What are they saying about Matthew?; David Aune, ed., 2001, The Gospel of Matthew in Current Study; and Daniel Gurtner and John Nolland, eds., 2008, Built Upon the Rock: Studies in the Gospel of Matthew.

central theoretical argument concerning Matthew's use of a particular inclusio. Once the broader use of the literary device in the biblical literature is established, Matthew's use of inclusio in his own Gospel will be submitted. This will demonstrate that Matthew is not only aware of the literary device but effectively puts it to use in his own writing.

Because the research project will have considered the various terms used and definitions propounded in scholarship for inclusio and also explored the use of inclusio throughout biblical literature, including in the Gospel of Matthew, criteria for determining the presence of an inclusio can then be catalogued. Additionally, the purpose of inclusios will have come into focus and can be expounded.

The last and most important section of this chapter, before giving the summary and relevance of the argument, will be to lay out the case for the large inclusio with references to "sins" at the beginning and end of Matthew's Gospel account, Matt 1:21 and 26:28. The way that this argument will be justified is by determining whether or not these passages meet the criteria for an inclusio that will have previously been set forth.

3.1 The Various Terms for the Literary Device of Inclusio

Anyone seeking to accurately interpret the biblical materials must take into account in their reading strategies the literary nature of those materials, even though New Testament scholarship has focused on these features only in recent decades.[19] Nevertheless, certain features, such as inclusio, have been recognized for a much longer time (Bullinger, 1898:245-249; Wyckoff, 2006:478). It is to this literary device that the research now turns its attention, beginning with a discussion of the various terms used for this feature or those terms related to it.

The classic work on literary figures of speech employed in the Christian Scriptures which has never really been surpassed is the text by E. W. Bullinger (1898) titled, "Figures of Speech Used in the Bible." In this text, Bullinger supplies a handbook of over two-hundred literary features in the Bible. For each, he defines the device, provides the biblical references where the device is present, and explains the usage. One of the more helpful features of Bullinger's text is the index of biblical references in the back. So, for example, a reader may look in the index to see if the verse he is studying is

---

[19] See the New Interpreter's Dictionary article on "Literary Interpretation, NT" in (Sakenfeld, 2009). Also, consider: "The New Testament is inherently literary at the levels of both form and content. . . . At the level of form, it shows its literary allegiance by the prevalence of literary genres, a high degree of artistry, special resources of language, and the presence of unifying master images (Ryken, 1987:22).

referenced. If it is in the index, then a figure of speech is likely present in the passage.

Bullinger, not surprisingly, does have a section on the literary device of inclusio. He labels it, in the first place, as epanadiplosis. Bullinger categorizes "Epanadiplosis" under the heading and subheadings of, "Figures Involving Addition—Affecting Words—Repetition of the Same Word—In the same Sense" (Bullinger, 1898:xxii-xxiii).[20] The alternative words listed by Bullinger include encircling, inclusio, and cyclus (Bullinger, 1898:245). The writer supports the use of the Greek term ἐπαναδίπλοσις by saying that the word "means *a doubling upon again*" (Bullinger, 1898:245).

Epanadiplosis is also referenced by others (DeMoss, 2001:51; Mickelsen, 1984:196). DeMoss does not define the term but only points the reader to "anaphora" (DeMoss, 2001:51). Mickelsen, on the other hand, does submit a simple definition of epanadiplosis: "This term describes a situation where an important word is repeated for emphasis" (Mickelsen, 1984:196). By stating that this refers to a "situation," Mickelsen gives the researcher the opportunity to use the term in a wide range of interpretive scenarios. In other words, Mickelsen leaves room for an interpreter to find epanadiplosis in a broader set of scenarios than just a doubling of a word at the beginning and end of a sentence.

On a similar note, "Epanalepsis" is often used as a synonym, or even as a heading for several subcategories (Quinn, 1993:102; Watson, 2013:830-831). Eminent academic of rhetoric Arthur Quinn categorizes under the banner of repetition uses the terms epanalepsis as well as inclusio (Quinn, 1993:102). Epanalepsis is defined by Quinn simply and straightforwardly as, "repetition of the beginning at the end" (Quinn, 1993:102). However, the writer uses what seems to be a broad and simple term for the use of repetition within a sentence in particular. He writes, "we could end a sentence or clause with the same word or phrase with which we began it" (Quinn, 1993: 87).

Another literary term highlighted as an alternative word for epanadiplosis, previously mentioned above, is "anaphora" (DeMoss, 2001:18). This has been defined as "a reference back to a previous context by the repetition or the inclusion of a word or phrase (ἀναφορά, 'a carrying back'). The anaphoric article, for example, points back to something stated or implied in a previous context. In rhetoric, anaphora occurs when successive clauses begin with the same word or group of words. . . . Also known as epanadiplosis and epanaphora" (DeMoss, 2001:18). However, anaphora seems to refer to the repetition of words at the start of successive clauses.

Encircling and cyclus are also used as synonyms for inclusio, both referring to the circular nature of the literary structure. Bullinger says that these

---

[20] For the full article, see "Epanadiplosis" (Bullinger, 1898:245-249).

terms may be used "because the repetition conclude[s] what is said, as in a circle" (Bullinger, 1898:245).

In addition to the terms given in Bullinger's treatment of the literary figure (epanadiplosis, encircling, inclusio, and cyclus) are synonyms such as bracketing, enclosing, envelope structure, intercalation, and more contemporary terms such as bookending and sandwiching.

Of course, all of these words are very similar since they are all attempting to describe the same occurrence. Bracketing and bookending are helpful words because they convey the idea that what comes at the beginning and at the end in some way help to hold the whole structure together. What is contained within is important, but what comes first and last is equally significant.

The next two names which may be listed are similar, enclosing and envelope structure. If the words bracketing and bookending communicate the importance of the first and last parts themselves, these two names express the value of what is contained within the brackets. On envelope structure, one scholar asserts, "The two related terms that use 'envelope' (structure/figure) give us an interesting metaphor" (Longman, et al., 2008:323). The metaphor helps one to picture contents within a package.

Intercalation is a literary term that may be used at times for inclusio but typically refers to the composition of one story in the middle of a different story. Tate defines it as, "The technique of sandwiching one story or block of material within another story or block" and goes on to elaborate with, "Since the relationship of the two is generally not explained, the reader is forced to ask questions about the significance of the relationship" (Tate, 2006:179). This arrangement constructs an A1, B, A2 pattern. Sometimes in the related literature this device is labeled "frame story" (Tate, 2006:145). Intercalation and inclusio are best understood as two different but closely related literary devices. The biblical interpreter can apply many of the same hermeneutical principles to inclusios that one would apply to intercalations. However, there are stark contrasts. As Tate observes, "Intercalation as a literary device prompts certain questions from the reader without supplying any definitive answer. Consequently, intercalation is a literary device that involves the reader in determining meaning" (Tate, 2006:179). Inclusio as a literary device also prompts certain questions from the reader yet does seem to supply more conclusive answers. The answers are folded within the inclusio. Intercalation is a related term to inclusio but is not exactly the same because it is usually employed to describe the occurrence of "inserting" something within the brackets. For example, a frame-story when a narrative is inserted inside of another narrative is intercalation in a specific sense, but there is the purpose of inclusion more broadly because the inserted narrative is enveloped by the broader narrative.

There are numerous terms used to designate the literary occurrence of repeating a word or phrase at the beginning and end of a section. Some designations may be better than others. Encircling, cyclus, enclosing, and enveloping are all terms which attempt to describe the circular and embracing nature of the device. Bracketing, bookending, and sandwiching are all names used to express the structural nature of the literary device. The section of text is held together in some sense by this literary structure. Epanadiplosis may be used generically as in Bullinger's description but is often synonymous with epanalepsis, anaphora, and epanaphora. Anadiplosis, it seems, is often used to refer to the repetition of words at the end of phrases or sentences. These labels all appear to refer to something somewhat different than inclusio, even if they are related terms. Rather than at the beginning and end of a sentence or passage, scholars typically employ these terms to designate the occurrence of the repetition of the same word or phrase at the beginning of successive lines. Intercalation is a related term to inclusio but is not exactly the same because it is usually employed to describe the occurrence of "inserting" something within the brackets. Some have even termed the device "distant parallelism," especially so in Old Testament studies and poetry, in particular (Wyckoff, 2006:477).[21]

While there are several different expressions used for the literary and rhetorical device, inclusio appears to be the most common term employed in biblical studies (Longman, et al., 2008:323; Chapman, 2013:1). For the purpose of this research project, "inclusio" will be the term of choice to designate the literary occurrence that accomplishes two main ideas. First, there is an enveloping nature of the device where the contents between the first and the last are highlighted. Second, there is a structural nature to the device where what is said at the first and last are highlighted. Both the outer brackets and the inner contents are important to the main point the author is making.

The broader category to which inclusio and these related terms is assigned is "repetition" (Bullinger, 1898). On the idea of repetition in literature, Ryken affirms, "All of literature relies on various forms of repetition, but the Bible has even more of it than most literature, probably because so much of the Bible was originally oral literature. In poetry this urge for repetition takes the form of parallelism and rhetorical patterns. There is an equal abundance of repetition in the stories of the Bible, Jesus' parables and discourses, and the epistles" (Ryken, 1984:195). The most basic notion involved in an inclusio is reiteration. Repetition can take on many different forms in literature (and in speech, for that matter), but in the case of inclusio the repetition comes at the beginning and end of a sentence, section, or book. With the terms and concepts in mind, then, one can turn to defining exactly what an inclusio is and do so with the nuances of these related terms.

---

[21] (Wyckoff, 2006:478) notes in footnote 4, "Inclusio structures are also called 'frame', 'envelope figure', and, in rare cases, 'distant parallelism' Regarding the latter term, see Dahood 1972:80-81, where it is used to describe conventional word-pairs that have been split and placed at the extremities of a poem."

3.2 Various Definitions of Inclusio

The definition and the uses of inclusio are rarely ever given any thorough treatment in the literature of biblical studies but are typically referenced in brief without explanation (Chapman, 2013:1; Nel, 2015:2).[22] The fullest elaboration of the literary device of inclusio is usually given in the literature of Old Testament studies and in the area of the wisdom literature, in particular. Consider the following: "As is often the case with terminology in Hebrew poetics, the same phenomenon can have more than one name in the scholarly literature. Inclusio is the most common term used, but envelope structure or envelope figure is also found" (Longman, et al., 2008:323).

There is debate over exactly what is an inclusio. There are various definitions of the term and literary feature. Rehearsing the definitions given by several scholars may be helpful before giving the working definition for this current research project. The reader will notice that many scholars use the expression and define it in terms of one sentence or a small passage. Of course, the idea of an inclusio at the beginning and end of a work has already been presented as possible. Before someone shrugs off the possibility that there is such a thing as a "large inclusio," that is, an inclusio bracketing a large section or the entirety of a biblical book, they should consider the work done by Old Testament scholars and also those working in the New Testament as well (Decaen, 2021:57-58).[23]

One may begin the discussion of a definition for the term inclusio by considering inclusio within the greater framework of symbolism in the Bible.[24]

---

[22] E.g. Marius Nel: "The prologue itself is linked to the epilogue (26:1–28:20) by an inclusio formed by the announcement that God would be present in the ministry of Jesus (1:23), which echoes the promise of the resurrected Jesus of his continuing presence in the church (28:20). This inclusio provides a frame for the interpretation of Matthew's extended διήγησις (3:1–25:46) of Jesus' words and deeds. In the prologue, the identification of Jesus as the saviour of his people (1:21) also foreshadows the declaration by Jesus (26:28) that he would save his people from their sins by giving his life as an offering. The literary frame provided by the prologue and epilogue of Matthew thus clearly emphasises that forgiveness is an important motif in its διήγησις (Nolland 2005:380)" (Nel, 2015:2). Some explanation is provided but very little. This is a scholarly insight worthy of further development.

[23] Consider footnote 5 by (Decaen, 2021:57) and his summary statement: "It begins to appear that even such macro structures were not uncommon among the NT writers, so one might second guess the widespread conviction that Matthew was not equally ambitious. . ." (Decaen, 2021:57-58).

[24] "Symbols represent a connection that can be perceived and apprehended only when one enters the system of symbols and participates into it, and thus when one abandons the critical distance that, since the Enlightenment, biblical scholars thought

Symbolism connects ideas within the biblical text with one another. Symbolism also connects the biblical text with the reader or hearer. The symbolism of a biblical text "can be described. But a detached description of the biblical symbolic score is missing the symbolism. It is only when we account for the way in which this symbolism is performed that we can recognize how this text connects its readers (or hearers) to an ultimate reality" (Sakenfeld, 2009).[25] The overall structure of a biblical book, including the use of inclusio, speaks to a grand reality. It represents something larger than the literary device itself or the mere words employed. A macro inclusio, especially, means to convey an all-inclusive message to the reader (Tucker, 2008:588).

To give an initial definition from the immediately preceding source, within the context of symbolism, it is asserted, "A most common literary device in biblical books is the inclusio, where the beginning and end of a section are similar, thus 'including' the intervening material as if between bookends. As a triadic literary device, the inclusio highlights both 1) the relationship between the bookends—which have parallel features (that signal them as forming an inclusio) but also differences (thus an inclusio can be viewed as underscoring the 'inverted parallelism' between its bookends)—and 2) the center of the inclusio, in which case it is viewed as a 'chiasm' (often involving progressive concentric inclusios)" (Sakenfeld, 2009).[26] This opening definition highlights the two most important elements of an inclusio. First, the two sentences or passages at the beginning and end both repeat the same thought, thus emphasizing a main point. Second, the content included within the structure is also emphasized as important to the message of the structure. Moreover, the writer briefly states the similarities between inclusio and chiasm, affirming that they can be closely related and reminding the reader that they may be interpreted in much the same way. Notice, furthermore, that this particular definition states that an inclusio occurs at the beginning and end of a "section." This is an important nuance. Other scholars will define the device as occurring at the beginning and end of a sentence or paragraph. This initial definition provided gives a broader view.

DeMoss also allows the figure to happen in a "section," stating, "A literary framing device in which the same word or phrase stands at the

---

they needed to maintain so as to develop a truly critical interpretation. Yet, in a postmodern perspective attentive to communication theories and to the ways readers/hearers produce meaning with a text or discourse (semiotics), the critical study of symbolism can be envisioned" (Sakenfeld, 2009:Symbolism). Digital: Olive Tree Bible Software. No page numbers.

[25] (Sakenfeld, 2009:Symbolism.A.). Digital: Olive Tree Bible Software. No page numbers.

[26] (Sakenfeld, 2009:Symbolism.B.2.). Digital: Olive Tree Bible Software. No page numbers.

beginning and the end of a section. Sometimes called bracketing" (DeMoss, 2001:71). This brief definition also seems to refer to the more technical aspects of the literary device. Inclusio as a literary device, structurally speaking, frames or brackets a section of writing.

E. W. Bullinger's definition for this figure of speech is simple but sound: "The Repetition of the same Word or Words at the beginning and end of a Sentence" (Bullinger, 1898:245). After breaking down the roots of the Greek, ἐπαναδίπλοσις, to begin explaining the term, the writer goes on to say, "It means *a doubling upon again*, and the Figure is so called because the same word is repeated at the beginning and at the end of a sentence" (Bullinger, 1898:245). The term inclusio is incorporated into Bullinger's discussion when he writes, "The Latins called it INCLUSIO, *inclusion*: either because the first word of the sentence is included at the end, or because of the importance of the matter which is thus included between the two words" (Bullinger, 1898:245). Bullinger provides a straightforward and effective definition. However, one will notice that the author classifies the figure as taking place at the beginning and end of a "sentence." This definition does not seem to leave room for wider uses of inclusio and certainly not for macro inclusios. The core of this definition is that inclusio involved "repetition," and the importance of the brackets as well as the contents is once again underscored.

Quinn defines inclusio plainly as "repetition of the beginning of a passage at its end" (Quinn, 1993:102). This simple definition reiterates what has been seen in other definitions. Inclusio involved repetition, and it occurs at the beginning and end. Quinn defines the borders of inclusio to a passage. This is broader than Bullinger's limit to a sentence but not as wide-ranging as Tate's definition below. Furthermore, Quinn uses the term inclusio to refer to a specific epanalepsis. He elaborates, "The use of an epanalepsis to mark off a whole passage is called an inclusio" (Quinn, 1993:88).

Another simple definition is given by Tate who inserts some nuance. Of the inclusio, which he affirms as having application in the realm of literature as well as rhetoric, he defines it as a "device by which textual material is framed by the same OBJECT or words at the beginning and end. Many biblical scholars argue that the framed textual material must be seen as a thematic unity" (Tate, 2006:176). Tate gives the broadest scope by simply not delimiting the device at all. He leaves it open-ended in its function. Moreover, the author nuances the meaning of the literary device as conveying, through its structure, a thematic unity.

Furthermore, the definition given by Chapman is helpful. He defines inclusio as "the intentional repetition of clearly recognizable elements at the beginning and end of a composition or one of its parts" (Chapman, 2013:2,

71-73).[27] Adding the distinction that the repetition is "intentional" is imperative. There may be countless inadvertent repetitions throughout a literary work. The focus of this research, however, is the intentional applications. One way of deducing that the repetition is intentional will be "clearly recognizable elements." While not all inclusios are created equal and some are more obvious than others, a close reading of a text which has an inclusio should be clearly recognizable to the reader. The last item of note in Chapman's definition is his understanding that an inclusio can be employed for an entire composition or of one of its smaller parts. Again, inclusio is not only limited to a sentence or small section, although it can be and often is used in that way, but occurs in larger structures also.

Thinking primarily of the Old Testament use, surely, Corley and Huey define inclusio as a "Poetic device whereby the opening word or theme reappears at the end. The first word may include the overall meaning of a number of words that follow it, or the first concept in a series of poetic concepts or units is restated in the final unit" (Corley and Huey, 1983:103). This is a helpful definition because it does not limit the use of inclusio to only a repeated word of phrase but allows for a "theme" from the beginning to reappear at the end. Inclusio, then, can be employed by the author or speaker but also discovered by the reader or hearer through the use of the same word, phrase, or idea at the beginning and end of the bracketed material. To restate in the final unit something previously introduced is inclusio. As a poetic device, one may conclude that the author is not only conveying a main idea but also adding artistic beauty to his or her work.

Another work which defines inclusio as a "structural device" and works from the viewpoint of poetry is the one by Klein. This scholar defines inclusio as, "framing a poem by repeating words or phrases from its opening lines at its conclusion. This repetition provides a unity and finality the poem would not have otherwise" (Klein, et al., 2004:303). While it is understandable that an author working with poetic literature will think of literary devices in those terms, inclusio should not be limited to poetry. The device certainly frames poems, at times, but it is also used in prose. Moreover, as previously mentioned, the term is also used as a rhetorical device from ancient times until the present day. Thus, the definition submitted by Klein is too limited. However, it does provide benefit to the current project by affirming that the device allows for an open-ended use rather than a sentence or small section of material. The author also helps by stating that the repetition of an inclusio provides something that the literary writing would be lacking otherwise. Inclusio provides unity and finality, he writes. This is an significant aspect of the literary device that should not be overlooked by the reader.

---

[27] Chapman also helpfully suggests a Latin term to use for the material enclosed within the inclusio: "The term *includitur* will be used to describe the enclosed material within the inclusio" (Chapman, 2013:2).

In the dictionary article on the "Old Testament as Literature," Sandra Gavett defines inclusio as repetition of a key word or theme which attracts readers' attention to the main theme. Inclusio functions as a frame to illustrate the main emphasis contained within it. Inclusios occur in shorter sections and longer ones (Gavett, 2000:812-815). Gavett states what scholars rarely do on this point: inclusio can occur in long sections. This is likely included in the definition because of passages such as Ecclesiastes 1:2 and 12:8, which is mentioned by the author.[28] Such a conspicuous use of a macro inclusio forces itself upon the reader so that one cannot conclude that the literary device is limited to only a sentence or small section. The scholar also highlights that the repetition is of a "key" word or theme. In doing so, the "main theme" is highlighted. Rather than using the definite article, this project offers a more humble statement that an inclusio calls the reader's attention to "a" main theme. So then, an inclusio accentuates a main point by the words or theme conveyed in the brackets themselves but also by the contents within the brackets.

In a separate article in the Eerdmans Dictionary of the Bible on oral composition by Casey Davis (2000:991-992), the scholar writes, "The primary characteristic of oral composition is the use of formulaic and thematic style. . . . Repetition, as evidenced in structural patterns such as inclusio and chiasm, has to this point been the major emphasis of most oral biblical criticism. Forms of repetition include sounds, grammatical constructions, words, and topics. Repetition can be used to group elements into high frequency blocks to indicate units or be fashioned into inclusio and chiasm to show structure. Especially in the case of word and topic repetition, they can be spread over large blocks of material to designate major structures." Inclusio is meant to show structure, and the writer admits that it can be used to designate major structures. The new addition that Davis supplies to the understanding of an inclusio is that the reiteration can take on many different forms. Davis says that sounds, grammatical constructions, words, and topics can all be repeated and thus form an inclusio.

Much like the discussions relayed above by Klein as well as Corley and Huey, Longman writes from an Old Testament perspective, especially thinking of the use of inclusio in poetry. Giving another straightforward definition, Longman writes, "The inclusio delimits a poetic unit, providing a strong sense of beginning and closure. Thus the term inclusio indicates that everything that is found between the two occurrences is 'included' in the unit. The two related terms that use 'envelope' (structure/figure) give us an interesting metaphor" (Longman, 2008:323). Certainly, the related term of "envelope" gives the reader an illustration of what is meant by an inclusio. Something is contained inside, and there are limits outside. Longman has given a nuance that has not

---

[28] This Old Testament passage is briefly surveyed in section 3.5 "The Use of Inclusio in Old Testament Literature."

been quite seen in the previous descriptions of the literary device when he says that inclusio provides a "strong sense" of beginning and closure. In using an inclusio the biblical author "brings things home" and "ties things up." There is a definitiveness and conclusiveness to the message when the device is employed. Once again, a definition is provided which states that the material within the brackets is stressed as important to the overall message.

In a broader discussion of inclusio, Longman (2008:323-324) mentions the relationship of inclusio to other literary devices in Old Testament poetry such as "refrain." He states that inclusio and refrain are similar except that inclusio only occurs twice, at the beginning and end of the unit. Longman writes, "An inclusio is a repeated phrase or a whole line that stands at the beginning and end of a poetic unit." The presence of inclusio is most definite for the reader when the repetition involves the whole line. He also discusses how some scholars wrongly use the term, in his estimation. They use it when only one word or even one root word is repeated. He thinks this is an unwarranted stretch. The function of inclusio is said to be obvious and straightforward in that it delimits a unit of text "like an envelope delimits a tax by containing it." This frame structure evokes coherence. Not only is the frame valuable, signified by the outer brackets, but the content often points to a central subject in the section of text. So then, "The inclusio opens and closes the poem and provides the mood throughout." It also summarizes what the author wants to say in that section. And just so the reader does not begin to think that the inclusio is constrained to poetic literature, Longman writes, "Ecclesiastes demonstrates that an inclusio can operate in a prose context. Indeed, there are no literary devices that are exclusive to poetry, though they may find a heightened and intensified use in poetry."[29]

After reviewing the various definitions of inclusio by numerous respected scholars, a few things may be summarized in conclusion. First, inclusio is a repetition. Second, the repetition may be of a key word, phrase, or idea. Third, the repetition may occur in a sentence, a small literary section, or in larger units even to include entire biblical books. Fourth, inclusio is employed to give structure, to highlight main messages, and to use the content within the brackets to support the main idea. Lastly, the varied definitions and distinctions between the biblical scholars on inclusio demonstrates that there is flexibility in the use of inclusio. Therefore, there should be flexibility in the biblical reader's awareness and understanding of the literary device.

3.3 My Own Definition of Inclusio

One may begin to gather the meaning of an inclusio from the various terms themselves which are used of this literary feature. The preceding survey

---

[29] The content of this entire paragraph conveys and discusses the ideas of (Longman, et al., 2008:323-325).

of definitions in the scholarly materials also helps to decide an understanding. However, a streamlined working definition is in order for the current discussion. Considering the various terms used and the definitions supplied by several scholars, the following working definition is offered: An inclusio is a literary and rhetorical device of repetition employed for several reasons including to give structure and to highlight main points and is recognizable because the same idea, even the same words at times, are repeated at the beginning and end of a sentence, section, or book.

Is there such a thing as a large inclusio? The goal of this book is to demonstrate that very possibility. Casey Davis notes: "Especially in the case of word and topic repetition, [inclusios] can be spread over large blocks of material to designate major structures" (Casey Davis, 2000:992). Several scholars echo this opinion.[30] Examples of large or "macro" inclusios will be supplied in subsequent sections.

3.4 The Use of Inclusio

The reader of Scripture does well to remember that, "The style of the Bible is an oral style. The prevalence of dialogue and biblical narrative is unique in ancient literature. But the Bible is everywhere filled with voices speaking and replying. To read the Bible well is to become a listener, either literally or in one's imagination" (Ryken, 1984:196). The literary use of inclusio may have originated in the ancient oral tradition (Davis, 1999:88; Chapman, 2013:119). Matthew's Gospel is assumed to have originated in an oral tradition, as were all of the canonical Gospels (Carson and Moo, 2005:79-85). In this way, the device was probably a form of repetition used to make the main point of the passage more memorable (Chapman, 2013:104; Foley, 2019).[31] Several other uses of inclusio besides this original use of memorability will also be delineated below.

Considering the text as it stands presented and not the speculations of redaction theorists (e.g. Gundry, 1994), one may consider the literary nature of the feature. Writing on the subject generally, Randolph Tate affirms, "Literary

---

[30] See Decaen, 2021:57-58; Chapman, 2013:2; Gavett, 2000:812-815; Longman, 2008:323-324.

[31] Oral traditions "use special languages and performance arenas while employing flexible patterns and structures that aid composition, retention, and reperformance" (Foley, 2019:Britannica). The point here is not that the entirety of the Matthean Gospel was necessarily memorized and recited verbatim before being composed in written form. However, it is reasonable to conceive of the types of patterns and structures used in a majority-oral society also being used in written form. Repetition, and inclusio specifically, are helpful to oral traditions but also to written ones, especially those of a religious nature. Religious texts are meant to be catechetical, from one disciple to the next and from generation to the next.

devices at the disposal of authors are used to enhance the reading experience by engaging the reader in a variety of ways" (Tate, 2006:199). Just as rhetorical devices served certain purposes in the oral tradition, like the abovementioned repetition for memory's sake, so also do literary devices enhance the reading experience in diverse respects. This section covers some of those ways.

Tate defines a literary device as, "A strategy or apparatus employed by an author to enhance the reading experience and to engage the reader and making inferences about meaning. These literary devices may be rhetorical, as an issue of structure and plot, or more direct, as in figurative language. . ." (Tate, 2006:200). Later, Tate offers insight into the idea of rhetoric, especially as used in written form, by saying that it is "the art of composition for the purpose of persuading. Therefore, rhetoric implies that there are guidelines or rules of form and structure for effective composition" (Tate, 2006:322). So, the reader of the Matthean Gospel is right to be aware of rhetorical and literary elements in the composition and structure of the work, even the overall structure (Decaen, 2021:57). The previously documented sources have shown that rhetorical and literary devices have been employed from ancient times until the current day. This is the way that writers communicate to their readers. These devices make for effective communication. With his written words, the author intends to teach certain doctrines or convince his readers of a particular message. Often, he is trying to accomplish both simultaneously. In order to do so, literary devices and those coming from the art of rhetoric become useful tools. They help the writer to convey his message, but they also help the reader to understand what the main points are and to comprehend the overall message(s).

With the broader context of literary structure and devices in mind, the use of inclusio may now be specifically considered. What may be called micro-inclusios would be more easily recognizable because of the proximity of the opening and closing brackets, but macro-inclusios may also be found (Decaen, 2021:57-58). Sometimes the presence of an inclusio is obvious and apparent to the majority of readers. On other occasions, the literary device is less apparent, yet one may argue that subconsciously a less-apparent-inclusio still has an effect on the reader (Furnam, 1986:351-357).[32] One may argue that even if the reader is not aware of the inclusio at all, the device may still accomplish what the author intended. The reader does not need to know the technical jargon and the scholarly literature concerning a literary device for it to work. This is

---

[32] A student of the biblical text should be alert to the literary features but also careful not to find literary devices where they are not actually present (Wyckoff, 2006:478). This is sometimes difficult to determine, even for biblical scholars. "Not all scholars or readers will agree with every other reader's identification. Sometimes repetitions are incidental and not an intentional echo back to the beginning of a unit" (Longman, et al., 2008:324). So then, one must be alert but also cautious in reading the text. The book intends to help the reader of Matthew's Gospel to do both.

demonstrated by the simple fact that the literary structures and devices of the Scriptures have worked to be memorable, meaningful, and persuasive for centuries before the "discovery" or study of the devices was even considered.

The most common examples of inclusios are in the Psalms, likely because of their poetic and musical nature which is conducive to repetition. Nevertheless, inclusios are found throughout the Scriptures. In fact, several inclusios have been observed within the Gospel of Matthew. This fact will be demonstrated and discussed in later sections, and several examples will be supplied in each case.

Inclusios are sometimes overlooked by present-day readers. There are understandable reasons for this oversight. English translations of the Hebrew Old Testament and the Greek New Testament do not always preserve the structure or verbiage so that modern readers can recognize the inclusios (Chapman, 2013:119; Bullinger, 1898:249). These are not always apparent in translation. Chapman notes, "The original authors of the Bible were skilled performers who wrote for aural audiences. Sadly, due to distance, ignorance, or perhaps even scholarly apathy, elements of their art of have been ignored, neglected and temporarily lost" (Chapman, 2013:119).

For an example of the lack of clarity in translation, one may look to the Old Testament. Consider the passage in Gen 9:3. The NKJV translates: "Every moving thing that lives shall be food for you. I have given you all things, even as the green herbs." The NASB translates: "Every moving thing that is alive shall be food for you; I have given everything to you, as I gave the green plant." However, as noted by Chapman, "Everything" is the very first and very last word of the verse. He writes, "[T]his should be considered a strong inclusio, because (1) the word כל (everything) is exactly repeated, (2) it has been intentionally positioned precisely at the beginning and end of the verse, and (3) the repeated word is unique in the verse, not used again within the *includitur*" (Chapman, 2013:81). The NIV is at least one English translation that preserves the obvious inclusio: "Everything that lives and moves about will be food for you. Just as I gave you the green plants, I now give you everything." Of the meaning of the inclusio, Chapman explains, "Therefore, this inclusio is primarily meant to provide emphasis, highlighting the fact that everything (כל) is now permissible to eat" (Chapman, 2013:82).

Another New Testament example of an inclusio that often gets lost in translation is highlighted by Bullinger (1898:249). Paul says in Gal 2:20, "I have been crucified with Christ; it is no longer I who live, but Christ lives in me; and the life which I now live in the flesh I live by faith in the Son of God, who loved me and gave Himself for me." However, the Greek text actually says, "Χριστῷ συνεσταύρωμαι· ζῶ δὲ οὐκέτι ἐγώ, ζῆ δὲ ἐν ἐμοὶ Χριστός·" Bullinger offers his own translation to highlight the inclusio: "Christ, I have been crucified-together-with, yet I live; and yet it is no longer I that live, but, in me, Christ" (Bullinger, 1898:249). English translations typically do not maintain the inclusio in translation. One is quick to state that the reason the passage is translated so is because it makes for good English. However, the reader of the Greek text is able to see the inclusio and to learn from it the emphasis that the inspired writer places on Christ. The inspired Greek text places Christ in the place of priority and emphasis, while the English text, because of its grammatical rules, inadvertently places more emphasis on Paul, or the reader who imagines himself or herself in the place of Paul.

Inclusio is an enduring literary feature used in all types of literature from all sorts of places. A couple examples are offered by Quinn in his book, *Figures of Speech*. Consider the words of Stephen Crane recited by Quinn: "Do not weep maiden, for war is kind. Because your love turned wild hands toward the day and the affrighted steed ran on alone, do not weep. War is kind" (Quinn, 1993:88). Also reflect upon the poem of TS Eliot, one of the great writers of the twentieth century, likewise retold by Quinn: "O hidden under the dove's wing, hidden under the turtle's breast, under the palmtree at noon, under the running water at the still point of the turning world. O hidden" (Quinn, 1993:89). Both examples that Quinn submits display the use of inclusio in literature outside of the Christian Scriptures. So, to reiterate, inclusio is a feature that has been used in literature of all kinds for centuries.

Longman clues the reader into a few important items in reference to inclusios: "[I]nclusio delimits the preamble and points to a major theme" (Longman, 2008:325). Moreover, "Close readers will notice other instances of full and partial repetitions, and it will help them sense units as well as detect major themes" (Longman, 2008:325). There are a variety of uses, then, for the literary device of inclusio. It helps both the writer and the reader. For the writer, it helps him or her to structure the section or book, to convey the main message, and to highlight the supporting themes for that main message. For the reader, it helps him or her to sense the cohesion of the section or book, to realize and grasp the main message, and to find the supporting themes throughout the well-structured work.

Inclusio makes use of primacy and recency (Furnam, 1986:351-357). Primacy is the principle which states that words at the beginning of a speech or written document are more memorable.[33] Recency, on the other hand, is the principle that words at the end of a speech or document are more memorable.[34]

---

[33] "This refers to the process by which early information colours our perception of subsequent information. The common sense notion that first impressions are the most compelling is not always correct. First impressions may count most because subsequent information is more difficult to absorb—although recent information may be remembered most clearly" (Scott, 2014:Primacy). Internet. No page numbers.

[34] "A recency effect is the tendency for individuals to be most influenced by what they have last seen or heard, because people tend to retain the most complete knowledge about the most recent events" (Scott, 2014:Recency). Internet. No page numbers.

Inclusio makes use of both of these principles by bracketing the text with the same words or ideas at both the beginning and the end.

As seen above, there are many uses of inclusio in literature. The following sections will provide examples throughout the biblical corpus and discuss the uses therein. Assuredly, more uses of the important literary device will be displayed and discussed.

3.5 The Use of Inclusio in Old Testament Literature

The literary feature of inclusio is one that is employed often by the inspired authors of Scripture to great effect. Inclusio is recognized by contemporary scholars and has been so for some time (Chapman, 2013). While the prevalent feature is often observed, it is rarely well-defined or its effects thoroughly detailed. The previous sections of this chapter have detailed that point and have sought to give definition to the literary device. Now, the chapter may give attention to practical uses of inclusio as several examples are cited throughout the scriptural corpus.

Inclusio is a common literary feature in Hebrew literature (Longman, 2008:323-325; Chapman, 2013; Wyckoff, 2006). The Old Testament is known for long narrative sections, parallelism in its poetry, and other noteworthy literary characteristics. One should add to that list of distinctives the device of inclusio. There are numerous examples of it. A few are provided below with commentary.

A micro inclusio is formed in Gen 39:1, "Joseph had been taken down to Egypt" and "who had taken him down there." A larger inclusio is formed for the whole chapter in Genesis 39:2-3 and 39:21-23, "The Lord was with Joseph, and he was a successful man" and "the Lord was with him; and whatever he did, the Lord made it prosper."

Another is found in 1 Sam 3:1 and 21, "Now the boy Samuel ministered to the Lord before Eli. And the word of the Lord was rare in those days; there was no widespread revelation" and "Now the boy Samuel ministered to the Lord before Eli. And the word of the Lord was rare in those days; there was no widespread revelation."[35]

Yet another is found in Ruth 1:6 and 22, "Then she arose with her daughters-in-law that she might return from the country of Moab" and "So Naomi returned, and Ruth the Moabitess her daughter-in-law with her, who returned from the country of Moab."[36]

Psalms 1:1 and 2:12, "Blessed is the man" and "Blessed are all those who put their trust in Him." These two parallel phrases have caused many

---

[35] (Klein, et al., 2004:303) gives this as "prose examples" in a footnote.

[36] (Klein, et al., 2004:303) gives this as "prose examples" in a footnote.

commentators to think that the first two psalms were intended by the author and/or editors of the psaltery to be taken together. The first line of Psalm 1 along with the last line of Psalm 2 bind these two psalms together and bracket their content. From the opening section of the Psalms, which were purposefully placed here at the front although they were not the oldest psalms composed, the reader/worshipper learns, among several things, that the Psalms are didactic and welcome the worshipper into the "blessed" life.[37]

Psalm 8:1, 9 delivers a classic example of inclusio in the psalms (Wyckoff, 2006:477-478). The phrase, "O Lord, our Lord, how excellent is Your name in all the earth" is repeated verbatim at both the very beginning of the hymn and at the very end. When looking at the inclusio of Psalm 8, Klein suggests that the inclusio is important for two reasons: (1) The inclusio signals the main theme, and (2) the inclusio indicates that the reader must interpret the content within the bracket by bearing that main theme in mind. "In other words, they illustrate or amplify it" (Klein, et al., 2004:303).

A similar example from the Psalms is the inclusio created at the beginning and end of Psalm 118. The line, "Oh, give thanks to the Lord, for He is good; for His mercy endures forever" is given verbatim as the opening and closing lines of the famous song. The point of the psalm is to thank God for his saving works and to invite others to join in that thanksgiving. The content of the psalm, those verses "included" within the brackets, serves to support that main idea of thanksgiving and God's goodness. In doing so, examples and reasons are given for God's goodness and the needed response of thanksgiving on the part of the believer.

The book of Proverbs opens with a neat and straightforward micro inclusio. Solomon states in Prov 1:2 that his purpose in writing the Proverbs is for the reader "to know wisdom and instruction" and then in Prov 1:7 he affirms, "fools despise wisdom and instruction." Wisdom and instruction are said to be, from the very opening lines, the main point of the Book of Proverbs. The young man needs to hear and obey the wisdom and instruction of his father rather than despising it like the fools.

The prophet Jeremiah conveys a series of macro inclusios in his work. The prophet begins and ends his published oracles in Jer 1:1-2 and 51:64, "The words of Jeremiah the son of Hilkiah, of the priests who were in Anathoth in the land of Benjamin to whom the word of the Lord came" and "Thus far are the words of Jeremiah." The passage in Jer 51:64 does not constitute the very last words of the entire book. There is one more chapter that follows, but that final chapter relays historical notes rather than Jeremiah's sermons. So then, one may reasonably state that the entire book of Jeremiah is bracketed by a macro inclusio which conveys the main idea that the Lord spoke through the prophet Jeremiah.

---

[37] Moses' song numbered as Psalm 90 would predate Psalms 1-2 by a few hundred years.

Jeremiah 1:10 and 24:6 form another macro inclusio within the largest one, "See, I have this day set you over the nations and over the kingdoms, to root out and to pull down, to destroy and to throw down, to build and to plant" and "For I will set My eyes on them for good, and I will bring them back to this land; I will build them and not pull them down, and I will plant them and not pluck them up." This macro inclusio expresses one of Jeremiah's main ideas that God is sovereign over history and the nations and is working out his purposes in Judah's Babylonian captivity.

In Jer 1:11 and 24:3 there is yet another macro inclusio with similar question and imagery language: "Moreover the word of the Lord came to me, saying, 'Jeremiah, what do you see?' And I said, 'I see a branch of an almond tree'" and "Then the Lord said to me, 'What do you see, Jeremiah?' And I said, 'Figs, the good figs, very good; and the bad, very bad, which cannot be eaten, they are so bad.'"

Amos is famous for the continual repetition at the beginning and end of prophetic revelations (e.g. Amos 1:3-5). Several of the brief disclosures begin with, "Thus says the Lord" and then end with, "Says the Lord." The prophet makes clear throughout his work that what he is declaring is not his own wisdom or opinion, but a word revealed to him from the Lord.

The example from the book of Ecclesiastes will serve as an appropriate conclusion to this section on the use of inclusio in Old Testament Literature. Solomon crafts a macro inclusio to bookend his entire work. In Ecc 1:2 and 12:8, the author writes, "'Vanity of vanities,' says the Preacher; 'Vanity of vanities, all is vanity'" and "'Vanity of vanities,' says the Preacher, 'All is vanity.'"[38] On this bracketing, Longman states, "Ecclesiastes demonstrates that an inclusio can operate in a prose context. Indeed, there are no literary devices that are exclusive to poetry, though they may find a heightened and intensified use in poetry. . . . The effect of the repetition is that it leaves the reader in no doubt as to Qohelet's ultimate conclusion that the search for meaning in the world 'under the sun' is meaningless. This inclusio and its importance for discerning the message of the book of Ecclesiastes is recognized by many interpreters today" (Longman, 2008:323-324).

3.6 The Use of Inclusio in New Testament Literature

There is no surprise that inclusio is also a common literary feature in the New Testament documents as well. The New Testament authors were Jewish men themselves and more than well-acquainted with the Old Testament writings. Their thinking and writing would have been heavily influenced by what they perceived to be the inspired Word of God in the First Testament Scriptures. The Gospel of Matthew, the document most central to this

---

[38] Also see (Gavett, 2000:812-815).

research, is a prime example of this fact. Repeatedly, the author, with the relevant quotations cited, describes how events surrounding the life of Jesus Christ or deeds performed directly by him are fulfillments of Old Testament Scriptures.[39] Burridge enlightens readers with more figures, "Matthew has about 60 references of quotations from the Old Testament" (Burridge, 2014:76-77). So then, the Gospel of Matthew is steeped in the words, ideas, and theology of the Old Testament. The same is true of the remainder of the New Testament to varying degrees.

The Gospel of Mark is well known in biblical studies for the so-called "Markan sandwich" (Edwards, 1989). This occurs several times through the text, especially in narrative passages. Edwards comments thus about the literary pattern, "Mark begins story A, introduces story B, then returns to and completes story A." He goes on to say, "These inserted middles have been variously indentified as intercalations, interpolations, insertions, framing, or, in German, as Schiebungen or Ineinanderschachtelungen. A more graphic description, and one I prefer, is to refer to Mark's A-B-A literary convention as a sandwich technique" (Edwards, 1989:193-194). An example of this feature is found in Mark 5:21-24 where the narrative begins concerning the healing of Jairus' daughter. That narrative is interrupted by Mark 5:25-34 when the when with the issue of blood is healed. Finally, the narrative picks up where it left off at Mark 5:24 and in Mark 5:35-43, the story is concluded concerning the healing of Jairus' daughter. Edwards asserts that this technique occurs nine times in the Gospel of Mark (Edwards, 1989:193). On the sandwiching technique, Edwards argues, "The technique is, to be sure, a literary technique, but its purpose is theological; that is, the sandwiches emphasize the major motifs of the Gospel" (Edwards, 1989:196). There is a sort of bracketing effect that takes place with this technique, even if it is not exactly an inclusio. There is, however, more evidence of inclusio in Mark's Gospel. For example, there is a "doubling upon again" of Jesus being identified as "God's Son" at both his baptism and at his crucifixion. Mark 1:11 records at Jesus' baptism, "Then a voice came from heaven, 'You are My beloved Son, in whom I am well pleased.'" Then, at the crucifixion of Christ, Mark 15:39 records a Roman centurion exclaiming, "Truly this Man was the Son of God!" More explicit inclusios in Mark would consists of the macro inclusio concerning Peter in Mark 1:16 and 16:7 showing Peter's prominence in Mark's Gospel account; Mark 1:3-6 and 1:9-13 about John's baptism in the wilderness and Jesus' relation to it; and a double inclusio of Mark 1:16–20, 21–22 with 2:13, 14–15 recounting Jesus' teaching the multitudes and many following him.

The Gospel of Luke contains what appears to be a macro inclusio. Luke 1:2 begins the Gospel account with, "just as those who from the beginning were eyewitnesses and ministers of the word delivered them to us" and Luke 24:48 concludes the Gospel with, "And you are witnesses of these

---

[39] Matt 1:22; 2:6, 15-16, 23; 4:15-16; 8:17; 12:17-21; 13:14, 35; 21:4; 27:9-10.

things." Thus, the Gospel of Luke is framed by an inclusio emphasizing the great responsibility placed upon the disciples who witnessed all the things concerning Jesus' suffering, death, and resurrection. They were witnesses to the actual events, to the understanding of these things from the Old Testament Scriptures, and had, thus, been given the great responsibility of preaching repentance and forgiveness of sins to the nations on the basis of their witness to these facts concerning Jesus Christ.

John 1:1 and 20:28 also form a macro inclusio for the Gospel of John.[40] John 1:1 begins with the theological doctrine: "In the beginning was the Word, and the Word was with God, and the Word was God." John 20:28 concludes the Gospel with the practical confession of the believer, the confession that the apostle wants to engender in his readers: "Thomas answered and said to Him, 'My Lord and my God!'" The macro inclusio creates a start-to-finish depiction of conversion. Jesus Christ has come and accomplished all that he has and revealed God to the world, and now men and women are only left to respond, preferably with the same confession and doxology of Thomas.

The canonical Gospels are not the only New Testament documents to employ inclusios. The Pauline documents do as well. A couple micro inclusios may be offered as examples. Consider Rom 8:25 which begins and ends with hope when it says, "Hope that is seen is not hope." Likewise, Phil 4:4 begins and ends on the theme of joy when readers are commanded, "Rejoice in the Lord always, and again I say rejoice." The main body of the book of Colossians seems to be bookended by a fairly large inclusio. In Col 2:6-7, the apostle writes, "As you therefore have received Christ Jesus the Lord, so walk in Him, rooted and built up in Him and established in the faith, as you have been taught, abounding in it with thanksgiving." Then, in Col 4:5-6, the apostle echoes that first passage, "Walk in wisdom toward those who are outside, redeeming the time. Let your speech always be with grace, seasoned with salt, that you may know how you ought to answer each one." James Dunn goes so far as to say, "The exhortation to 'walk in wisdom' (ἐν σοφίᾳ περιπατεῖτε) is an effective summary of one of the main emphases of the letter, forming an inclusio with both 1:9-10 (ἐν πάσῃ σοφίᾳ . . . περιπατῆσαι) and 2:6-7 (ἐν αὐτῷ περιπατεῖτε)" (Dunn, 1996).[41] If Dunn is correct, then the inclusio in

---

[40] "All of this falls within another inclusio: two of the clearest statements in the NT about the 'divinity' of Jesus (1:1; 20:28). Within this inclusio, all statements about 'God,' if explicitly or implicitly linked to the Son, are correct (including 1:18 and 4:24), but those which are not so linked are mistaken (e.g., 8:41-42, 54; 9:16; 16:2), or inadequate (9:29)" (Sakenfeld, 2009:NT View of God, G.1.). Digital: Olive Tree Bible Software. No page numbers.

[41] (Dunn, 1996:Col 4:5). Digital: Olive Tree Bible Software. No page numbers. Also see commentary on the links between these key passages in (Pao, 2012:295).

Colossians is an even better example of a macro inclusio. The passages all refer to the "walk" of the Christian disciple. Believers are to carry themselves in a certain way within the community of faith and also among those who are outside the church, meaning unbelievers.

The book of Hebrews uses a passage from Jeremiah in Heb 8:8-12 and Heb 10:16-18 to create a bracket. This inclusio highlights the new covenant established by Jesus Christ. In this covenant there is forgiveness of sins and the Lord himself writes his law on the hearts of his people.

The book of James similarly provides yet another example of a micro inclusio. In Jas 2:14, the writer begins his point with the rhetorical question, "Τὶ ὄφελος." He also ends the point with the same phrase in Jas 2:16, "Τὶ ὄφελος;".[42] What he means by this is something like "What does it profit?" or "What good is it?" Peter Davids remarks on verse 16: "He concludes with the same expression found in 2:14, τί τὸ ὄφελος ("what's the use?"). In doing this he produces a type of *inclusio*: catch-phrase statement, statement repeated as an example, catch-phrase" (Davids, 1982:122). Why Davids refers to the literary device on this occasion as a "type of inclusio" is not exactly clear. The example is a solid one of an actual inclusio in the New Testament text.

So then, there are several uses of inclusio throughout the New Testament. Examples of inclusios have been shown in the Gospels, Paul's letters, and the general epistles. The apostles of Jesus Christ were uniquely inspired to write the 27 documents comprising the church's New Testament Scriptures. The apostles were thoroughly knowledgeable of the Old Testament Scriptures, fully acquainted with the literary devices employed therein, and evidently sophisticated in thinking and skillful in writing. The authors of the New Testament documents made good use of inclusio in their writings in order to teach their audiences, to make their points more memorable, and to emphasize central Christian principles.

3.7 The Use of Inclusio in the Gospel of Matthew

The Gospel of Matthew has a complex and sophisticated compositional structure. It has been said, "That Matthew was a skilled literary craftsman no one denies. Disagreements over the structure of this gospel arise because there are so many overlapping and competing structural pointers that it appears impossible to establish a consensus on their relative importance" (Carson and Moo, 2005:134). If one were to concede that the author of the Matthean Gospel were well-acquainted with the Old Testament, then it would be a logical conclusion that the figures of speech, literary and rhetorical devices, and structures of various Old Testament writings were recognized and appreciated by that author. Matthew must have known the recurring literary

---

[42] Some manuscripts read, "τί τὸ ὄφελος;".

device of inclusio. He quotes extensively from the Old Testament (Burridge, 2014:76-77; Viljoen, The Torah, 2018).

Several examples of inclusios in Matthew can be given. An initial example is Matt 4:23 and 9:35 which says, "And Jesus went about all Galilee, teaching in their synagogues, preaching the gospel of the kingdom, and healing all kinds of sickness and all kinds of disease among the people" and "Then Jesus went about all the cities and villages, teaching in their synagogues, preaching the gospel of the kingdom, and healing every sickness and every disease among the people." The repetition found in these two passages provides structure and cohesion to the narrative account. The inclusio helps to summarize and transition from one part of the narrative to the next. The threefold ministry of preaching, teaching, and healing that Jesus carried out in the Galilean villages is highlighted by this inclusio.

The Sermon on the Mount provides another example. The famous sermon begins with the Beatitudes in Matthew 5 and is bracketed by an inclusio. The first Beatitude in Matt 5:3, "Blessed are the poor in spirit" and the last Beatitude in Matt 5:10, "Blessed are those who are persecuted for righteousness' sake" are both followed by the same promise: "For theirs is the kingdom of heaven." Carson calls the inclusio a "stylistic device" and remarks, "This means that everything bracketed between the two can really be included under the one theme, in this case, the kingdom of heaven" (Carson, 1982:16). This inclusio frames the Beatitudes and points the reader to the central theme of kingdom living. Readers are signaled to the fact that the Beatitudes describe citizens of the kingdom of heaven and all the divine benefits the accompany that citizenship.

A second example of inclusio in the Sermon on the Mount is found at Matt 5:17 and 7:12 using "the Law and the Prophets" phrase. In Matt 5:17, Jesus is recorded as saying, "Do not think that I came to destroy the Law or the Prophets. I did not come to destroy but to fulfill." Then, in Matt 7:12, the Lord is recorded as saying, "Therefore, whatever you want men to do to you, do also to them, for this is the Law and the Prophets." Referring to the entirety of the Old Testament, this inclusio bookends the main part of the Lord's message. The Sermon on the Mount is seen as an expositional sermon as Jesus extensively quotes and explains Old Testament Scriptures within this frame. Blomberg acknowledges the inclusio when he comments, "With its reference to 'the Law and the Prophets,' 7:12 ties back in with 5:17 and provides a frame to bracket the body of the sermon" (Blomberg, 1992:131). A central point of the Sermon on the Mount is therefore made obvious by the inclusio: The Lord Jesus has come to accurately interpret the entirety of the Hebrew Scriptures.

A final example, and one that is almost universally recognized, is a very large inclusio that bookends the whole Matthean Gospel. Many commentators have remarked on Matt 1:23 and 28:20 as a macro inclusio (Sakenfeld, 2009; Angel, 2009:527; Hagner, 1995:888-889; Gundry, 1994:597; Harrington,

1991:415; Boxall, 2019:51).[43] This particular inclusio, many have said, was constructed in order to show the prophecy and fulfilment of the Emmanuel theme (Carson, 2010:669; Wilkins, 2003:958; Hagner, 1995:888). In the beginning, Matthew tells the reader that the angel declared the newborn Jesus to be "Emmanuel, God with us;" and at the end, the Risen Lord Jesus himself says, "I am with you always." Consider the following summary on this point: "Matthew's Gospel begins with the prophecy that the Savior's name would be 'Emmanuel, that is, 'God with us," (1:23, in which the author has linked Isa 7:14 and Isa 8:8, 10 together) and it ends with Jesus' promise to be with his disciples forever. The Gospel of Matthew thus forms an inclusio about Jesus in his relationship to his people that suggests his deity" (NET, 2003:1744).

While it is reasonable to conclude that Matt 1:23 and 28:20 form a macro inclusio around the entirety of the Gospel of Matthew, it is also likely fair to argue that the theme highlighted by this specific inclusio is not the only main theme in the Gospel. The mission of Christ is more than simply "God with us." It is certainly not less than that idea, but it is also more than that. The mission of Christ, as conveyed in Matthew's Gospel, must include the meaning of the cross, or, at least, one would assume so. The remainder of this chapter sets out to argue for another book-long, macro inclusio that may be even more significant than this well-accepted one.

3.8 The Purpose of Inclusios

Following the sections above of the various definitions of inclusio and my own definition, the use of inclusio in both Old Testament and New Testament literature as well as the use of the literary device in the Gospel of Matthew, the question may now be asked and answered: What, then, is the purpose of an inclusio? The subsequent paragraphs in this section will catalog the numerous purposes of inclusio.

First of all, repetition is used because, "The original authors of the Bible were skilled performers who wrote for aural audiences" (Chapman, 2013:119). The inspired writers of Scripture knew their culture and audiences. They wrote for the ear and for memory. Their documents are didactic, so they wanted the lessons to be memorable. To do so, they took full advantage of the principles of the primacy and recency effects (Foley, 2019:Britannica). What is said or written at the beginning and end is most memorable for the audience.

Another decidedly important aspect of the device of inclusio is to give structure to the literary work. Consequently, the passage or book is accorded maximum cohesion by the structure of the inclusio. The material is better

---

[43] "In Matthew the twofold affirmation of the divine presence in Jesus (1:23 and 28:20) form an inclusio for almost the whole Gospel" (Sakenfeld, 2009:NT View of God, G.1.). Digital: Olive Tree Bible Software. No page numbers.

organized and more easily understood through carefully devised and finely written structures. Accordingly, the relation of materials is demonstrated. Moreover, one might reasonably determine that if an entire book is bracketed by an inclusio, then those brackets must call attention to an essential message for the entire book.

The inclusio can also give literary and theological beauty and style that standard prose may miss without symbolism and express literary features (Chapman, 2013:119; Piper, 1986). This point of the purpose of inclusios is linked to the last about structure. Literary devices make manuscripts more enjoyable to read and effortlessly appreciated. Like many other structural and literary features, once an inclusio is discovered, the reader likely will experience joy at the discovery and the artistic beauty of the work of God through the Holy Spirit inspired authors. There are several other purposes for inclusios, as this section exhibits, but readers of the Christian Scriptures should not pass over the beauty of the God-breathed literature but can appreciate it for beauty's sake.

One of the more obvious and useful purposes of inclusio is to inform the reader of a significant theme. Repetition is highly effective to highlight an important topic. Inclusio is used to summarize an argument and to emphasize. A main point or multiple central issues are made clear through its use.

To link from the previous point, sometimes viewed similarly to chiasms, inclusios may point to the passage(s) and theme(s) at the center of what is bracketed. This could be used to highlight the main idea of the section that is contained within the brackets but summarized in the wording of the bookends themselves. What comes between the two brackets is "included" in that unit of thought and can be the main point itself or can support the main point.

Inclusio tells the reader how the material should be read. Piper notes, "The value of seeing this is that it warns us against treating any little piece of the section in isolation. Matthew is the writer here, and he is putting his material together in a particular way. He is the inspired author, and we should care about how he chose to put things together. That is the way he gets across his meaning" (Piper, 1986).[44] The reader of Scripture should not read any section in isolation. There are broader points to be ascertained. The fullest knowledge of any given passage is found in the wider context. Structure and other literary features help the reader to discover not just a small point here or there but all that the author intends to convey to the audience.

Lastly, an inclusio is a marker and tool. In the simplest understanding of the literary feature, inclusio is a device or tool available to the writer. The author uses the tool to indicate to the reader that something has happened. One does well to remember that there were no paragraph or chapter breaks in

---

[44] Internet. https://www.desiringgod.org/messages/the-beatitudes-and-the-gospel-of-the-kingdom. No page numbers.

the original. Defining literary markers were beneficial for the writer and for his or her audience.

3.9 The Criteria for Determining the Presence of an Inclusio

After investigating the various definitions of inclusio propounded by the scholarly community and examining the different uses of inclusio in the biblical literature as well as the purpose of inclusios, in general, one may begin to detect the appropriate function of the literary device and prepare a list of criteria by which to determine if a biblical author is making use of inclusio.

Chapman (2013:73-79) outlines in impressive detail a sophisticated system of criteria and evaluation. He suggests that students of the Scriptures should think of inclusios in terms of a sliding scale.[45] Some inclusios are stronger and some are weaker. Stronger inclusios are based on exactness, positioning, and uniqueness. The more exact the repetition, the stronger the inclusio. On positioning, the closer the repetition is to the actual beginning and end of a section or book, the stronger the inclusio. On the third criterion of uniqueness, Chapman writes, "As a general rule, the Biblical authors make the repeated elements of the inclusio more prominent by avoiding these elements within the enclosed material and in the surrounding material. . . . Therefore, a unique repetition makes a stronger inclusio" (Chapman, 2013:76). In utilizing these key factors, one may measure the strength of an inclusio. The scholar cautions that some repetitions are so weak that they may not even be categorized as inclusios at all. Chapman does provide secondary factors in helping to determine an inclusio but notes that they are not as definitive. He considers items such as the length of the repetition, the unity of the enclosed content, and other delimiters such as formulaic sayings.[46]

How does one know that what he or she is noticing in a text is an inclusio? Criteria may be established to help the reader ascertain the presence of an inclusio. Chapman has provided a useful discussion, but I will now put forward my own set of criteria that will be used in the book at hand. The following set of questions will be asked of any given passage in question: Is there repetition at the beginning and end? Is the same word or phrase repeated at the end from the beginning? Is the same idea or set of ideas conveyed again? Does the potential inclusio stand out from the surrounding text or come as a surprise to the reader? Is the saying unique?

Repetition at the beginning and end of a passage or book is the most basic element of an inclusio. If a reader realizes that something is being repeated at the close of a section that was first introduced at the beginning,

---

[45] Also see (Wyckoff, 2006:481) on this discussion of a "sliding scale."

[46] The content of this entire paragraph conveys and discusses the ideas of (Chapman, 2013:73-79).

then there is a good chance that an inclusio has been encountered. There will be a sense of circling back, summarizing, and wrapping up.

Specifically, the repetition that comes at the beginning and end of a small or large section will often repeat the same word or phrase. Sometimes a synonym will be used but that makes for a weaker inclusio. The presence of the literary device is most obvious when the exact same word is repeated. If an entire phrase is repeated verbatim, then inclusio is highly likely.

Even if the bracketing at the opening and closing does not include the repetition of a word or phrase, it could contain the repetition of the same idea or set of ideas. This also makes for a strong inclusio. The parallel could possibly be of a key theme rather than simply the echo of a word.

Sometimes an inclusio will not fit the context or is a surprise. This is yet another sign that an inclusio is present. By introducing a surprise into the text, the content of that disclosure is emphasized for the reader. The reader (or listener) has his or her attention renewed and focused. An inclusio often stands out from the surrounding context because the author is resuming a previously disclosed word, phrase, or idea.

Sayings that are unique to the author's work are a further indication that the author is forming an inclusio. There are internal and external considerations to be made on this point. If the writer only uses a keyword at the beginning and end of a section or book but does not use the word or phrase anywhere else within the body of the section or work, then there is a strong possibility an inclusio is intended. Alternatively, if no other biblical author uses the keyword, key phrase, or main idea, then a compelling argument can be made for an inclusio. In the case of the inclusio in Matthew, the former point does not stand but the latter does and is maybe the most significant point. The idea of salvation from sins and the forgiveness of sins is made not only in the inclusio but also throughout the Gospel. This, accordingly, is support for the thesis. However, looking externally, the Gospel of Matthew provides two unique sayings which are not found in the other canonical Gospels: "He will save his people from their sins" and "Shed for many for the forgiveness of sins." Depending on one's view of the dating of the Gospels, this point will be more or less significant, but the point of the distinctiveness of the two passages is significant either way.[47]

Consequently, for the purpose of this research project, the following criteria will be used to judge whether or not a passage employs an inclusio:

---

[47] If Matthew was produced first, then one may wonder why the other Gospel writers, dependent to a certain degree upon the First Gospel, did not reproduce the two sayings. If Mark came first, then Matthew likely inserted the unique sayings into the beginning and ending sections of his Gospel purposefully to create an inclusio. As to the significance of the inclusio in comparison and contrast with the other Gospels, the former would be weaker and the latter stronger. However, the significance stands in either case.

Repetition at the beginning and end; same word or phrase repeated; same idea or set of ideas conveyed again; something outstanding or surprising about the passage; and the uniqueness of the wording or idea.

3.10 The Inclusio with Reference to "Sins" at the Beginning and End of Matthew's Gospel

The texts of Matt 1:21 and 26:28 which form a macro inclusio both contain phrases which are unique to Matthew's Gospel (Viljoen, 2020:1; Blanton, 2013:393). One scholar comments: "The prologue itself is linked to the epilogue (26:1–28:20) by an inclusio formed by the announcement that God would be present in the ministry of Jesus (1:23), which echoes the promise of the resurrected Jesus of his continuing presence in the church (28:20). This inclusio provides a frame for the interpretation of Matthew's extended διήγησις (3:1–25:46) of Jesus' words and deeds. In the prologue, the identification of Jesus as the saviour of his people (1:21) also foreshadows the declaration by Jesus (26:28) that he would save his people from their sins by giving his life as an offering. The literary frame provided by the prologue and epilogue of Matthew thus clearly emphasises that forgiveness is an important motif in its διήγησις" (Nel, 2015:2).[48]

Several scholars have acknowledged the connection between Matt 26:28 back to Matt 1:21.[49] However, no commentators seem to have elaborated upon the connection. Moreover, the thesis is that Matthew intended to provide an inclusio. This is not an accidental connection or a simple connection. The argument is that it is purposeful and provides a central explanation of Matthew's message about the mission of Christ and the meaning of the cross. Thus, in the ensuing paragraphs, the potential inclusio of Matt 1:21 and 26:28 will be detailed. The attempt will be made to demonstrate how these two passages meet the previously established criteria for an inclusio.

The first criterion concerns the question of repetition. Is there something repeated at the beginning and end? As one reads through the Matthean Gospel, one sees that there is something that stands out from the text at both the beginning and end of the book and is repeated. In both Matt 1:21 and Matt 26:28, the reader finds two intriguing passages or sayings. The two passages seem to be similar in many ways, and this is the first clue that it may be an inclusio that one has encountered.

---

[48] Nel footnotes (Nolland 2005:380). The reference must be to Nolland's acknowledgment that, "The 'bracketing' effect of 1:21 and 26:28 establishes sin and its forgiveness as key concerns for Matthew."

[49] E.g. Nel, 2015:2; Nolland, 2005:380; Carson, 2010:603; Carter, 1998:62; Ham, 2000:62; France, 2007:994; Bruner, 1990:967; Przybylski, 1980:106.

The second criteria to consider is whether or not the same word or phrase is present in both passages in question. In this case, there is only one word that is presented in both passages. The word is "sins" (ἁμαρτίαι). While at first the reader may think that one word is inconsequential, yet several items should be evaluated. First, not only does the word appear in both passages, but the term is given in the plural in both cases. Second, the word "sins" is a critical and loaded term in the biblical corpus. Third, the word is linked to the mission of Jesus Christ. So then, the student of Matthew sees that the first two criteria for an inclusio are met by Matt 1:21 and Matt 26:28.

The next criterion to consider is whether or not the passages convey the same idea or set of ideas. The first passage claims that "she will bring forth a Son" and names the Son, "Jesus." The second passage does not express this idea precisely, but it does give the parallel: "My." The Son, Jesus Christ himself is the one speaking in the first person. So then, the person of Jesus is present in both passages. The first passage also communicates the idea of salvation from sins. Does the second passage do this same thing? Yes, in the idea of the forgiveness of sins. The idea is present in both passages.

The fourth criterion proposed which should be evaluated in relation to Matt 1:21 and 26:28 is that sometimes an inclusio will not exactly fit the context or comes as a surprise to the reader. This would be a sign that the segment is an inclusio. To say that the phrases or ideas in these two passages of Matt 1:21 and 26:28 do not fit their context would not be quite right. However, it seems reasonable to affirm that in both passages there is a surprise. The claim in Matt 1:21 that the newly conceived Son would "save his people from their sins" comes as a surprise and gives reason for the reader to be intrigued and to search the rest of the Gospel to see exactly how Jesus will fulfill this prediction. The saying in Matt 26:28, this Jesus' blood "is shed for many for the forgiveness of sins" also comes as a shock to the reader. When considered in light of Matt 1:21 which had set the pace for the entirety of the Gospel, the reader is surprised all the more that Jesus will save from sins by the shedding of his own blood. Thus, both passages, at the beginning and end of the book of Matthew, have an element of surprise.

The last criterion to inspect is the question of the uniqueness of the sayings to the passage or book. The reference to sins is not unique to the brackets but can be seen in multiple prose passages as well as narratives throughout the book. The same is true of salvation and forgiveness. These ideas and even the exact words are referred to not only in the brackets but also throughout the Gospel account. In fact, later chapters of this book will argue that the passages that discuss sins and forgiveness and salvation are enclosed within the brackets and serve to support the main idea conveyed in the inclusio brackets. So then, the terms and ideas of the brackets are not unique when looking internally at the Gospel of Matthew. However, the two passages in question, Matt 1:21 and Matt 26:28 both contain sayings which are externally unique to Matthew. The other Gospel writers do not include the sayings:

"[Y]ou shall call His name Jesus, for He will save His people from their sins" (Matt 1:21), and "For this is My blood of the covenant, which is shed for many for the forgiveness of sins" (Matt 26:28).

In the case of the macro inclusio in Matthew, this last criterion is maybe the most significant point. Both the Matt 1:21 and Matt 26:28 passages contain sayings which are unique within the Matthean Gospel and unique to Matthew when compared with the other two Synoptic Gospels. Only Matthew provides the explanation in the birth narratives of Jesus' name because "He will save His people from their sins." Furthermore, only Matthew provides in the context of the Last Supper the words of Jesus Christ that his blood "is shed for many for the forgiveness of sins." The reader of the Gospel of Matthew can easily pick up on the exceptionality of these two verses, and the student of the canonical Gospels will also notice the distinctiveness of the Matthean Gospel at these points. The uniqueness of these two passages is likely the strongest argument for a macro inclusio.

One may argue that Matt 26:28 is not the precise end of the book. This is true, strictly speaking. There are two and a half more chapters of narrative after this scene. However, the passage does seem to be a closing section before the Gospel's epilogue. Everything that needed to be documented and explained concerning Jesus Christ to set the reader up for the finale of his crucifixion and resurrection comes to a culminating point at the end of Matthew 26. The mission of Christ that was first predicted in Matt 1:21, "He will save his people from their sins" is finally interpreted straightforwardly by Jesus himself in Matt 26:28, his blood will be "shed for many for the forgiveness of sins." There is a full circle, a wrapping up, a climax point. The idea was first birthed in the opening sections of the story and now comes to maturity in Jesus' interpretation of the meaning of the cross. All that is left to relay after Matt 26:28 are the historical facts of these things coming to pass.

After thoroughly reviewing the potential inclusio of Matt 1:21 and 26:28 through the five previously established criteria of repetition at the beginning and end; same word or phrase repeated; same idea or set of ideas conveyed again; something outstanding or surprising about the passage; and the uniqueness of the wording or idea, one can reasonably conclude that these two passages constitute the brackets of a macro inclusio. One may now consider the significance of the literary device in Matthew's Gospel. If one accepts the validity of this inclusio, then: (1) The Matthean Gospel has a unique perspective on the mission of Christ and the meaning of the cross amongst the four canonical Gospels. Matthew has a distinctive approach to explaining Christ's significance. (2) This has implications for the doctrine of man as well. Man's condition. Man's depravity. (3) We learn the meaning of "he will save his people from their sins." (4) We have cause to look back through the whole of the Matthean Gospel with an eye toward better seeing this "major theme."

Now that the inclusio of Matt 1:21 and 26:28 has been reasonably authenticated, Matthew's purpose in using the inclusio may be considered. The first point seems obvious. Matthew has used the inclusio to make the main point of Christ's mission to forgive sins by his death on the cross most memorable. Taking advantage of what is now known as the primacy effect, Matthew set the stage for the main point of the mission of Christ in the opening section of his Gospel (Pitrowski, 2013:35). Then, making the most of what is now called the recency effect, Matthew circles back to that opening section at the end of the book to show that the meaning of the cross is bound up with the mission of Christ to "save his people from their sins." He will do this by shedding his blood on the cross for the forgiveness of sins.

Matthew gives structure to his Gospel with these two bookends. There is a coherence infused in the literary work by the framing. Then, as the reader thinks back over the content of the whole book, he or she better understands how the *includitur* supports the structure of the inclusio. Chapters four and five of the book will examine the *includitur* and elaborate on the connections to the brackets of Matt 1:21 and 26:28.

There is little doubt that the reader of the Matthean Gospel will grasp the literary beauty when the macro inclusio is detected and considered. Matthew's main point is demonstrated artistically through the literary feature. The theological beauty of the mission of Christ and the meaning of the cross is creatively displayed in the structure that the inclusio furnishes.

The main idea of the mission of Christ culminating in the meaning of the cross is highlighted by the outer brackets of the inclusio themselves. The main idea, or at least one of the main ideas of the First Gospel, is emphasized by the repetition at the beginning and end. Since the entire book of Matthew is bracketed, the important message of the entire book is well accentuated.

An inclusio gives structure to a literary passage or book. This has been reviewed in preceding sections and paragraphs. The brackets themselves highlight a main idea. What is also vital to note is that the *includitur*, the intervening material that is included within the brackets, is also highlighted. An inclusio does not, of course, require that the content within the brackets use the exact same terminology or phraseology, although it could. However, what does need to be repeated, is the same idea. An inclusio is a literary device slightly different from straightforward repetition. What is enclosed in the envelope structure needs to support the main idea conveyed in the outer brackets. So, as will be described in the next two chapters of the book, the intervening material that is included within the brackets of Matt 1:21 and 26:28 should support the structure and theme of the macro inclusio.

Matthew is telling his readers how his Gospel account should be read. Through the use of inclusio, he is pointing his audience to a main idea of the salvation from sins through the forgiveness that Jesus Christ offers through his shed blood on the cross. In a skillful and creative way, Matthew is, in essence, saying to the reader, "Read my entire Gospel account with the understanding in mind of salvation from sins by the forgiveness offered through the shed blood of Christ." When the reader hears the repetition in the closing bracket in Jesus' words, "shed for many for the forgiveness of sins," he or she may also hear Matthew saying, "Go back and read the Gospel again with this in mind." The reader is being told: What happens next (the crucifixion and resurrection) is the fulfillment of Christ's mission, and you already know ahead of time the meaning of the cross, that is, salvation from sins by the forgiveness offered through Christ's shed blood.

Lastly, Matthew surely uses the inclusio as a marker and tool. He is sectioning off the main bulk of his Gospel as a thorough prelude to the climactic events of Christ's death on the cross and his impending resurrection. All of what is written in the first 26 chapters are leading up to the summation of the last two and a half chapters, and Matthew tells the reader this in the beginning, Matt 1:21, "He will save his people from their sins." He then reminds the audience of this main idea before the reader comes to the concluding section of the Gospel.

3.11 Summary and Relevance of the Argument

In familiarizing New Testament students with the Gospel of Matthew, Carson and Moo (2005:162) propose a mental exercise. They want the reader to imagine that the Matthean Gospel "suddenly disappeared." The question is, what would be missing from the New Testament? What contribution(s) would be left out? The sweeping summation from Carson and Moo is, "If Matthew suddenly disappeared, much of its material would still be found, more or less intact, in Mark and Luke. In that sense, Matthew cannot be said to make the same sort of independent contribution that Hebrews or the Apocalypse does, for example" (Carson and Moo, 2005:162). However, the argument here is that Matthew does make exceptional contributions, even if they are of a different sort from other New Testament documents. The point is granted that Matthew has much of the same material as the other Synoptics. Arguing otherwise would be difficult. Yet, the reader of the New Testament and the whole of the Christian Church would be worse off without Matthew's Gospel and his above-explored inclusio. The inclusio itself provides two significant statements exclusive to the First Gospel.

Joseph surely had very little initial understanding of what was meant by the saying, "For he will save his people from their sins." The same was likely true for the original readers of the Matthean Gospel and is to be expected for many readers of the Gospel today. The claim here is that the reader cannot fully grasp the statement from Matt 1:21 until he or she reads the words of the Lord Jesus Christ in Matt 26:28, "My blood shed for the forgiveness of sins." The two passages are purposefully linked together by the author in an inclusio so that the reader more fully understands the mission of Christ and the meaning of the cross.

Citing Carter's thoughts on this connection in Matthew may be helpful presently. While not designating the passages as an inclusio and not elaborating extensively, he writes of the connections, "For the audience, this saying with the words 'the Son of Man has come' in 20:28 is, thus, a further interpretive clue about Jesus' life and mission. In the context of the previous six 'I have come' sayings the audience under- stands this seventh saying to mean that Jesus performs his divinely commissioned purpose of saving from sins not only in his deeds and words but also in his death. This understanding will be confirmed in 26:28 when he identifies the passover cup as 'my blood of the covenant poured out for many for the forgiveness of sins' (ἁμαρτίαι), the key word deriving from 1:21. His resurrection from the dead (chap. 28) in accord with his predictions (16:21; 17:23; 20:19) makes God's presence available to disciples 'all the days' (πάσας τὰς ἡμέρας, 28:20), in accord with his God-given mission of manifesting God's presence as Emmanuel (1:23)" (Carter, 1998:62). Carter articulates well the essence of the First Gospel. He sees the relationship of the various texts and pulls them all together.

So then, to restate the viewpoint of the book, it has been concluded that Matt 1:21 and 26:28 are deliberately linked together by the inspired author of the Gospel. Reading one without the other will not give the reader the fullest meaning of the mission of Christ and the meaning of the cross. Subsequent chapters will delve into exactly what is the mission of Christ and exactly what is the meaning of the cross.

While it is true "that a neat, coherent Christology may not emerge from the gospel" (Tuckett, 2001:119), it is reasonable to find a very helpful interpretive key given to the reader by Matthew in this inclusio (Nolland, 2005:380). One can best understand Matt 1:21 after realizing and exploring the connection that Matt 26:28 makes with it. "He will save his people from their sins" by shedding his blood. Salvation comes by forgiveness in Christ Jesus. The mission of Christ is most fully comprehended through all of the Matthean Gospel, including all of the narrative, didactic, and prose passages, by discovering and applying the macro inclusio. The meaning of the cross is most easily apprehended and appreciated with the knowledge of the inclusio. Interestingly, the Lord Jesus himself in Matt 26:28 interprets the prophecy concerning his mission.

While some highlight the Emmanuel/Great Commission passages of Matt 1:23 and 28:20 as an inclusio to demonstrate that God has come near in the person of Jesus, what may be of more significance is the large inclusio of Matt 1:21 and 26:28. This inclusio emphasizes the significance of Jesus' mission and the meaning of his cross. The bracketing that Matthew generates explains the meaning of Christ's mission and his cross, that is, the forgiveness of sins. Important to note in support of this view is that both passages refer to sins (and even in the plural, one might add). Furthermore, the strength of this thesis lies in the fact that both passages are unique to Matthew's Gospel. The Matthean literary feature could be called a panoramic inclusio because of the all-encompassing nature of the literary device.

The aim of this research project is not to answer the question, and there is no space to pursue this line of thinking here, but one may begin to consider whether or not the two macro inclusios in Matthew's Gospel (Matt 1:21 and 26:28 as well as Matt 1:23 and 28:20) are meant to combine to express one main idea (Kunjanayil, 2021). This would be a thesis to pursue in further research. The proposition would go something like this: The two macro inclusios in Matthew's Gospel combine to communicate the main idea that God is with us to save us from our sins.

The thesis of the work at hand is that the Gospel of Matthew has a unique Christological perspective which is highlighted by a large or "macro" inclusio. The inclusio is labeled large because, rather than bracketing a single pericope, as most commonly done, this one forms at the beginning and end of Matthew's Gospel account. The bulk of the Matthean Gospel, then, "connects the dots" with various supporting verses according to this theme. Within the structure of intercalation, the author employs parallels, contrasts, miracles, controversies, parables, and more to develop his major theme (Tate, 2006:425). These supporting episodes will be analyzed in the subsequent chapters.

The mission of Christ and the meaning of the cross are definitively highlighted by the inclusio of Matt 1:21 and 26:28. The bulk and heart of the Matthean Gospel are explained and emphasized by the inclusio. The mission of Christ was to save his people from their sins. This is presented in the opening passages of the Gospel account. Christ fulfilled the missional prediction by shedding his own blood for the forgiveness of sins, as the closing bracket elucidates. This is the meaning of the cross. This is what happened in the suffering and death of Christ. Matthew is demonstrating why Jesus came and why he had to die, his mission and the meaning of his cross.

There has been debate over exactly what is an inclusio. There are various terms used and definitions offered for the literary feature, as shown above. Some may even deny that there is such a thing as a large inclusio, that is, an inclusio bracketing a large section or the entirety of a biblical book. However, the thesis of this project is that Matthew actually does employ a macro inclusio for the entirety of his Gospel account.

Now that the inclusio of Matthew 1:21 and 26:28 and its significance has been shown to be a plausible feature of the book, the remaining chapters of this study will turn to investigating the *includitur*, or body, of the Matthean Gospel with an eye toward better seeing the mission of Christ and the meaning of the cross as salvation and forgiveness of sins. Although Tate references the Gospel of Mark, the principle is applicable to the Gospel of Matthew as well: "Although we are told directly that Jesus is the Messiah and the son of God, we can discover what these titles mean only in the context of [the] story" (Tate, 2006:426). It is only when one takes the material within the brackets in light of the bookends themselves that one understands fully what the author of the Matthean Gospel meant to convey.

Chapter 4: The Forgiveness of Sins in Matthew's Gospel

The forgiveness of sins is a distinctive doctrine of Christianity. From the first Christian sermon in Acts 2 and down to the present, this doctrine has been proclaimed by countless Gospel preachers.[50] The complexity of Christian doctrine and the long history of interpretation have established the idea that God was in Christ saving the world from sin through the forgiveness secured by his death as a foundational Christian principle.

The fact that several scholars have noted the theme of forgiveness in Matthew and yet there has been little systematic treatment of the subject in Matthean studies is acknowledged by Nel and agreed upon here (Nel, 2015:1). To help remedy the situation, this chapter aims to catalog the passages within Matthew that pertain to the subject of the forgiveness of sins and then to expound upon each of them. The criteria used to determine key texts on which to comment will be the following: a passage that is part of the opening or closing brackets of the large inclusio; a pericope that deals directly with the problem of sin; a text that refers explicitly or even implicitly to the subject of forgiveness, actually employing the term or conveying the notion; and any pericope that speaks to the mission of Christ, including any "I have come" statements. Moreover, special interest will be given here in chapter four to demonstrating the connections of each of the passages expounded upon concerning the forgiveness of sins to the macro inclusio advanced in the previous chapter of the book.

4.1 Matthew 1:21 Jesus: He will save his people from their sins

The section which constitutes the first half of Matthew's macro inclusio is Matt 1:21. The text is distinctive in multiple ways. Jesus Christ's mission is clearly stated at the very beginning of the book ("he will save"). That mission of Christ is explicitly connected to salvation from sins ("he will save his people from their sins"). Thus, the mission of Christ is made plain, and the theme of salvation (and, arguably, forgiveness) takes prominence from the start of the Gospel because of this verse. Moreover, the angelic message of Matt 1:21 is unique to Matthew (Viljoen, 2020:1; Blanton, 2013:393). The other two Synoptic Gospels do not record the narrative, and the content of the message is not relayed in the same way in any other book of the New Testament. Matthew alone provides this central introductory announcement from on high.

---

[50] See Acts 2:38, in particular.

When the reader enters, "The account of the life of Jesus Christ, the son of David, the son of Abraham,"[51] Joseph is already found to be betrothed to Mary. This was, in effect, a legal marriage, even though the union had not been consummated (Carson, 2010:99; Keener, 2009:89). During this time, Mary is already found to be with child. The Evangelist quickly adds theological commentary: She was found with child "of the Holy Spirit." Thus, at this point in the narrative, Joseph is mulling over the thought of secretly divorcing Mary. In the midst of that distressing episode, God intervenes through an angelic messenger. Matthew uses one of his favorite terms to catch the reader's attention: ἰδού ("behold"). The word is often used to mark surprising elements in the narrative and in connection with an act of God's intervention, especially angelic encounters in the early chapters of Matthew's Gospel.[52]

An angel of the Lord appears to Joseph in a dream to speak forth God's revelation to him. Dreams were a well-known means of revelation from above in Jewish tradition (Boxall, 2019:50). In a published article, focusing on later chapters in Matthew, Viljoen says more generally of angels in the First Gospel: "Angels play a significant role in the characterisation of Jesus in Matthew's Gospel. Matthew does not tell who the angels are or how they relate to the Father. He assumes knowledge of Jewish angelic traditions among his readers. However, he adds new perspectives on the relation of the angels with Jesus, which enlivens his portrait of Jesus" (Viljoen, 2020:6). From opening to closing in the Matthean account, angelic activity is conspicuous. Viljoen is certainly right in his assertions concerning Matthew's recording of the role of angels in the life and ministry of Christ. Angels are a part of the mission of Christ in interesting and impactful ways. What Viljoen claims is not any more obvious than in the passage recorded in Matt 1:20-21. An angel of the Lord plays the significant role of explaining the virginal conception and origins of Jesus Christ. This revelatory role of the angel in the very first chapter begins to add new perspectives and to enliven Matthew's portrait of Jesus, to echo the words of Viljoen. The angel tells Joseph that God is at work, there is no reason to fear, Mary should be taken as his wife, the Son conceived in her is of the Holy Spirit, he is to be named Jesus, and the mission and purpose of Jesus, the Son, is to save his people from their sins. Matthew's portrait of Jesus is already taking shape in vivid ways in this first angelic revelation.

The statement that she will bring forth a "Son" is also significant. The new Son, Jesus Christ, is connected back to the patriarchs as the son of Abraham and the son of David (Matt 1:1). Through this genealogy, as the Son, Jesus is also associated with Israel and her history (Matt 1:2-17). Moreover, the Son is most immediately linked with Joseph who is addressed by the angel as "Joseph son of David" (Matt 1:20). The link with Joseph as his adoptive father

---

[51] See Matt 1:1 and the BDAG entry on γένεσις (2000:192-193).

[52] E.g., see Matt 1:20, 23; 2:1, 9, 13, 19; 3:16; 4:11.

is especially important in making Jesus a son of David.[53] As the next two verses of Matt 1:22-23 confirm, the Son, Jesus Christ, is also fully identified with God. Jesus' sonship is divine sonship. Gundry attests that divine sonship is a prominent theme in Matthew (Gundry, 1994:24).[54]

Joseph is to give the Son his name. Joseph will be the adoptive father (Keener, 2009:86). The legal realities of adoption today are similar to those of ancient times but not precisely the same. In ancient times, adoption was common, especially for one who did not have an heir (also see Gen 15:2; 16:2; 30:3). The Romans had laws concerning adoption (Wansink, 2000:990-991). Maybe the most famous adoption in history is Julius Caesar's adoption of Octavian (later, Emperor Augustus) (Moo, 2002:47). Adoption does not seem to have been as prominent in the Jewish community though, but it did take place. For the adoptive father to name the child only adds to the significance of the legal and familial responsibilities he assumes for the child (Turner, 2008:67). To name the child is to demonstrate authority over the child but also to take responsibility for him. Joseph will be accountable for raising Jesus. Joseph is addressed in Matt 1:20 as a son of David. As stated above, this must be to reinforce what Matthew has already told the reader: Jesus is a legitimate descendant of David. Thus, Gibbs comments, "Because the heir of David will take Mary as his wife even though the child in her womb is not his own, this will bring Jesus into the royal line of David" (Gibbs, 2006:106). A son of David adopts the Son of David.

The name "Jesus" had a long history in Jewish tradition, dating all the way back to the first famous "Joshua" (Exod 17:9; see Gibbs, 2006:107).[55] Dale Allison states: "'Jesus,' a name common among Jews before the rise of Christianity, derives from Hebrew yeshuaʿ (יֵשׁוּעַ), from yshʿ (ישׁע), meaning 'to help' or 'to save.' This is why Matt 1:21 glosses 'Jesus' with the words 'he will save his people from their sins'" (Sakenfeld, ed., 2009).[56] To these points, one might add the comments of Hagner: "The Greek form of the name *Iesous*, which was translated into Latin as *Jesus*, is the same as the Hebrew *Yeshua* (Joshua), which means 'Yahweh saves' (Yahweh is typically rendered as 'Lord'

---

[53] Gibbs provides a helpful paragraph on the significance of Jesus as "Son" (Gibbs, 2006:106).

[54] Matthew replaces Isaiah's name with a note that the statement come from the Lord. Also see Matt 2:15 "for the same phenomenon in the only other fulfillment-quotation containing a reference to Jesus as "a son" (Gundry, 1994:24).

[55] Reflecting on the biblical name "Joshua" (i.e. Jesus), Turner points out, "In the NT, Moses's successor Joshua is viewed as a type of Christ (Heb. 3-4)" (Turner, 2008:67).

[56] Article on "Jesus Christ." Digital: Olive Tree Bible Software. No page numbers.

in the OT)" (Hagner, 1993:19). The editors of the NET Bible affirm: "It was a fairly common name among Jews in 1st century Palestine, as references to a number of people by this name in the LXX and Josephus indicate" (NET, 2003:1687). So then, the name "Jesus" means "Yahweh saves" and had a rich tradition in the Jewish world (Quarles, 2017:21). While the newborn would often be named immediately upon birth, the formal introduction of the infant to the community along with the announcement of his name would have been at the time of his circumcision (Hagner, 1993:19).[57] Joseph received the angelic directives for the naming of the Son long before his birth, much less his circumcision. Joseph and Mary have the name months in advance.

Fathers and mothers intended for the names of their offspring to have significance (Keener, 1993:48; Hagner, 1993:19). Culturally, names had meaning. Sometimes the circumstances surrounding the child's arrival would be the basis for the child's name.[58] Other times, parents envisaged the child's character and destiny (Hagner, 1993:19).[59] There was certainly significance in the fact that parents named their children. Furthermore, there was meaning in the names they selected. However, arguing from the lesser to the greater, if God gave the name for the child, the name and destiny of the person was thought to have greater value (Keener, 1993:48). Those newborns were "considered to be particularly important and righteous people" (Davies and Allison, 1988:210).

What is the meaning that is conveyed by the name "Jesus," the name God expressly reveals? As already stated, the name "Jesus" means "Yahweh saves" or "Yahweh is salvation." Thus, "The saving character of Jesus . . . is aptly evoked by his name" (Davies and Allison, 1988:209). God elects the child's name to reveal the purpose of his mission (Chamblin, 2010:199). This child, conceived of the Holy Spirit of God, will be on mission to save his people from their sins, primarily through the forgiveness of sins (Matt 26:28).

The further elaboration upon the name cannot be missed: "For he will save his people from their sins." Quarles comments, "The clause introduced by γάρ shows why the name is appropriate" (Quarles, 2017:21). The Son's name and the meaning of it becomes foundational to the rest of the Matthean Gospel (Chamblin, 2010:146; Nel, 2015:2; Kunjanayil, 2021:22). The amplification is a partial quotation of Ps 130:8 (Pitrowski, 2013:33; Newman,

---

[57] See Gen 17:12-14; Lev 12:3; Luke 2:21.

[58] See Gen 4:1; 16:11; 17:17-19; 25:25-26.

[59] Gen 4:2, 25; 5:29.

1988).[60] Turner provides a helpful summary of the background: "The angel here alludes to Ps. 130:8, where Israel is exhorted to trust in Yahweh's unfailing love because Yahweh would redeem Israel from all their sins. Thus Jesus, already shown to be the miraculously conceived Son of God and about to be revealed as 'God with us,' is portrayed as Yahweh's agent in effecting this eschatological salvation" (Turner, 2008:67).

In the phrase "He will save," the "He" is emphatic. The Greek text states: αὐτὸς γὰρ σώσει, "He himself will save." Numerous commentators note the emphasis (Davies and Allison, 1988:210; Gibbs, 2006:99; Obsorne, 2010:77; Quarles, 2017:21; Hagner, 1993:19). The question is the meaning that the author intends. Osborne thinks it "means that Jesus alone can bring eschatological salvation to humankind" (Osborne, 2010:77). Furthermore, Chamblin is surely right to conclude: "This opening instance of sōzō [save] will prove to be foundational for all further references to Jesus' saving works" (Chamblin, 2010:146).[61] Speaking to Matthew's storyline, Kingsbury comments: "In relation to his mission, Jesus is 'saving,' 'authoritative,' and utterly 'certain' that he is accomplishing God's purposes. The single most fundamental character trait ascribed to Jesus is the power to save, as the angel declares to Joseph: '. . . you shall call his name Jesus, for he will save his people from their sins' (1:21)" (Kingsbury, 1988:12).[62] So again, the mission of Christ and the meaning of the cross begin to germinate here in the opening bracket of the macro inclusio. Throughout Matthew's διήγησις, the theme will sprout and grow.[63] By the time the reader makes it to Matt 26:28, the closing bracket of the macro inclusio, the theme will have fully developed and then will produce its fruit in the epilogue, chapters 27-28.

Matthew seems to use the future tense specifically as the "predictive future" when quoting the angelic announcement in this verse. The predictive future can be defined this way: "The future tense may indicate that something will take place or come to pass. The portrayal is external, summarizing the action: 'it will happen.' The predictive future is far and away the most common use of this tense" (Wallace, 1996:568). While this use of the future tense is the most common, it also seems the most appropriate for an angelic message from

---

[60] Although, Pitrowski provides an appealing alternative: "Ezekiel 36:28b-29a; 37:23b, however, provides a more convincing and more fruitful conceptual background for Matthew's programmatic verse" (Pitrowski, 2013).

[61] "Matthew 1:21 is programmatic for the entire Matthean narrative" (Pitrowski, 2013:35).

[62] Also see (Kingsbury, 1988:45-46).

[63] The term διήγησις is used by (Nel, 2015) to refer to the "long narration" or the bulk and main body of the Gospel book.

God foretelling the mission of Christ. The angel says, Mary "will give birth," and Christ "will save" his people. Under the sovereignty of God, these things are sure to occur and have effect. Joseph could be confident of it. Of the certainty, Repschinski writes, "The formulation itself leaves no room for speculation. It is an announcement of what will take place in the future. Joseph is not given a choice. He is told what will happen to Mary and what he has to do with the child" (Repschinski, 2006:254). The first-time reader or hearer of Matthew's Gospel, of course, could take courage that God was at work in the arrival and then unfolding life and mission of the Son. The long-time student of Matthew reads the prediction knowing with certainty that it was fulfilled but also with the full knowledge of exactly how it was accomplished: The cross of Christ (Matt 20:28; 26:28; 27:26, 32, 35, 50).

Contra Carter, salvation from Roman occupation or oppression is not what was needed (2001:75–92), and, per Chamblin, the necessary salvation was "not 'from their enemies,' nor 'from every social ill or physical affliction or mortal peril'" (Chamblin, 2010:146). Quite the contrary, the angel affirms that the Son will save his people from their own sins. Rescue from sins is what the people needed. One might say, "Jesus came to deliver his people from personal sin and thus to deliver them from its judgment" (Keener, 1993:48). Moreover, Davies and Allison emphasize the religious and moral nature of Christ's saving work (Davies and Allison, 1988:210; also see Gibbs, 2006:107). According to Gibbs, forgiveness is included in salvation, but the salvation that Jesus brings or secures is much more. It also entails "healing and full eschatological restoration" (Gibbs, 2006:107). "He comes to save his people — body and soul — from their sins" (Gibbs, 2006:107).[64] If the mission was to save the people from their personal offenses against God and the just punishment of them through forgiveness in the first place, one might also reason from there that the "rescue from sins" encompasses much more beyond that initial stage.

In guiding translators, Newman notes that "save" is sometimes translated as rescue, redeem, and set free, but suggests that it is better to make clear in the translation that Jesus will rescue people from the situation or effects of sin and even from God's punishment because of their sins (Newman, 1988).[65] The interpretative nature of his translational suggestions should be recognized, yet his points are helpful to translators. However, the scholar's theological conclusions go awry when he comments: "It would not be right, either, to translate *save* as 'forgive.' Jesus will not forgive his people, but rather will bring about God's forgiveness" (Newman, 1988). To say that Jesus will

---

[64] Also see Novakovic who makes this point (2003:69–75), and consider: "Perhaps, then, Matthew thought that Jesus saved his people from their sins in a variety of ways" (Davies and Allison, 1988:210).

[65] Digital: Olive Tree Bible Software. No page numbers.

bring about God's forgiveness is fair enough. The problem, as readers of the New Testament know, is in stating that "Jesus will not forgive his people." The word σώσει, it is true, should be translated as "he will save" in the sense of deliver or set free rather than "forgive" (Perschbacher, 1990:399; BDAG, 2000:982), but numerous passages challenge the theological comment that Jesus is not meant to be the one to forgive his people.[66] In New Testament theology, Jesus Christ is typically seen as the agent of God's forgiveness.[67] Nevertheless, as God incarnate, Jesus is seen as forgiving sins directly at times. Moreover, as Repschinksi puts it, "Throughout his Gospel Matthew prefers the verb ἀφίημι in connection with the forgiveness of sins. It is probable, though, that Matthew was persuaded to use σώζειν in 1:21 because of the possibility of the wordplay on the name of Jesus" (Repschinski, 2006:255). Matthew likely saw a clear connection and even overlap of the terms ἀφίημι and σώζειν.

What are "sins"? In the study of Classical Greek thinking and usage, ἁμαρτία is often considered a "misjudgment" or even a "tragic flaw" in someone's (usually even a hero's) character, but many scholars, interpreting Aristotle and the Greek Tragedies, are coming to believe that the Greeks thought of the term and idea as more of an error or mistake rather than a character defect (Leftkowitz and Romm, 2017:xx, 811; BDAG, 2000:50). New Testament usage is distinctive, pulling its background from Old Testament notions more so than Greek Tragedies. Thus, the BDAG defines the biblical term as follows: "A departure from either human or divine standards of uprightness—sin (with context ordinarily suggesting the level of heinousness)" (BDAG, 2000:50). Other glosses for the term given by BDAG include "a state of being sinful, *sinfulness*," and "a destructive evil power, sin" and notes that Paul uses the term almost in personal terms, and Hebrews uses it as the power that deceives humanity and leads to destruction (BDAG, 2000:51). Quarles also highlights the personification of "sins": "The statement seems to personify 'sins,' portraying them as enemy combatants who have captured people and keep them as hostages or slaves until Jesus rescues them. The statement is likely an allusion to Ezekiel 36:28–29; 37:23 and is linked to the prophet's promise of a new Exodus and new covenant" (Quarles, 2017:21). Louw and Nida define the term under the subdomain of "sin, wrongdoing, guilt" as, "to act contrary to the will and law of God" (Louw and Nida, 1988:1.773). The term has been translated and defined in various ways (Newman, 1988). Matthew tends to view the term as a separation from God in need of remedy because of a man or woman's wrongdoing.[68] Nolland provides a helpful overview of Matthew's

---

[66] See, for example, Matt 9:2; Luke 7:48; 23:34.

[67] Acts 2:38; Eph 1:7; 4:32; Heb 9:15, 28; 1 John 1:7-9; et al.

[68] See Matt 1:21; 3:6; 9:2; 12:31; 26:28; etc. Also see (Osborne, 2010:77; Newman, 1988). "Salvation in Matthew can refer to deliverance from physical danger, illness,

usage: "What might be involved for Matthew in being saved from sins can be clarified by looking at his later references to 'sins': John the Baptist's ministry provokes the confession of sins (3:6); Jesus himself forgives sins (9:2, 5, 6); his blood is finally 'poured out for the forgiveness of sins' (26:28; cf. 20:28). Also pertinent is Jesus' orientation to 'sinners' in 9:10-13; 11:19, and perhaps also his call to greater righteousness in 5:20" (Nolland, 2005:99).

As noted previously, "Jesus came to deliver his people from personal sin" (Keener, 1993:48). The sins are individual, particular, and manifold.[69] Yet, the state of sinfulness is experienced by all of his people. As one scholar comments: "That it is 'his people' whom Jesus will save from their sins brings to the fore here the corporate dimension of forgiveness and its connection with the covenant (as in 26:28)" (Nolland, 2005:99). Moreover, the sins are against God and are under his righteous judgment. "The translation of this sentence will then be something like 'He will rescue his people from the effects of their disobeying God'" (Newman, 1988).[70] Jesus is seen as coming to deal with the sin problem. He will save his people from their offenses against God which have resulted in the just wrath of God against them.

One last matter in this passage should be assessed in relation to the forgiveness of sins. Those in need of Jesus' saving work are referred to as "his people." Who are these people? The people are thought to, in some sense, belong to Jesus. Gibbs boldly assumes: "That 'the people' are called his, that is, Jesus' people, places the Christ in the position of God himself" (Gibbs, 2006:107). If this is the case, then an answer may be more readily available. All people belong to God in some sense (Deut 10:14; Ps 24:1). Of course, those chosen by him from among the nations belong to him in a special sense (Deut 7:6; Ps 100:3). Yet, can it simply be assumed that this places the Christ in the position of God himself, as Gibbs asserts? The Scripture does teach, for example in Isa 43:11, "I, I am the Lord, and besides Me there is no savior." God alone is savior, and God is at work in the events recorded in Matthew 1. Additionally, the Emmanuel passage of Matt 1:23 makes clear that the Son is to be understood as embodying God's presence. Therefore, connections leading to Gibbs' assumption are possible but without a fuller exploration into the matter, one cannot say for certain that Matthew intended his readers to draw this conclusion simply from the phrase "his people." Unfortunately, Gibbs does not provide any elaboration on this interpretive notion.

The question is still at hand: Who are these people who belong to Jesus, the people he will save from their sins? The interpreter is faced with two

---

and death (Matt. 8:25; 9:21-22; 24:22), but salvation from sins is the focus of the angel's announcement here" (Turner, 2008:67).

[69] Note the plural: ἁμαρτιῶν.

[70] Digital: Olive Tree Bible Software. No page numbers.

primary options, it seems, for the meaning of "his people." The term, λαός, can refer to Israel (Luz, Matthew 1-7, 2007:121; Repschinski, 2006:256; Keener, 2009:97; Newman, 1988) or the Church, now including the broad "people of God" (Davies and Allison, 1988:210; Osborne, 2010:77; Hagner, 1993:20; Turner, 2008:68; Brown, 1993:131).[71] This research project settles with the latter interpretation, primarily because of the overall thrust of the Matthean Gospel.

Throughout Matthew, λαός seems to refer to Israel. Although, the Lord Jesus declares in Matt 21:43, "Therefore I say to you, the kingdom of God will be taken from you and given to a nation bearing the fruits of it." Because of this passage, it is concluded, "So the majority of commentators are probably correct to identify 'his people' with the ecclesia of both Jew and Gentile" (Davies and Allison, 1988:210). Over against Luz and echoing Davies and Allison is Turner who comments, "It is perhaps significant that the allusion to Ps. 130:8 substitutes 'his people' for 'Israel'. . . . [I]t is more likely that this expression implies the biblical-remnant concept of a genuine Israel within national Israel" (Turner, 2008:68; also see Green, 1992:157).

Therefore, the "people" who are "his" are likely all his disciples. This would include the original twelve, crowds of Jewish disciples, countless disciples from the nations, and all future disciples (Matt 28:18-20).[72] His people are also those from the past who looked forward to the work of God, even the coming of the Messiah (Matt 8:11). Indeed, Jesus of Nazareth came from a dysfunctional family line. So, when the angel tells Joseph to name the Son "'Jesus,' because He will save his people from their sins," this is likely even a backward look at Jesus' own family tree. The people in need of salvation are all those who belong to him by faith from ages past to centuries ahead.

The student of Matthew's Gospel learns quickly that Matt 1:21 is foundational to Matthew's presentation of Christ, his mission, and the meaning of his cross. Not only is the text foundational, but it will reveal significant echoes throughout the work. Marius Nel has written, "Every mention of Jesus' name in the διήγησις therefore reminds the reader of his mission to save his people from their sins" (Nel, 2015:2).[73] In fact, every time the reader or hearer encounters the name "Jesus" throughout the rest of the Gospel account, the

---

[71] This is not meant to oversimplify the issues put to categorize the main interpretive camps. The assertion of Repschinski is well-respected: "The precise meaning of λαός in Matthew's Gospel is a matter of intense debate" (Repschinski, 2006:255).

[72] For a more thorough discussion on the matter of the identity of "his people," see (Repschinski, 2006). Note that Repschinski draws a different conclusion, believing "that in his saving activity Jesus will be taking possession of his people, and this people is Israel" (Repschinski, 2006:256).

[73] For more work on forgiveness in Matthew, see (Nel, 2013) and (Nel, 2017).

reader will harken back to the words of the heavenly angel "he will save his people from their sins."

Therefore, Luz is prepared to comment, "This provisional high point of the story makes a christological messianic statement. It first speaks of Jesus' meaning in the context of Jewish expectation: that the Messiah will be the savior of his people is a common Jewish hope. The statement, however, that he will save the people 'from their sins' is unusual as a Jewish hope. This reflects the Christian experiences with Jesus. Matthew in particular has a special interest in the forgiveness of sins that happens through Jesus and continues to be effective in the church" (Luz, Matthew 1-7, 2007:95). What was predicted from the very conception of the child had lasting ramifications in the experiences of the early Christians down to current days.

4.2 Matthew 6:12-15

The Sermon on the Mount is the most famous sermon ever delivered. The text is also a central part of the makeup of the Matthean Gospel. At the heart of the Sermon is the so-called Lord's Model Prayer. In the section on prayer, Jesus teaches about the nature of forgiveness. Not only does the Lord Jesus teach his followers to pray about issues of forgiveness, but he even elaborates on the point after the model is provided. Significantly, "The petition on forgiveness is the only clause of the prayer which is singled out for comment at the end (vv. 14-15)" (France, 2007:249).

Contrasting with those who take the reference to debts in Matt 6:12 to mean only financial deficits (e.g., Overman, 1996:98; Wright, 1997:55-56), the context seems to speak to a broader sense of moral indebtedness to God and between people. Several commentators understand the line to mean something like moral transgressions (Nolland, 2005:290; France, 2007:249-250; Keener, 2009:223). In this context, the word refers to sins generally (Carson, 2010:206). Of course, this could include financial debts and much more. Yet, Blomberg is likely correct when he comments straightforwardly, "Spiritual debts to God are first of all in view" (Blomberg, 1992:120).

So then, "debts" and "transgressions" are both accurate translations, but transgressions may be the best choice here so as not to confuse the contemporary reader who would limit debt to financial burdens. After an in-depth study of this passage to decide whether or not Matthew means monetary debts, Nel concludes, "it does not appear that he regarded the remission of monetary debts as a precondition for receiving forgiveness from God in the Lord's Prayer. . . . In order to make it clear that Matt 6:12 does not refer to the cancellation of monetary debts it should therefore he translated as 'and forgive (ἀφίημι) us our transgressions (ὀφείλημα), as we ourselves have forgiven our transgressors (ὀφειλέτης)'" (Nel, 2013:102-103).

Verses 12-15 seem to function together as a unit of instruction on forgiveness (Carson, 2010:206).[74] There is even a possibility that all the lines should be read together on the same subject on forgiveness. If so, one might read the Lord's words as saying, in essence, "And, Father, forgive us our transgressions, as we ourselves forgive our transgressors. And do not put us to the test, we ask, but deliver us from the evil of unforgiveness—For if you forgive others their wrongdoings, your heavenly Father will also forgive you, but if you do not forgive others their wrongdoings, neither will your Father forgive your wrongdoings." Again, this is only a possibility and may be worth a more thorough exploration at another time.

Verses 14-15 certainly reinforce what Jesus taught his followers to pray in verse twelve. With the repetition, the reader learns just how important forgiveness is for the Christian community (Carson, 2010:209; Hagner, 1993:152). This does not mean that we can earn forgiveness by forgiving others (Carson, 2010:207; Hagner, 1993:152). What it does reveal is that God will only forgive the kind of person who is sorrowful and truly repentant (blessed are the poor in spirit); the kind of person who forgives others (Hagner, 1993:152). Just as we need forgiveness from God, and God enjoys forgiving us, so do others need our forgiveness, and we should emulate God in extending forgiveness to them. Surely, "a close parallel is maintained between God's forgiveness and ours. . . . [O]ur concern, like God's, is to be with personal relationships" (France, 2007:250).

The one who is said to be on mission to save his people from their sins (Matt 1:21) includes in the heart of his most prominent sermon an encouragement toward forgiveness as a part of a regular prayer life. The follower of Christ and worshipper of God is to think on matters such as forgiveness, seek forgiveness for oneself, and extend forgiveness to others. Forgiveness is to be a mark of the Christian community, those who belong to the one who has come to save his people from their sins.

4.3 Matthew 9:2, 5-7, 12-13 The Son of Man has power on earth to forgive sins

Matthew, by inspiration of the Holy Spirit, narrates in chapter nine one of the few recorded descriptions of Jesus declaring someone's sins forgiven. In chapter one of his Gospel, Matthew recounted to the reader what the angel said to Joseph, Christ's adoptive father. The messenger said, "And she will bring forth a Son, and you shall call his name Jesus, for He will save his people from their sins." This was Jesus' mission on earth—to save his people from their sins. As indicated earlier, Jesus is normally understood to be the mediator of God's forgiveness, but, as God incarnate, he is sometimes seen

---

[74] "The first three petitions stand independently from one another. The last three, however, are linked in Greek by 'ands'" (Carson, 2010:206).

as directly forgiving sins himself. He often acts authoritatively as only God can. For this reason, his opponents accuse him of blasphemy.[75] The text of Matt 9:2 is one of those occasions. Again, this is in keeping with Matt 1:21 that he himself will save his people from their sins. The one said to be the Savior from sins is now actively forgiving the sins of a man, and he does so on the basis of faith.[76]

Capernaum had become the Lord's new hometown (Matt 4:13). He had settled by the Sea of Galilee. Matthew records three sets of miracles that happen on each side of the Lake. He healed a leper with only a touch (Viljoen, 2014, Healing). He healed the centurion's servant without even seeing the boy. He also healed Peter's mother-in-law of a fever. He then cast out many demons with only a word. He calmed the storm on the sea. Then he cast out numerous demons from two men and into a herd of swine. Matthew's arrangement of the narratives demonstrates that he is building up evidence to demonstrate Jesus' divine authority. In the Matt 9:2ff passage, the onlookers recognize that Jesus is claiming for himself the authority of God, especially to forgive sins.

4.3.1 Matthew 9:2

After demonstrating Jesus' authority over disease and demons, Matthew now shows that Jesus even deals with sin. Osborne provides a reminder of what sin is: "'Sin' refers to that basic self-centered aversion toward God's laws, and sin clearly throughout the OT was the cause of God's wrath poured out on the nation of Israel" (Osborne, 2010:77).[77] By grouping these several episodes together, Matthew makes evident that the forgiveness of sins is spiritual warfare. He is on mission to deal with sin. Destructive demonic activity, debilitating diseases, and dangerous storms are all a part of the disorder in the creation that instigated the mission of Christ to come into the world to save his people from their sins.

To heal a sickness is one thing. To have the power to deal with sin, the core cause of mankind's problems, is a whole other thing (Viljoen, 2014, The Law). Gibbs notes that, "Sin ultimately is the root of all human suffering and need. The sin of Adam and Eve brought the curse of death, sickness, and every malady upon the human race. . . . Jesus speaks to the root cause of all need, and he invites this person to be brave, for even as he is encountering Jesus, Jesus is in the act of forgiving his sins" (Gibbs, 2006:459). Matthew

---

[75] E.g., Matt 9:3; 26:65.

[76] "The forgiveness of sins reminds the reader of the angel's prediction that Jesus would save his people from their sins" (Turner, 2008:248).

[77] Osborne goes on to say, "Christ alone has provided the antidote for sin once-for-all (cf. Matt 3:6; 9:9–13; 11:19; 20:28; 26:28; Heb 7:27; 9:12, 26, 28; 10:10)" (Osborne, 2010:77).

wraps Jesus' mission, authority, and compassion all together in this captivating episode. The ministry of Jesus pierces far deeper than surface level social or moral improvement—even to the depths of humanity's problems, namely, sin.

The narrative recorded at the beginning of Matthew 9 is the well-known account of the men who lowered their paralytic friend through the roof (Mark 2:3-12; Luke 5:18-26). As he retells the narrative, Matthew does not provide the details of the friends going to the roof because they could not get past the crowds, removing the roofing tiles, and lowering their friend down in front of Jesus. In fact, Matthew does not indicate any particulars of the setting including the detail that he was indoors, likely in a house (Nolland, 2005:379). Matthew is focused on one point: Jesus' authority and power to forgive men their sins. The dialogue is key to grasp the point that Matthew is making, which is why many of the details of the incident are excluded (France, 1985:165; Luz, 2001:26). The author of the First Gospel deems it crucial to his message to address the subject of the forgiveness of sins. He made this clear in Matt 1:21 and now demonstrates Jesus beginning to fulfill that description in Matt 9:2. The fundamental nature of the mission of Christ is put on full display in this passage.

Jesus states clearly and emphatically his authority to forgive the sins of mankind. He does so autonomously (Antwi, 1991:23). The main point in this passage is authority (Nolland, 2005:380). Jesus claims to have the authority to forgive sins, usually seen in the Scriptures as only the prerogative of God (Ps 32:5; 49:7-9, 15; Isa 1:18; 55:7; Dan 9:9). Apparently, Jewish tradition believed that even the Messiah could not forgive sins (Antwi, 1991:23).[78] In his presence and even while he speaks, forgiveness of sins is being conferred through Jesus' own authority and on the basis of no other person or thing (Gibbs, 2006:456). Not only does Jesus declare the man's sins forgiven, but he addresses the man as "son" (or "child") which puts Jesus in the place of authority.[79] Thus, Turner comments, "When these verses are taken with other Matthean texts (6:10; 16:19; 18:18; 28:18), Jesus's future universal authority is implied" (Turner, 2008:249).[80] The reader learns that Jesus' mission to save from sins, which will culminate in his atoning death, also includes healing from various maladies (Davies and Allison, 1988:210). The reader notes that healing, or what might

---

[78] At the same location, see Antwi's footnote 24 with references to Jewish tradition.

[79] Gk. τέκνον. Some would say the label "son" simply means that the man was younger than Christ (Blomberg, 1992:153). Morris claims that it was just "a warm and friendly form of address" (Morris, 1992:215). However, the language of "son" or "child" was often used by those in authority toward those in their care (e.g., John 13:33; Gal 4:19; 1 Tim 1:2, 18; 1 John 2:1, 12-13, etc.).

[80] Turner follows (Nolland, 2005:380) here who says, "Once again the focus is on the authority of Jesus, now exercised in yet another realm."

be deemed "saving," is connected to the forgiveness of sins. Jesus has authority over illness but also over the root cause of illness which is sin (Gibbs, 2006:459). He delivers folks from the surface level issues and also from the internal ones, from the immediate and the perpetual problems.

The Lord Jesus himself links faith with forgiveness. Apparently, the vast majority of translations render the phrase in the middle of verse 2: "When Jesus saw their faith." However, Gibbs translates the line as: "and because Jesus saw their faith" (Gibbs, 2006:454). If Gibbs is correct, his rendering of the phrase would provide an even more explicit connection, even a causal link, of faith to forgiveness. Thus, in Matt 9:2, the Gospel reader learns that the one said in Matt 1:21 to be on mission to save his people from their sins comes in the authority to do so and brings about that salvation through the forgiveness of sins when someone trusts in him (i.e., faith). Not only can the healed man "take heart" (or "be of good cheer") because his sins were forgiven but every reader of the First Gospel can be encouraged that the forgiveness of their sins is available through faith in the Lord Jesus Christ.

4.3.2 Matthew 9:5-7

Matthew does not relay what Jesus' foes said in reply, if anything, to the question, "Which is easier to say?" Maybe the question was rhetorical (France, 2007:346; Davies and Allison, 1991:92). Jesus, however, makes his response to the question abundantly clear. Neither healing nor forgiveness could be offered from any other person. Nevertheless, Jesus is revealed to be more than capable of bringing about both (Antwi, 1991:27). In a dramatic manner, an argument is made from the greater to the lesser, from the difficult to the easier. Jesus is shown to perform the more demanding act in healing the man (a claim that had to be immediately proven) and is simultaneously justified in pronouncing the judgment: "Your sins are forgiven." The healing is the proof of forgiveness (France, 2007:346). Jesus can both heal the effects of sin and sin itself. This is important. In the thinking of ancient Judaism, sin and sickness were tied closely together (Carson, 2010:101; Davies and Allison, 1991:93; cf. Viljoen, 2014, The Law).[81] Some sins have immediate and direct effects in people's lives while others are more indirect. The reason people suffer at all is because they live in a fallen world. A theological point made often in the Scriptures is that even if people have lived upright lives and pursued the things of God's kingdom, they may still suffer in this age because it is "fallen."[82]

---

[81] "[I]n the biblical perspective, sin is the basic (if not always the immediate) cause of all other calamities" (Carson, 2010:101).

[82] Gen 3:14-19; John 16:33; Rom 5:12; 2 Cor 12:7-10; and could Job also be viewed this way?

The Son of Matt 1:21 was said to save his people from their sins. Now, this same one claims to be the Son of Man and to have authority on earth to forgive sins.[83] The title "The Son of Man" is defined and understood by the Christian tradition in the words of Jesus himself. On this point, the words of Jesus as he employs the term "are decisive for Matthew and his readers" (Luz, 1992:8). This Son of Man, therefore, is the divine figure with authority, power, dominion, and glory. He receives worship and reigns over the nations. Jesus is not only claiming but exhibiting a glimpse of that heavenly authority on earth. Considering the inclusio, and especially the closing bracket of Matt 26:28, the student of Matthew's Gospel knows that Jesus' authority is based not only on his essence as God but also on the forgiveness of sins secured by the shedding of his blood for many. The one coming on the clouds of heaven is the same one who has authority on earth to forgive sins and secures that salvation of his people by his own precious blood.

4.3.3 Matthew 9:12-13

The proverb Jesus communicates in reply to the question of verse eleven may have been one that was well-known, but one cannot know definitively (Nolland, 2005:386). The phrase appears innocent enough as it stands, but considering the tension between Christ and the Pharisees, this statement becomes an indictment of their counterfeit "righteousness." The quotation from Hos 6:6 is important in the Matthean development of Jesus' arguments with the Pharisees (Viljoen, 2014:214). In fact, Viljoen believes that the Matthean community may have even had conflict with some sort of Pharasaic component years after Christ's ministry (Viljoen, 2015:214). Jesus' statement in 9:13 is ironic (Gibbs, 2006:471; Luz, 2001:35). Christ says, "Those who are well have no need of a physician, but those who are sick." In making this statement, Jesus is not endorsing the Pharisees as "well." Instead, he is criticizing them for *supposing* that they are well, spiritually and morally speaking. In the first place, Jesus agrees with the Pharisees' assessment of his company by categorizing them as the "sick," but the Lord's views diverge quickly from the Pharisees because he sees them as "needy and able to be helped, rather than as contaminated and spurned" (Nolland, 2005:386-387). Jesus' point, over against the notions of the Pharisees, is that through healing, indeed even his saving work, the sick can be made whole (Nolland, 2005:387). Cutting through the irony, the reader realizes "that all Israelites — indeed, all people — [are] sinners and all [are] in need of the saving work of Jesus, who had come, and who was to be named Jesus, because 'he himself will save his people [all, not just some of them!] from their sins' (1:21)" (Gibbs, 2006:468).

Thus, it is true of all those who encounter Jesus that "Their salvation must begin with forgiveness, with cleansing from sin. But Jesus' salvation does

---

[83] See Dan 7:13-14. Also see (France, 1998:288-292; Davies and Allison, 1991:43-52).

not stop with forgiveness offered to a paralytic. Jesus' authority to forgive sin extends over all the effects of sin as well" (Gibbs, 2006:459). Jesus is laying claim over all. His mission is for all. As one will soon see, he comes to call sinners, that is, all those who come to the realization that they are sinners (Matt 5:3 "poor in spirit").

After the proverb, Jesus cites a Scripture from the prophet Hosea (Hos 6:6). While the Pharisees often position themselves as the experts, teachers, and ones in authority, Jesus challenges them to become learners (Nolland, 2005:187). They needed to revisit an important passage from the Scriptures. The emphasis lands on "mercy" (Nolland, 2005:387). For those claiming to be "healthy," they should know well that mercy is required in their interactions with others. They are to follow God's merciful example.[84] Mercy and forgiveness are intrinsically tied together by the back-to-back episodes of Matt 9:1-8 and 9:9-13. God forgives, and his people are to forgive. God is merciful, and his people are to show mercy. The mission of Christ, so focused on the forgiveness of sins, encompasses the healing of the paralytic and the eating with tax collectors and sinners. In both cases, the sins of the recipients of Jesus' attention and ministry are made clear.[85] In both cases, Jesus' awareness of their sins and dealing with that crucial problem is made obvious. In fact, it might be said that Jesus is the most mindful of the sins around him.

Some commentators rightly point out the connection of Matt 9:13 to Matt 1:21 and 26:28 (Gibbs, 2006:468, 473; Carter, 1998:55-57). The language of "coming" points to Jesus' mission, and the idea of "calling sinners" directs readers to the meaning of the mission. This last phrase of Matt 9:13 reiterates once more that the mission of Christ is to save his people through the forgiveness of sins. Carter asserts that this verse "concludes a sequence of three scenes (9:1-13). Various factors lead the audience to understand this sequence as one exhibiting Jesus' forgiveness of sin" (Carter, 1998:54). He goes on to conclude, "Thus, 9:1-13 demonstrates that by his actions and words Jesus enables others to encounter the saving presence of God. By attention to the passage's thematic emphasis and to the four words ἁμαρτία (with its cognate ἁμαρτωλόι), Ἰησοῦς, ἀφίημι, and καλέω, the audience pondering the 'I have come' saying in 9:13 recalls Jesus' mission and interprets his words and actions in that divine perspective" (Carter, 1998:57). The narratives of Matt 9:1-13 prove to be not only in accord with the message of the forgiveness of sins of

---

[84] "Jesus, like God, heals and forgives (Ps 103:3; cf. Matt 8:17; Isa 53:4)" (Carter, 1998:54).

[85] "From the repeated words 'sins' (ἁμαρτίαι, 9:2,5,6) and its cognate 'sinners' (ἁμαρτωλόι, 9:10,11,13), it sees that sinners are the focus of Jesus' mercy. These same words, almost absent from chaps. 2-8, lead the audience to recall God's commissioning Jesus to save from sins (ἁμαρτιῶν, 1:21)" (Carter, 1998:56).

the macro inclusio of Matt 1:21 and 26:28 but to be robust support of that major theme.

4.4 Matthew 18:11 The Son of Man has come to save that which was lost

The saying attributed to Jesus in Matt 18:11 was likely not original to the context of the parable of the lost sheep in Matthew's account (Carter, 1998:46). Several scholars provide strong arguments against the inclusion of the saying including Metzger and the editors of the New English Translation notes. First, contemplate Metzger's annotations: "There can be little doubt that the words ἦλθεν γὰρ ὁ υἱὸς τοῦ ἀνθρώπου (ζητῆσαι καὶ) σῶσαι τὸ ἀπολωλός are spurious here, being absent from the earliest witnesses representing several textual types (Alexandrian, Egyptian, Antiochian), and manifestly borrowed by copyists from Lk 19:10. The reason for the interpolation as apparently to provide a connection between ver. 10 and verses 12-14" (Metzger, 1994:36). Also consider the notes provided by the NET editors: "The most important mss (ℵ B L* Θ* f1, 13 33 892* pc e ff1 sys sa) do not include 18:11 'For the Son of Man came to save the lost.' The verse is included in D Lmg W Θc 078vid lat syc,p,h, but is almost certainly not original, being borrowed, as it were, from the parallel in Luke 19:10. The present translation follows NA27 in omitting the verse number as well, a procedure also followed by a number of other modern translations" (NET, 2003:1719).

At the outset of the current project, the researcher determined to consider the biblical text as it is presented. While there seems to be a consensus in the scholarly community as to the misplacement of Matt 18:11, the current book will give comment on the saying nonetheless since it appears in some texts. The saying may not belong at Matt 18:11 but almost certainly belongs to the canon of New Testament Scripture (France, 2007:684).[86]

The idea that the saying was awkwardly inserted before this passage rather than after may be overstated (France, 2007:684). In fact, one could make a case that the saying forms a transition from verse 10 into the parable of the lost sheep and serves as an appropriate and helpful heading over the parable. The message of the parable is that an owner of sheep is right and good to seek after a sheep that has gone missing. That is exactly what the saying of Matt 18:11 states. Jesus' mission to seek and save the lost is also right and good. This is his central pursuit, so, actually, the saying "is Jesus' mission succinctly defined" (NET, 2003:1864).

The idea of pursuing the lost in order to save them fits suitably with the opening bracket of the macro inclusio, Matt 1:21. The Son will save his

---

[86] See esp. Luke 19:10 but also Matt 9:13; 10:6; 15:24; 18:12; Luke 5:32; 15:1-32; 19:56; John 3:17; 12:47. The saying seems to be based on Ezekiel 34 and comes in many different forms throughout the Gospel accounts.

people from their sins. Here, in Matt 18:11, Jesus refers to himself again as the Son of Man and says that he has come to save that which was lost. Salvation, through the forgiveness of sins, is the mission of Christ (Matt 1:21; 9:2, 13; 18:11; 20:28; 26:28; etc.).

4.5 Matthew 26:28 Christ's blood shed for many for the forgiveness of sins

What is true of Matt 1:21 is also true of Matt 26:28, that is to say, the content of this verse is unique among the four canonical Gospels (Moo, 1983:306; Carson, 2010:603; Hagner, 1995:771). Thus, Bruner has affirmed, "Only Matthew has this phrase about forgiveness of sins in the Lord's Supper. We recall that Matthew, unlike Mark and Luke, did not want to see even John's baptism invested with forgiveness (contrast Matt 3:1 with Mark 1:4 and Luke 3:3): only Jesus and Jesus' people (through him) can give forgiveness, and Jesus gives it to them especially in the Lord's Supper" (Bruner, 1990:967). Several commentators note in passing the connection between Matt 1:21; 20:28; and 26:28 (Carson, 2010:603; Gibbs, 2006:107; Hagner, 1995:773; Turner, 2008:68). The fact that both Matt 1:21 and 26:28 contain phrases concerning the mission of Christ which are exclusive to Matthew provides solid support for the proposition that a macro inclusio is formed by the two passages. Furthermore, Matt 26:28 is the climax of the message of the forgiveness of sins in the First Gospel. All that remains after this point in the narrative is for Jesus to accomplish what has been forecasted and described. To replicate the analogy that was utilized before, the mission of Christ and the meaning of the cross began to germinate in Matt 1:21, the opening bracket of the macro inclusio. Throughout Matthew's διήγησις, the theme has sprouted and grown. When one makes it to Matt 26:28, the closing bracket of the macro inclusio, the theme will have fully developed and then will produce its fruit in the epilogue, chapters 27-28.

In the context of a Passover Meal and what is normally called the Last Supper, Jesus takes up a cup from the table and says, "This is my blood." From the time that those words were first spoken, it seems that the church has debated the exact meaning of the phrase. Writing from an Evangelical perspective, the current work will not attempt to contemplate, much less rehearse, the various interpretations but will simply hold to the understanding that the cup from which the disciples are all told to drink *represents* Christ's blood. Consequently, the meaning of the words "this is my blood" is deep and substantive but remains figurative.

The Jews celebrated the Passover with four cups of wine, and Jesus modifies the meaning of the third cup (Blomberg, 1992:390; Carson, 2010:601). Just as the Jewish historical tradition up to this point explained symbolism throughout the Passover meal, Jesus transfigures the meanings and points the meaning of the cup to his blood—the blood which will be shed on the cross. Blomberg explains that each of the four cups had a meaning which was linked to a line of Exod 6:6-7, and the cup Jesus holds up at this point was tied to the promise that God would redeem the people (Blomberg, 1992:390). A deep, important, and dynamic symbolism takes place as the disciples drink of the cup (Hagner, 1995:772). They are in some sense participating in the blood and its atoning effect (Hagner, 1995:772). At this point, the cup looks ahead to what will happen at Calvary. Every time the meal is celebrated after the crucifixion, the cup will look back to the procurement of the forgiveness of sins on the cross and every other spiritual blessing which flows out from that event.

The significance of the blood is expounded upon with three different phrases. The first is the "blood of the covenant." The background of the phrase is likely Exod 24:8 (Carson, 2010:602; Blomberg, 1992:391).[87] In the Old Testament context, Moses highlighted the significance of the covenant between both the Lord and the people of Israel. The prophet sprinkled the blood of the sacrificial animals on the altar which was the place of God's presence. Furthermore, Moses not only threw blood on the altar, but he also showered it upon the people. In the New Testament context, the blood will be shed upon the cross, much like the altar, but this time instead of the blood being upon the people, the contents of the cup will be imbibed. What was outward upon the people will now be internalized.

The discerning reader might also think of Lev 17:11 at this point, which teaches that the life is in the blood. Blood is representative of the life of the person (or animal). The sprinkling of blood was actually the graphic "pouring" of blood. The animal sacrifices of the Old Covenant were didactic, intending to serve as reminders for the people's sins (Heb 10:3). The people were to hold out until the coming sacrifice of the Christ. The pouring of blood, then, was a reminder of their own sins and the promise that the Lord would provide a solution to the problem of sin.

The word "New" is not included in some of the best manuscripts (Blomberg, 1992:391). "Nevertheless the newness is clear from the Old Testament allusions" (Blomberg, 1992:391). Some writers think that the newness "is to be presupposed" (Hagner, 1995:773). Moreover, the term is a part of the Lukan account at Luke 22:20. The reader familiar with the Old Testament will also be drawn in mind to Jer 31:31-34 (Ham, 2000:61). As Green puts it, "The newness of this era is marked in a different way by the interpretive sayings of Jesus at the Last Supper. By his use of the words 'covenant' and 'forgiveness of sins' in the same breath (26:28), Jesus interprets his mission against the backdrop of Jeremiah 31:31-34. 'The time is coming,' Jeremiah proclaims, when the Lord will make a 'new covenant.' That time has

---

[87] In addition to Exod 24:8, the phrase is also found in the OT in Zec 9:11 and then in the NT in Heb 9:18-22 (esp. 20). Blood and covenant are found together in the Old Testament in only these two passages (Carson, 2010:602).

come, according to Jesus. In his death he inaugurates the new order of salvation" (Green, 1992:157). With the notable Jeremiah passage in the background, the reader is safe to assume that the Lord Jesus was referring to a New Covenant whether he used the word "New" or not (Quarles, 2017:315-316). The Mosaic Covenant is not being renewed. Instead, a New Covenant is being initiated. Carson explains: "Jesus understands the violent and sacrificial death he is about to undergo . . . as the ratification of the covenant he is inaugurating with his people, even as Moses in Exodus 24:8 ratified the covenant of Sinai by the shedding of blood" (Carson, 2010:602).

The second elaborative phrase for the meaning of Christ's blood is "shed for many" or commonly, "poured out." The word ἐκχυννόμενον (from ἐκχέω) means something like liberally dispense or to emit copisouly (Perschbacher, 1990:132). His blood is shed for many for the forgiveness, or remission, of sins. The shedding of the blood of Jesus is the basis for the forgiveness of sins in the First Gospel (Gundry, 1994:528). Jesus' words concerning the pouring out of his blood direct the disciples, and later readers by extension, back to the atonement sacrifices in the temple (Hagner, 1995:773) and ahead to his own violent yet atoning death (Moo, 1983:130; Bruner, 1990:966).[88] The cup is pointing forward to the cross. The forgiveness of sins will be secured there. Combining the ideas of both Matt 20:28 and 26:28, the reader of the First Gospel may conclude that, "Matthew teaches that Jesus saves his people by shedding his blood as a ransom, which frees them from the bondage of their sins" (Turner, 2008:488).

To state the matter directly, "The deliverance from sins is in a much more profound, moral sense and depends finally upon the pouring out of Jesus' blood (26:28)" (Hagner, 1993:19). Without the shedding of the blood of Jesus Christ there is no deliverance from sins. A New Covenant is ratified by the shedding of his blood and forgiveness of sins is secured.

The idea of his blood being shed for "many" causes the reader to think back to Matt 20:28 where Christ said the Son of Man would give his life a ransom for many. There, forgiveness that is offered to "the many" echoes Isa 53:4, 10, 12 (Hagner, 1995:773). In fact, Jesus is probably thinking of Isaiah 53 throughout this narrative sequence and seeing himself as the Suffering Servant (Carson, 2010:604; Moo, 1983:127-132, 306; Bruner, 1990:966). The importance of Isaiah 53 in the episode is difficult to overemphasize. Carson gives three reasons at this point to connect Jesus to Isaiah's Suffering Servant: (1) "Blood of the covenant" calls to mind "a covenant for the people" in Isaiah 42:6; 49:8; (2) "Poured out" may reflect Isaiah 53:12; and (3) "For many" recalls the work of the Servant in Isaiah 52:13–53:12 (Carson, 2010:604). Gibbs notes that "many" is in Isaiah 53 five times and also in Matt 20:28 and 26:28, and he

---

[88] "'Poured out, ekchunnomenon,' is a present-tense participle with future force and may be rendered 'that (soon) will be poured out' (Jeremias, Euch., 178f)" (Bruner, 1990:966).

thinks that this speaks to a widely applicable atonement (Gibbs, 2006:107). The word may resonate with Isa 53:12 specifically, which says of the Servant that "he bore the sins of many" (Moo, 1983:306).[89] Many "is probably used in the Semitic sense of 'all' (as it is, e.g., in Rom 5:15, 19) and may point to the underlying Hebrew or Aramaic spoken at the meal" (Hagner, 1995:773). The word seems to be over against a "few." A great number of people will be beneficiaries of his shed blood.

Green also points out another intriguing note: "[W]e may observe the shift in Jesus' role as savior. In 1:21, 'he will save *his* people from their sins,' but in 26:28 his blood 'is poured out for *many* (i.e., 'all') for the forgiveness of sins.' The time of Israel's ultimate rejection of Jesus is a time of death, but death leads to life, a new era of salvation for the nations (28:18-20)" (Green, 1992:157). While there is more there than can be commented on at this point, suffice it to say that "his people" (Matt 1:21) are now seen as "many" (Matt 26:28). There is a broadening of the scope of Christ's mission.

The third and final descriptive phrase of the blood of Christ is that it is for the forgiveness of sins. Of course, this phrase brings together all of the theology of the mission of Christ and the meaning of the cross that has been propounded throughout Matthew's Gospel. At this point, the reader comes to a climax. The climax is not one of narrative or events or emotions but one of instruction. For the narrative climax there is still the cross and resurrection. Yet, for the climax of theological elucidation in the Gospel book, Matthew uses these words: "For the forgiveness of sins." Not only does the phrase bring the reader to a climax of theological elucidation concerning the mission of Christ and the meaning of the cross, but the saying now brings the reader full circle, thus forming an inclusio with Matt 1:21.

Thinking again of the Old Testament background, Moo writes, "Forgiveness is undoubtedly to be understood as a result of the Servant's bearing of sins [Isaiah 53], but is not as explicit as in Jeremiah 31" (Moo, 1983:306). These two OT passages are significant to the message of Matt 26:28 but not nearly as important as the inclusio itself. Looking ahead from Matt 1:21 to 26:28, Turner commented, "Forgiveness is accomplished by Jesus's gift of himself as a ransom for sinners in sacrificial death, as exemplified in the elements of the Last Supper (20:28; 26:26-30)" (Turner, 2008:68). The salvation from sins promised in Matt 1:21 is now explicitly seen as forgiveness of sins through the shedding of Christ's blood, that is, his death (Matt 26:28). Throughout church history and until the return of the Lord, the Lord's Supper, and Jesus' words of institution in particular, has interpreted the mission of Christ and the meaning of his cross.

Bruner provides a solid explanation of Jesus application of the cup: "The blood brings forgiveness. Jesus wants the forgiveness of sins—his point

---

[89] Moo thinks that Jer 31:34 could also be in the background of the idea of "many" ('for I will forgive their iniquity and remember their sins no more') (Moo, 1983:306).

in coming (1:21; 9:2; 20:28)—to be palpably and not just invisibly with his disciples. So much does *forgiveness* mean to Jesus that he wants to give it a perpetual place inside his church" (Bruner, 1990:967). Thus, as stated above, throughout history, whenever and wherever believing churches have gathered to participate in the Lord's Supper, they have had applied to them both the understanding and the benefits of the forgiveness of sins through the shed blood of Christ. Bruner goes on to say bluntly, "And [Jesus] places his forgiveness not in an unmovable thing (like the Kabalah in Mecca), but inside a meal, 'a moveable feast' where people are" (Bruner, 1990:967).

As demonstrated in the points above, the fact that both Matt 1:21 and 26:28 contain phrases concerning the mission of Christ which are exclusive to Matthew provides solid support for the proposition that a macro inclusio is formed by the two passages. Moreover, Matt 26:28 has been shown to speak to *how* Jesus will "save his people from their sins." The explanation is that he will "shed his blood for many for the forgiveness of sins." Over against the Temple cult or any other Jewish tradition, Jesus made the claim during his ministry and certainly in his death to personally embody the means by which forgiveness of sins may be attained (Antwi, 1991:27).

The macro inclusio combines to communicate that the mission of Christ is the salvation from sins through the forgiveness that will be procured by his blood. The meaning of the cross, then, is starting to come into focus. The next chapter will explore the relationship between the macro inclusio and the meaning of the cross along with the supporting passages throughout the Matthean Gospel.

4.6 Chapter Four Conclusion

This chapter has sought to demonstrate that the forgiveness of sins is one of the primary themes in the First Gospel. Flowing out of the first bracket of the large inclusio (Matt 1:21) are at least two essential pericopes on the subject of forgiveness of sins. The Lord's Model Prayer in the Sermon on the Mount includes a petition about forgiveness and an instructive elaboration of the Matthean community on the subject of forgiveness. There in Matt 6:12-15 both sin and forgiveness are discussed. The passages found at Matt 9:2, 5-7, and 12-13 concerning the Son of Man having power on earth to forgive sins have also proven to be crucial to Matthew's development of the theme. Again, sin and forgiveness are linked. Jesus was shown to not only claim to have authority in these matters, but he proved that he did with a miraculous display of his divine authority and power. Moreover, Matt 18:11, if original, also adds to the motif in the First Gospel where "lostness" is a symbol of sinfulness and from which people need to be delivered.

In the final analysis of this chapter, the thesis appears to hold. The two outside brackets which form the inclusio highlight the themes of salvation and forgiveness as well as several other passages included within the envelope structure. Matthew brings up the topic of forgiveness at several key points in his work. The evangelist explores the topic, showing concerns and needs, and explains how Jesus deals with the related problems.

The Matthean passages considered in this chapter have also been investigated in an attempt to prove their support of the macro inclusio of Matt 1:21 and 26:28. The researcher has endeavored to establish links from each of these passages within the envelope structure to the main brackets of the inclusio. In so doing, the thesis that Matthew has constructed a macro inclusio is strengthened.

Chapter 5: Sin and the Cross in Matthew's Gospel

The third chapter of the current book sought to demonstrate that Matt 1:21 and 26:28 form a macro inclusio for the entirety of Matthew's Gospel focusing on the mission of Christ and the meaning of the cross.[90] Chapter four explored the διήγησις of the Matthean Gospel to see if it supports the macro inclusio, particularly on the theme of the forgiveness of sins. The premise is that a macro inclusio is a bracketing structure that envelops the material within the whole book. If Matt 1:21 and 26:28 bracket the entirety of the Gospel to reveal the major theme of the forgiveness of sins through the death of Christ, then the contents of the book should fall under that category as well. In chapter four, the theme of the forgiveness of sins was investigated. All that remains now is to see if passages related to the cross of Christ within the διήγησις of the Gospel similarly connect to the macro inclusio.

Therefore, the aim of chapter five is to provide an account of the development throughout Matthew's Gospel of the death of Christ and the meaning of it which the inclusio highlights. In this case, the project turns to consider what Matthew understands about sin and the cross of Christ. An inclusio does not, of course, require that the content within the brackets use the exact same terminology or phraseology. Moreover, the inclusio does not demand that every passage relate directly to its brackets. As stated in chapter three, an inclusio is a literary and rhetorical device of repetition employed for several reasons including to give structure and to highlight main points and is recognizable because the same idea, even the same words at times, are repeated at the beginning and end of a sentence, section, or book. What is enveloped within the outer brackets of the inclusio, especially a book-length inclusio, will contain throughout the work echoes or pointers to the major themes highlighted by the brackets themselves. To state it slightly differently, what is enclosed in the envelope structure needs to support the main idea(s) conveyed in the outer brackets of the inclusio.

Thus, two of the passages that need to be explored on this point are the brackets themselves: Matt 1:21 and 26:28. These two passages were examined in the previous chapter but from a different angle. They will now be examined with a view toward sin and the cross. Alongside those two passages are several other texts from within the Matthean Gospel which will also be considered to see how they might connect to the theme and inclusio. Much like chapter four, the conditions used to determine key texts will be: a passage

---

[90] Throughout this chapter, the term "cross" is meant to refer to the actual place and means of Christ's death but also figuratively to his work of atonement.

that is part of the opening or closing brackets of the large inclusio; a pericope that deals directly with the problem of sin; a text that refers explicitly or even implicitly to the death of Christ (or the cross); and any pericope that speaks to the mission of Christ, including "I have come" statements. Once again, special interest will be given in chapter five to demonstrating the connections of each of the passages concerning the forgiveness of sins to the macro inclusio. Since both of the passages of the brackets were studied in the previous chapter, the examination here will focus specifically on their connection to Matthew's understanding of the meaning of the cross.

5.1 Matthew 1:21 Jesus: He will save his people from their sins

A thorough exploration of Matt 1:21 was put forth in chapter four. What is left to do in chapter five is to explore the relation of this verse to the cross of Christ. What does 1:21 have to do with the cross or sin being redressed in the death of Christ, specifically? As stated in the previous chapter, Matt 1:21 is foundational to Matthew's presentation of Christ, his mission, and the meaning of his cross. Not only is the text foundational to the Evangelist's theology, but the ideas conveyed in the verse reveal significant echoes throughout the work.

The announcement of Matt 1:21, the opening bracket of Matthew's macro inclusio, is that Jesus will save his people from their sins. Luz writes, "Matthew in particular has a special interest in the forgiveness of sins that happens through Jesus and continues to be effective in the church" (Luz, 2007:95). Now, the commentators Davies and Allison have it correct when they say that Matt 1:21 "is not very illuminating with regard to exactly *how* Jesus saves" (Davies and Allison, 1988:210). This is just a predictive or promissory statement, a foreshadowing of things to come. Yet, the fact must be admitted, and the commentators do concede, that the "atoning death must be in view" (Davies and Allison, 1988:210). The point that has been made in the project at hand is exactly what Nolland straightforwardly states when he writes, "What might be involved for Matthew in being saved from sins can be clarified by looking at his later references to 'sins': John the Baptist's ministry provokes the confession of sins (3:6); Jesus himself forgives sins (9:2, 5, 6); his blood is finally 'poured out for the forgiveness of sins' (26:28; cf. 20:28)" (Nolland, 2005:99).

In what sense can it be said that the naming of Jesus shortly after his conception is related to his messianic mission to die on the cross? One might consider the arguments of Millard Erickson (Erickson, 2000:44–49). The theologian highlights seven features of Matt 1:18–25, most notably the angel's words in verse 21, which suggest that Matthew is deliberately alluding to the story of Abraham in Genesis. For example, if Matt 1:21a "And she will bring forth a Son, and you shall call his name Jesus" alludes to Gen 17:19 "Sarah your wife shall bear you a son, and you shall call his name Isaac," then Matt 1:21b "for he will save his people from their sins" may allude to another part of the Abrahamic narrative, videlicet Gen 22:1-14. One can easily notice in the Genesis 22 account of the Akedah important themes echoed in Matthew such as sonship, mountain, offering, angels, death, and substitution. At the beginning of his Gospel account, Matthew may already be hinting at his Christological message of the Messiah's substitutionary and atoning sacrifice.[91]

David Turner accentuates the mission language in Matthew, especially in these early passages. For example, in referring to Joseph being instructed to name the boy Jesus, Turner thinks the name refers to the child's future mission. He states that the name Jesus "fits the predicted mission" (Turner, 2008:67). Moreover, Turner writes, "By naming Mary's son, Joseph will be accepting legal paternity. By naming him Ἰησοῦς, Joseph will be making a statement about Jesus's redemptive mission: 'He will save his people from their sins'" (Turner, 2008:67).

The grammar of the angel's words is telling in relation to the rest of the Gospel. The term σώσει from σώζω "to save" is not only in the future tense but likely is used as a predictive future (Quarles, 2017:21; Wallace, 1996:568). As a word from on high, the saying is probably more of a promise than a "mere prediction" (Quarles, 2017:21). The reader of Matthew's Gospel, in any case, would anticipate a fulfillment of the prediction at some point in the narratival unfolding. The believing reader waits for the promise to be realized. Unless one sees passages such as Matt 9:2 as the fulfillment, with Jesus simply stating that the sins of the person are forgiven, then one will have to understand the death of Jesus on the cross as the time and place when the promise of salvation from sins is effectuated. The development of the Gospel leads the reader more and more to this conclusion.

5.2 Matt 16:21-25; 17:22-23; 20:17-19; 26:1-2, 12

The following passages under section 5.2 are what might be labeled *mission* passages related to the cross of Christ. These passages declare the reason that Christ has come. Each of the passages listed will be expounded upon here in the chapter. In these pericopes, the Lord Jesus states explicitly his impending death. This was the mission of Christ.

One might identify Matt 9:15 and 12:40 as previous allusions to the death of Christ (Carson, 2010:427), but the saying of Jesus recorded in Matt 10:38 appears to be the background for the remaining passages wherein Christ

---

[91] Also see Matt 3:15, 17. The allusion to Genesis 22 may also be at work in other New Testament writings, for example, John 8:56 and Rom 8:32. Thus, the Akedah, or "The Binding of Isaac," appears to be an early Christian interpretive tool to understand the meaning of the cross of Christ. The Lord Jesus' death is seen as a fulfillment of the message to Abraham.

predicts his coming passion.[92] The saying concerning a cross in Matt 10:38 was surprising at this point in Jesus' ministry (Blomberg, 1992:181). After the resurrection, this saying and others like it will have fuller import and explanatory power but even at this point in the narrative the idea of crucifixion calls to mind a certain shame and pain of sacrifice (Carson, 2010:299). Moreover, several passion predictions will follow in the days ahead wherein Jesus will make clear that his mission relates to his cross. The way of Christ is death to self (Carson, 2010:299). Atonement by sacrificial death is the reason he came into the world. Christ's disciples will not make atoning sacrifices, but they will participate in that ministry (Matt 6:12-15; 18:21, 35; 16:19; 18:18). The connections to Matt 1:21 are not as obvious thus far but will begin to take shape over the next few chapters.

5.2.1 Matt 16:21-25

"From that time Jesus began" is a transitional phrase taken exactly from Matt 4:17 which marked another major progression in the Gospel narrative, and this time it marks the shift into the next main part of Matthew's Gospel to orient the reader towards Jesus' suffering and death before vindication (Hagner, 1995:478-479; Nolland, 2005:685). This is a significant turning point in the Gospel account (Kingsbury, 1991:7). Matthew has reached a decisive moment in the life and ministry of Jesus Christ. The suffering, death, and resurrection of Christ became a reverberating theme of Jesus' discipleship from this time forward (Carson, 2010:427).

The language of necessity is striking in this first prediction passage. Matthew uses the simple word δεῖ to say that Christ "must" or he "has to" go and suffer and be put to death (BDAG, 2000:213-214). The language of necessity, in Matthean Christology, appears to be the language of mission, and the mission of Christ is from on high, from God the Father himself (Nolland, 2005:686; Carson, 2010:428). In essence, Christ states that he has come to fulfill a mission (he will suffer and be put to death), and once the mission is complete, he will return to the one who commissioned him (he will be raised the third day).

The essentiality of going to Jerusalem to suffer and be killed is stated first here, but the elaboration of the necessity comes forth at Matt 20:28 and then is made explicit in Matthew 26 (France, 2007:631; Carson, 2010:428). Both the first disciples and all the readers of Matthew's Gospel since need to know that what was going to take place was in the plans and purposes of God.

Jesus teaches that he must: (1) Go; (2) Suffer; (3) Be put to death; and (4) Be raised. While the passion prediction here and the ones that will follow do not seem to point to particular Old Testament passages, "such statements

---

[92] Daniel Antwi even claims that Matt 12:1-8 is probably "the beginning of the tradition for atonement" (Antwi, 1991:21).

have increasingly been colored by the thought of Isa 53" (France, 2007:990). In addition to the several Old Testament themes already enunciated, one might also add Psalms 22 and 69 for background (France, 2007:631).

Peter speaks up for the group again as he rebukes Jesus for saying that he must be put to death. The disciples are still with Christ even though public sentiment has turned against him. The religious and political leaders have certainly taken their stand against Jesus. Yet, Peter is not willing to allow Jesus to go so far as to talk about being killed. Carson comments that the disciples understand full well what their teacher is saying but have a hard time believing that the Messiah will be executed, thus the disciples begin to think that Jesus is speaking only figuratively (Carson, 2010:428). This will lead to occasions of misunderstanding.

The application of this passage to the disciples and the readers comes already supplied in the text itself. Jesus teaches about what it means to follow him. Not only will Jesus have to go, suffer, be killed, and be raised, but there is a cross for each of his followers. The idea of the "discipleship of the cross" is "fundamentally important" (Luz, 2001:383). The mission of Christ is the mission of the Church, that is, to give of oneself for the sake of the world.

5.2.2 Matt 17:22-23

The reader got a glimpse of Christ's glory and coming kingdom in the transfiguration narrative, but the recounting of the episode regarding the demon-possessed boy reminds the reader why Jesus came and why he had to go to the cross. Sin had to be remedied. One should point out, though, that even in the glorious account of Christ's transfiguration on the mountain, the Lord explained, "But I say to you that Elijah has come already, and they did not know him but did to him whatever they wished. Likewise the Son of Man is also about to suffer at their hands" (Matt 17:12). The inner circle of disciples who witnessed these things may have been a bit confused at first, but Jesus makes clear that "Elijah, as forerunner, did not come to prevent the Messiah's suffering and death but to foreshadow it" (Blomberg, 1992:266).

The text of Matt 17:22-23 is a repetition in the Gospel narrative of the first passion prediction given in Matt 16:21. Jesus is heading to Jerusalem with his disciples following. The group has made its way back south from somewhere near Caesarea Phillipi and have gathered in Galilee which was, most likely, simply a brief stop in order to make preparations to travel on to Jerusalem for the Passover feast (Nolland, 2005:719). They will resume their trip in Matt 19:1. Jesus still has many things to teach them, including this prediction, and he must complete the mission by going to the cross and taking up his life again the third day.

This second prediction passage employs Son of Man language again. The first prediction passage beginning in Matt 16:21 and following used the title in relation to Christ's post-resurrection glory when he comes to judge the world. Here in Matt 17:22-23, the Son of Man label is attached to his coming rejection. Highlighting the play on words, Nolland comments that "the very figure who is intrinsically of great human significance is to be allowed [even "handed over"] by God to come under the power of the destructive will of humanity" (Nolland, 2005:720). The Son of Man will first be betrayed and killed and then will rise again in glory. Consequently, Matthean Christology is clear that suffering leads to glory. The mission of Christ leads to his exalted triumph by way of his death on the cross.

To be delivered or handed over (παραδίδωμι) can be used in the positive sense of entrusting something precious to someone or in the negative sense of betrayal or being legally condemned to death (BDAG, 2000:762). In this case, the latter is meant. Jesus will be handed over from one court and judge to the next and eventually delivered over to the executioners. And yet, as acknowledged above, Matthean thinking (and all of New Testament theology, for that matter), following Hebrew texts such as Isaiah 53, distinctly teaches that God is the one sovereignly orchestrating all events. Christ will be delivered over by evil men, but God the Father is also handing over Christ to death.

One might say, "The announcement of the suffering itself is short and terse" (Luz, 2001:411). This may be due to a desire to emphasize the shock of the declaration. Matthew apparently wants his readers to grasp the alarm and astonishment that the first disciples experienced when they heard the words.

The disciples' response has turned from denial to depression. They are so overwhelmed by the talk of death that they are deaf to the declaration of resurrection exultation. On the disciples' refusal to accept Jesus' prediction, displayed in their overwhelming sadness, Luz writes that "it contrasts with the clarity and decisiveness with which Jesus himself looks ahead to his dying" (Luz, 2001:411). The disciples may be disheartened and bewildered, but Jesus, the Savior from sins, is steadfast.

5.2.3 Matt 20:17-19

Another passion prediction comes in Matt 20:17-19. This is the third of Matthew's distinguished passages on the subject. Jesus predicts his coming suffering in Jerusalem. Nolland comments that the reader is reminded of "Jesus' goal in Jerusalem" or one might refer to it as his mission (Nolland, 2005:814). The reader notices that "going up" or "ascending" is repeated twice. Repetition in the New Testament is often employed for emphasis (Bullinger, 1898:189). The reader is nudged into bearing in mind the ascent to the holy city but also of Jesus' climb up the hill to the place of the cross. He is ascending to Jerusalem, and he is ascending to suffering.

As the passion predictions continue in the narrative sequence, one begins to conclude that, "What in 16:21 was announced is now already reality; the end is near" (Luz, 2001:539). The themes of the first two predictions are repeated but with greater precision (France, 2007:753). And again, the repetition increases the tension, not only for the disciples within the historical narrative but also for the reader.

Luz is right to assert that "This prediction of the passion already reveals, therefore, something of Matthew's understanding of the passion" (Luz, 2001:539). By differentiating these several passion prediction passages throughout the latter part of his Gospel, Matthew is building a case for the necessity of Christ's mission. He is demonstrating to the reader, as was Jesus to the disciples, that Christ was necessarily heading to Jerusalem to be put to death. This would be no accident but a sovereign act of God.[93]

Matthew records Jesus using the word παραδίδωμι once again. The idea of the term picks up the language of the famous Servant Song of Isaiah 53. God will do these things (Hagner, 1995:575). Christ will be rejected by men (Isa 53:3), yes, but it will be the Lord who lays on him the iniquity of us all (Isa 53:6). They will make his grave with the wicked and with a rich man in his death (Isa 53:9), but the Lord will be the one who crushes him and puts him to grief (Isa 53:10).

The only new ideas introduced in this passage that were not included in Matt 16:21 and 17:22-23 are the reference to the Gentiles and the specific reference to his mocking, scourging, and crucifixion (Blomberg, 1992:306; Hagner, 1995:576). Matthew records Jesus using the word σταυρόω, to crucify, specifically which has been said to be the most important term in all of the passion narratives (Hagner, 1995:576). Indeed, there is a sense of building up to a conclusion, so Hagner comments: "As the final infinitive in Matthew's series of three, σταυρῶσαι, "crucify," indicates the final climactic goal to be realized by Jesus in his earthly life" (Hagner, 1995:576). The promise of resurrection is made again here, as it was in the first two passion predictions (Hagner, 1995:576).

The context of this third prediction is fitting. There are bookends around the pericope that both concern the nature of Christ's messianic reign. The key sayings include: "the last will be first, and the first will be last" (Matt 20:16) as well as "whoever desires to become great among you, let him be your servant" and "whoever desires to be first among you, let him be your slave" (Matt 20:26-27). The Lord Jesus elucidates the nature of his messianic kingdom by pointing to his death. For his disciples to be great, they must follow his example. They must do what he does. This is stated explicitly and summarized well in Jesus' saying recorded in Matt 20:28, "The Son of Man did not come to be served, but to serve, and to give His life a ransom for many." This saying will be discussed in greater detail in section 5.3 below. The application for the church, of course, is to realize that the scribes and the prostitutes are both welcome in the kingdom. The pious and the peasants are on equal footing. The deathbed confessor will receive eternal life just the same as the lifelong believer.

---

[93] "Behind the passive verb is probably the divine will" (Hagner, 1995:575).

The rich and the poor have the same opportunity before God. Repentant Jews and repentant Gentiles, alike, share in the benefits of Christ's death and resurrection and are called to emulate their Savior.

5.2.4 Matt 26:1-2, 12

This is the last of the major Passion predictions in the Gospel of Matthew. The others were found at Matt 16:21; 17:22-23; and 20:17-19. At this point, the reader enters the steep ascent to the climax of the Gospel. In fact, it can be said, "Here the goal of Jesus' mission is realized. The death of Jesus on the cross is no surprise, nor does it indicate the failure of Jesus' mission. . . . Jesus in this narrative accomplishes the purpose for which he came into this world. . . . Though sinful men do their best to thwart the mission of Jesus, they accomplish the very purpose for which he came and thus fulfill God's will" (Hagner, 1995:749-750).

The Lord Jesus' prediction at the beginning of Matthew 26 is brief and straightforward. He repeats what he has said in previous announcements, including the element that he will be crucified. What is new in this prediction passage is the timeline. Christ says that after two days the Son of Man will be delivered up.

Of the last verse, Matt 26:12, the reader notes that Matthew places the narrative of the woman anointing Jesus thematically after Jesus' last passion prediction. This is a flashback to a week or so earlier when Jesus was staying in Bethany before the Triumphal Entry. This narrative takes place at the home of Simon the Leper. Many students of this passage conclude that Simon must have been healed by Jesus, otherwise lepers are usually banned from society (Blomberg, 1992:384).

Matthew leaves this particular woman unnamed, but John tells his readers that it was Mary of Bethany, the sister of Martha and Lazarus (John 12:3). The perfume was myrrh which may link back to the magi's gift (Blomberg, 1992:384). It was not typically used for anointing because it was an expensive perfume. Often, someone would be tasked with blessing guests as they arrived, just a small dab of the perfume on their foreheads, to honor the guests and to add an enjoyable aroma in the room (Keener, 1993:119). However, this woman does not put a simple touch of oil to Jesus' head, she breaks the flask of expensive perfume and anoints his head and feet. The Gospel of Mark tells readers that the value of this flask added up to nearly a year's worth of wages for the average worker (Mark 14:5). This woman spared no expense in honoring her Lord.

The Law teaches that since the poor would always be within the Israelite community, the citizens must always be ready to give generously (Deut 15:11). However, Mary is only able to do this anointing now because of the exact time and place she found herself in salvation history. Christ will not be with them much longer, and the poor will be with them always. She anoints

Jesus now, but the church will soon have to get back to generosity among its membership and beyond.

Determining just how much Mary really understood about Christ's upcoming Passion is difficult. Maybe she was one of a very small group who actually recognized that Jesus would be a Suffering-Servant-Messiah. She was one who sat under Jesus' teaching ministry and listened intently to his message. While she would have met every expectation by skipping out on the instruction Jesus offered, she chose the better part by sitting down and listening and learning and growing.

5.3 Matthew 20:27-28 The Son of Man [has come] to give his life as a ransom for many

The observant reader will notice that section 5.3 moves backwards in the Gospel narrative from where section 5.2 left off. This is because section 5.2 grouped Matthew's passion prediction passages together. The chapter now resumes the standard chronological outline. In Matt 20:27-28, the reader encounters one of the clearest examples of what Jesus (and thus, Matthew) thinks about his own mission. The Lord Jesus says, "The Son of Man did not come to be served, but to serve, and to give His life as a ransom for many." Carter counts this as the seventh ἦλθον statement in Matthew's Gospel and the final one about Jesus' mission (Carter, 1998:44, 60; also see France, 2007:763). Jesus states explicitly why he has come and a reason for which he has not come. He attests to the facts of his mission, "his deliberate goal" (France, 2007:763).

The messianic self-designation "Son of Man" is used by Jesus once more. This is his favorite title for himself and his mission. He used this title in Matt 9:6 in reference to his authority to forgive sins. The designation was repeated in Matt 12:40 when Jesus likens his death and resurrection to the account of the prophet Jonah. The textually disputed passage of Matt 18:11 recorded Jesus using the label in reference to his mission of salvation. The designation was used in all of the "prediction passages" outlined in section 5.2.[94] Matthew records the phrase of Christ's self-realization of the fulfillment of Scripture in 26:24. When Matthew records Jesus using this title, the reader

---

[94] This is opposing others who count Jesus using the title in only three of the four prediction passages (Carter, 1998:60). The reason to disagree here is that while the name is not in the prediction passage proper (Matt 16:21-23), Jesus does use the self-designation twice in Matt 16:27-28 which is in the same context as this first prediction passage. In fact, an even wider context in Matthew 16 should be acknowledged as playing a significant role in an interpretation of Matt 16:21. The pericope recounting Peter's great confession that Jesus is the Messiah is represented as a prompt for Jesus to begin defining his messiahship. Consider the link between Matt 16:20 into 16:21. His prediction of being killed leads into the next pericope about taking up a cross to follow him.

is reminded of the previous passages wherein it was utilized and are better equipped to understand the current passage (Carter, 1998:60).

Jesus' mission to save from sins, which was first prophesied in Matt 1:21, is here reinforced by three thematic aspects, according to Carter: (1) Jesus must die as compelled by God's will; (2) the one named "Jesus" because he will save his people from their sins is the one speaking in the passage; and (3) the idea of "ransom" draws the reader back to Matt 1:21 and the theme of God's faithful and merciful deliverance of his people (Carter, 1998:60-61). One can conclude from this passage, then, that "In the context of the previous six 'I have come' sayings the audience understands this seventh saying to mean that Jesus performs his divinely commissioned purpose of saving from sins not only in his deeds and words but also in his death" (Carter, 1998:62).

While the title induces pictures of grandeur in the imagination, Jesus quickly follows it by saying that the Son of Man "did not come to be served." This is striking in contrast to the standard messianic expectations (Matt 13:54-57; 16:1-4, 22-23; 20:20-22; 24:3) and notions of the Son of Man from the prophet (Dan 7:13-14). This Son of Man, a kingly and majestic figure, comes as a Servant-King. While most kings desire to be served, this one comes to work in behalf of his people. He exemplifies in his sacrificial death what it means to take the best place by becoming a slave for others (Matt 20:27).[95] Greatness is expressed in service (Nolland, 2005:824).

Thus, again, Jesus will not be served while on mission during his incarnation. In fact, the Son of Man will not even have a place to lay his head (Matt 8:20). Instead, Messiah has come to serve. Morris writes, "The verb διακονέω was used of waiting on someone at table, and from that came to denote lowly service in general. Jesus is using an interesting term to state quite firmly that he sought no great place for himself, but chose to serve in a humble capacity" (Morris, 1992:512). That humble capacity is specifically to give his life as a ransom. The Lord Jesus served in several different ways, especially through feeding multitudes and healing crowds, but the greatest service is to give one's life in behalf of others (Luz, 2001:546).

In this saying, Jesus interprets his crucifixion (Luz, 2001:546). His death will be for many, that is, a number of people much greater than just the apostles. Several will benefit from the sacrificial death of Christ. Thus, Green writes, "Jesus' mission is salvific, but he can open the way of salvation only by the sacrifice of his life" (Green, 1992:156).

Ransom (λύτρον) is the word often used for the price paid for the release of slaves but probably simply refers to the notion of substitution in this passage (Luz, 2001:546). The idea of an offering may also be included (Nolland,

---

[95] One may note again that Isaiah's Suffering Servant of the Lord is probably also in the background. For example, the prophet refers to the coming Messiah numerous times as the Lord's "Servant." Jesus fulfills the role of slave in his mission to serve his people through his sacrificial death on the cross.

2005:824). Again, substitution is an important concept wrapped up in the language of Jesus here (Wallace, 1996:365-367; Quarles, 2017:239). Exodus 30:12 adds context to the Hebrew idea of ransom, "When you take the census of the children of Israel for their number, then every man shall give a ransom for himself to the Lord, when you number them, that there may be no plague among them when you number them." Psalm 49:7-9 is another important reference on ransom, "None of them can by any means redeem his brother, nor give to God a ransom for him—for the redemption of their souls is costly, and it shall cease forever—that he should continue to live eternally, and not see the Pit." Phrases and ideas from Isaiah 53 are likely in mind here on the notion of ransom, including, "When you make his soul an offering for sin;" "For he shall bear their iniquities;" and "He bore the sin of many."

The phrase "to give his life" most likely refers to the Fourth Servant Song in Isaiah and particularly to Isa 53:10 which refers to the Servant's soul (or life) being made an offering for sin (Nolland, 2005:824; France, 2007:762).[96] Of course, this fits well with Matt 1:21 and the context of the Matthean Gospel. The price paid, the ransom, for that salvation from sins will be the very life of Jesus Christ.

Nolland is likely correct when he summarizes his thoughts on this passage by writing: "Admittedly, what exactly is thought to be involved in the Son of Man giving his life as a ransom for many remains quite imprecise" (Nolland, 2005:826). Furthermore, he is also accurate when he says, "Mt. 26:26-28 will provide us with related images which will freshly identify Jesus' death as the high point of the pattern of self-sacrificing service that characterized his ministry" (Nolland, 2005:826). In Matt 20:28, Jesus' death is evident by how and why that death is a ransom is not so clear. However, the passage fits within the themes that Matthew is developing throughout his Gospel. The theme takes fullest form in the closing bracket of the macro inclusio in Matt 26:28.

To add support to the idea that Isaiah is foundational for understanding the current passage, the phrase "for many" seems to allude to Isa 52:14-15; 53:11-12 (France, 2007:763). Jesus likely uses this language to continue to the references back to Isaiah 53 but also to contrast the *one* life that is given in behalf (ἀντὶ) of the *many*. This one life is special (Matt 1:21) and will be enough to pay (λύτρον) for the sins of many.

The saying found in Matt 20:28 fits smoothly within the envelope structure developed in the Matthean Gospel's salvation/forgiveness macro inclusio. The saying builds upon Matt 1:21, giving more information about the mission of Christ, but still does not say all that Matt 26:28 will reveal about the meaning of the cross.

---

[96] France seems firm on the point that Isaiah 53 is the background for the saying. Nolland is much less sure but leaves the possibility open and acknowledges the great number of scholars who take the position advocated by France.

Bruner draws a straight line between Matt 1:21; 9:2; and 20:28, asserting that Jesus' point in coming was for the forgiveness of sins (Bruner, 1990:967). Gibbs simply notes in passing the connection between Matt 1:21; 20:28; and 26:28 (Gibbs, 2006:107). Speaking to Matt 1:21, Davies and Allison see the associations as well and write, "The passion already comes into the picture, for it is at the crucifixion that Jesus pours out his lifeblood εἰς ἄφεσιν ἁμαρτιῶν (26:28). Thus, the entire Gospel is to be read in the light of its end. In addition, 1:21 makes clear from the outset that, notwithstanding Matthew's insistent demand for human righteousness, salvation is the gift of God. This fact will be reiterated in 20:28 and 26:28" (Davies and Allison, 1988:210).

Turner, though, makes much of the connections when he comments: "Matthew 20:28 recalls 1:21 and anticipates 26:28. In 1:21 it is stated that Jesus will save his people from their sins. This play on the meaning of the name Jesus indicates that Israel's root problem is not Roman occupation but sin. Matthew 20:28 shows *how* Jesus will deliver his people from their sins: he will pay a ransom that will free them from the bondage of alienation from God. In light of Isa. 53:10-12, the haunting question of Matt. 16:26 ('What will one give in exchange for one's soul?'), and the use of the preposition ἀντὶ (anti, instead of, in behalf of) in 20:28, Matthew teaches vicarious redemption: Jesus substitutes his own life for that of his people" (Turner, 2008:488). Matthean Christology is enriched with his inclusion of this Son of Man saying.

A beautiful theological summary from Green may be offered at this point. He remarks, "And this is where Matthew's christological portrait comes into focus. Jesus does not exercise his power as Messiah, Son of God to escape from death, but not because he lacks royal status or authority. Rather, Jesus exercises that power in unexpected ways; in obedience to God and in pouring out his life for others. The story of Jesus' death in Matthew is thus the story of his fidelity to God, his faithfulness to his mission and his willing solidarity with the pain and hope of his people" (Green, 1992:156).

5.4 Matthew 26:28 Christ's blood shed for many for the forgiveness of sins

While Matthew's retelling of the Lord's Last Supper is often overlooked when considering the subject (Ham, 2000:56), the student of the New Testament documents should not miss what Matthew has to say. The saying in Matt 26:28 is unique to Matthew and gives particular insight not only into Matthean Christology but also, for the Evangelical reader, into the historical Christian perspective on the meaning of the cross (Nel, 2015:7). The Lord Jesus told his followers what his death on the cross would accomplish. The events and sayings during the Last Supper give the explanatory foundation to the meaning of Christ's death. They are interpretive sayings (Green, 1992:157; Carter, 1998:62). As noted in the Chapter Four, this verse explicitly links Christ's blood with the forgiveness of sins, and so the culmination of the mission of Christ in Matthean Christology is now thoroughly tied to the meaning of his death on the cross.

To quote that uniquely Matthean remembrance again, the Lord says of the cup, "For this is my blood of the covenant, which is shed for many for the forgiveness of sins" (Matt 26:28). In these words, many have found profundity. For example, France comments: "There is thus a rich mixture of allusive elements in these words. The result is the most comprehensive statement in Matthew's gospel of the redemptive purpose and achievement of Jesus' death" (France, 2007:994). The whole Matthean Gospel, beginning at Matt 1:21, has been leading to this climactic point. Jesus now clearly states the meaning of the cross. Sins will be forgiven through his shed blood and thus, salvation will be accomplished.

As noted in the previous chapter, the Mosaic Covenant is not being renewed. Instead, a New Covenant is being initiated. Carson explains: "Jesus understands the violent and sacrificial death he is about to undergo . . . as the ratification of the covenant he is inaugurating with his people, even as Moses in Exodus 24:8 ratified the covenant of Sinai by the shedding of blood" (Carson, 2010:602). Christ "inaugurates the new order of salvation" (Green, 1992:157). The blood of Christ shed on the cross will be the beginning of a new epoch.

Luz thinks that the implied reader of the Matthean Gospel was not meant to hold any tension in the narratival unfolding but to be fully aware of what is taking place. In this way, once the reader makes it to this point in the narrative, then he or she only gains a deeper understanding of the passion, or what one might say is the mission of Christ and the meaning of the cross (Luz, 2001:540). The reader of the Gospel knows what is coming and can, thus, pay attention more closely in order to ascertain the details (Luz, 2001:540). When readers encounter the words of institution, "This is my blood," they will realize that his blood will be shed or poured out, that is, he will be put to death. They will also think of the divine plan of redemption to forgive their sins and save them when they encounter the words, "For the forgiveness of sins." The reader who has followed the Matthean developments will now know that Jesus will save his people from their sins by shedding his blood for their forgiveness. Jesus' death on the cross will be their salvation.

The word that Jesus speaks in reference to his blood is ἐκχέω which means something like "emitted in quantity" (Perschbacher, 1990:132; BDAG, 2000:312). The term is a clear reference to a decisive death (Hagner, 1995:773). The death is literal and physical and will be horrific, but the meaning of that death is metaphysical. "The blood that will flow from Jesus' death tomorrow will do cosmic duty" (Bruner, 1990:966). Furthermore, the phrase "shed for many" makes the reader think back to Matt 20:28. In that passage, forgiveness that is offered to "the many" echoes Isa 53:4, 10, 12. Gibbs notes that "many" is in Isaiah 53 five times and also in Matt 20:28 and 26:28 (Gibbs, 2006:107).

If Matt 20:28 began to show *how* Jesus will deliver his people from their sins, as previously noted above, then "Matthew 26:28 shows *when* Jesus will pay the ransom: the wine of the Last Supper is a sacred sign of the blood of Jesus, shed at his crucifixion for the remission of his people's sins" (Turner, 2008:488). Just as the healing of the paralytic man confirmed Jesus' authority to pronounce the forgiveness of sins (Matt 9:6), the death of Christ will prove his work of atonement to save his people from their sins (Matt 1:21) (Ham, 2000:62).

Hägerland also points out that the last supper narrative is influenced by Isaiah 53. Matthew extends Mark's formula, according to this author, by saying that Christ's blood of the covenant is poured out for many for the forgiveness of sins. He writes, "Here the link between Jesus' violent death and forgiveness is explicit" (Hägerland, 2012:74). Again, he affirms that Matt 26:28 "links explicitly" the Eucharist with forgiveness (Hägerland, 2012:125). The scholar believes, "It is not impossible that at least shortly before his execution — as opposed to during the main part of his career — Jesus had come to think of his death as salvific and even involving the forgiveness of sins" (Hägerland, 2012:74). Now, this is a more critical reading than what is affirmed in this book, but it does show that even a critical writer affirms the links fundamental to Matthean Christology. One should note that for a book length treatment of "Jesus and the forgiveness of sins," only two pages are dedicated to the passages of Matt 1:21 and 26:28. This amount of space is no doubt deficient for passages—two that are explicitly linked, even according to the author— that are acknowledged by the author himself as being significant to the theme of forgiveness. What seems to cloud the scholar's view on the subject and restrain him from elaborating upon the passages and the explicit link between Jesus' death and forgiveness as well as the connection between Matt 1:21 and 26:28 is the critical perspective. When one is suspicious of the received text, then conclusions are difficult to draw. For example, the writer states, "It must still be kept in mind how uncertain is the reconstruction of an original form of the tradition behind" the Pauline and Markan versions (Hägerland, 2012:74-75). What seems more plausible to the author is the conscious development of the themes by the Matthean author.

As mentioned in a few preceding sections, many scholars see Isaiah 53 as a significant interpretive key for the saying in Matt 26:28 (Bruner, 1990:966; Moo, 1983:306; Moo, 2002:130; France, 2007:994; Keener, 2009:630-631; Hägerland, 2012:74; Gibbs, 2006:107). Death, of course, is in view. Green observes, "[W]ith the servant motif Matthew expands the theological field of his portrayal of the passion. This is evident in Jesus' interpretive words at the Last Supper, where terminology such as 'on behalf of' and 'poured out for many' are reminiscent of the work of the servant and Isaiah 52:13–53:12. These sayings interpret Jesus' death as efficacious, thus showing how Jesus would 'save his people from their sins (1:21)'" (Green, 1992:156). Contemplating the thematic nuances of Matthew's concepts, Keener concludes, "Whatever this early tradition preserved, therefore, likely tells us much about Jesus' view of his mission. Jesus elsewhere spoke of the pouring out of martyrs' blood (23:35) in terms of death, guilt, and impending judgment, a theme Matthew develops further in 27:4, 25. But even if the gospel tradition also plays on the atoning value of martyrs' deaths (especially attested in 4 Maccabees) here, Jesus' death appears as more than that of a mere martyr in this earliest tradition. Jesus' probable allusions to Isaiah 52–53 . . . tell us a great deal about how Jesus viewed his own death" (Keener, 2009:630-631).

Both Matt 1:21 and 26:28 contain phrases that are unique to the First Gospel, which supports the idea that a macro inclusio is formed. As Carson perceives, a crucial literary and theological correlation with "v.28 is to be found in 1:21. It is by Jesus' death, by the pouring out of his blood, that he will save his people from their sins" (Carson, 2010:603). The large inclusio explains the meaning of the cross. The first passage lays the groundwork while the second explicitly communicates the meaning of Christ's death on the cross for the forgiveness of sins. Jesus does not direct his followers to think back to his manger in Bethlehem. He does not point his disciples to his Sermon on the Mount. He does not guide them to his healings or any other activity. When Jesus wants to teach his people about his mission, he leads them ahead to his death on the cross. Thus, one can comment, "Here again is evidence that for Jesus death was no unexpected event unrelated to his life and work. In his death Jesus' obedience to God is manifest, and in this the cross is comprehended as the heart of his mission to open the way of salvation to all" (Green, 1992:157). When believers eat and drink the commemorative meal, they remember Jesus' death at Calvary for the forgiveness of their sins. Bruner poignantly observes, "The blood that will flow from Jesus' death tomorrow will do cosmic duty. That saving blood is placed sacramentally in the cups of disciples" (Bruner, 1990:966). By the time Matthew gets to 26:28, his explanation of the mission of Christ and the meaning of the cross has now been fully developed. All that is left to do is bear the cross. The Lord Jesus will do that very thing in the next chapter of the Gospel.

5.5 Matthew 26:24, 31, 54, 56 Fulfillment of Scripture

Beginning with Matt 26:24 here in section 5.5 and the remaining passages discussed in sections 5.6 and 5.7, the research moves outside of what might be considered the envelope structure between the brackets of the large inclusio to material that is better categorized as part of the epilogue. In these passages the main themes of the inclusio and Matthean Christology on the whole are reiterated in order to reinforce that Christology. The way that Matthew presents several items around the time of the crucifixion and just afterward tells the reader what to think about the event. The reader is told the theological significance of the cross by means of the fulfillment of certain key Hebrew Scriptures, Jesus' actual words from the cross, and the immediate events that took place at his death. Each of these three areas will be explored in the next three sections. The book will now look at the first of these three, the fulfillment of particular Scriptures from the Hebrew prophets of old. The verses with reference to what was written before are found in Matt 26:24, 31, 54, and 56.

The first reference in this section to consider is Matt 26:24. Another Son of Man passage, Jesus says that he will go "just as it is written of him." The cross of Christ will be a fulfillment of Scripture. This more generic reference to the Hebrew Scriptures does not hone in on a particular passage. Thus, several Scriptures may be in mind, for example Ps 22:1, 18; Isa 52:13-53:12; and Zec 11:12-13; 13:7. God is sovereign. He knew long ago that this would happen. He was sovereignly orchestrating the events. Jesus knew that Judas would be his betrayer, and yet God is working in and through the rebellion of men to accomplish his saving purposes. What becomes clear is that "Jesus has predicted his betrayal and death not as the natural outcome of a political process but as the fulfillment of a scriptural pattern" (France, 2007:990). "His conviction that his suffering and death will fulfill a scriptural mandate is now made explicit and will be further underlined in vv. 31, 54, and 56" (France, 2007:990).

The next reference to what is written about Christ's death is Matt 26:31. This is a quotation from Zec 13:7 (Moo, 1983:173-224). The prediction is that when the Shepherd is struck, the sheep will be scattered. One can see, in the first place, that Jesus announces his suffering again, now in connection with his prediction that the disciples will all flee from him. Jesus is seen in light of the Zechariah passages as God's Shepherd, his close associate who will be struck by God himself, and the sheep are the people of God who are scattered when the shepherd is hit (France, 2007:998). The disciples will not stand by his side or come to his defense. The Lord demonstrated great emotional turmoil previously when he looked on the crowds of people and exclaimed, "They are like sheep without a shepherd" (Matt 9:36). He reserved his harshest critiques and warnings for those in places of authority and influence who led the people astray and worse. His mission, which would culminate in his atoning death and glorious resurrection, was to bring as many into his fold as possible so that he would be their Shepherd and they would be his sheep. The reader clearly sees that the betrayer was not the only one to exhibit human sinfulness and weakness that night. In fact, Jesus says, "All of you;" all of the disciples would demonstrate their human frailties. They will be "made to stumble" or "take offense" at Jesus. They will trip up over the things that will shortly take place as Jesus is brazenly betrayed, unjustly arrested and tried, and viciously crucified at the cries and hands of both the Jews and the Romans. Jesus quotes a messianic passage from Zec 13:7. Many commentators agree, "The meaning in the Old Testament context is not entirely clear. But Zechariah seems to imply that a day would come when God's appointed leader in Israel would be cut off and his people scattered" (Blomberg, 1992:393). What should be noticed, though, is the way that Matthew records the reference. A close reading proves that the quote begins with, "I will strike." No matter what the Jews would plot or what the betrayer would scheme or what the Romans ultimately would do—God is the one who was bringing these things about in his sovereign plan.

In Matt 26:54 the Lord Jesus acknowledges that the Scriptures say that he must be betrayed to death. This is God the Father's will (France, 2007:1014). What Scriptures were fulfilled at this point? The reference may be again to Zec 13:7-9, but Isaiah 53 and Psalms 22 and 69 are likely also at work (France, 2007:1014). Matthean Christology comes to into focus here, as Hagner comments, "From the evangelist's point of view, [the death of Jesus on the cross] is the fulfillment of scripture (26:54, 56), the fixed will of God, and the deliberate choice of the obedient Son of God" (Hagner, 1995:749).

Jesus had told the disciples in verse 54 that these events and his submission to them were fulfilling Scripture. Now in Matt 26:56 he also tells the multitudes there that the evil actions taken against him are a fulfilment of the Scriptures of the prophets. At this point, Isa 53:12 is relevant when the prophet declares, "He was numbered with the transgressors." Yet, many of the passages cited above are probably also still at work. While they think that they are doing away with Jesus, they are actually doing exactly what God had known and prophesied long ago.

5.6 Matthew 27:46 My God, My God, why have You forsaken Me

The so-called "Cry of Dereliction" is recorded in Matt 27:46. This passage is another notable one that is not included in the envelope structure of the inclusio detailed in this book. Yet, the saying does speak to Matthew's theology of the cross. When harmonizing the four canonical Gospels, this becomes the fourth saying of the Lord Jesus from the cross, and it is one that has garnered much discussion (Harris, 2016:56-59). If a scholar only looks at Matthew's Gospel, this saying is the only one of Jesus from the cross, which must mean that the episode was significant for Matthew (Morris, 1992:720). In fact, this is the first time that Jesus has spoken since he appeared before the Sanhedrin in Matt 26:64 (Nolland, 2005:1207). Furthermore, Jesus cries out loudly when speaking these words, so he must have wanted bystanders to hear his words (Morris, 1992:720). With these words, the reader gets a glimpse into the mind of Christ and what he was thinking about his own death (Nolland, 2005:1207). Moreover, the reader (and the original hearers) learns not only what Jesus thought about his own death but also what Jesus wanted others to know about his death.

Matthew records, "And about the ninth hour Jesus cried out with a loud voice, saying, 'Eli, Eli, lema sabachthani?' that is, 'My God, my God, why have you forsaken me?'" With the opening words of Psalm 22, Jesus finds two things: (1) He finds words to put to what he is feeling—despair, the brink of death, overwhelming agony, the wrath of God against sin; and (2) He finds the message that he wants conveyed to the people who stood around him and for generations of those who would learn of this historical episode. How should one interpret what was happening on the cross in the death of Christ? Look no further than Psalm 22.

Now, the question is how literally are the words of Christ from Psalm 22:1 to be taken (Brown, 1994:1045)? Understanding what the words mean is a "difficult problem" (Morris, 1992:720). Although Jesus was crucified and in great agony does not mean that he is not in his right mind to speak exactly what he wants to say. He is, in fact, strong enough to cry aloud these words (France, 2007:1075; Nolland, 2005:1207). Thus, he could still be strategic in what he conveys.

Psalm 22 is certainly at work in the episode. Some scholars have even pointed out that allusions have already been made to Psalm 22 leading up to and preparing the way for the Cry of Dereliction in Matt 27:35-36, 39, and 43 (France, 2007:1075-1076; Nolland, 2005:1207; Stern, 1992:84). Nolland admits that Psalm 22 and the Cry of Dereliction are special cases (Nolland, 2005:1207). He claims that the answer to the theological problem the reader faces is answered in the psalm itself, that answer being that "the abandonment is only temporary" (Nolland, 2005:1207).

Apparently, most scholars, at least in the Evangelical camp but also others, take the saying to mean that Jesus is suffering some kind of divine forsakenness. They say he must have felt somehow abandoned by God the Father (Morris, 1992:721-722; France, 2007:1076; Moo, 1983:271-274; Brown, 1994:1047-1051; Nolland, 2005:1207). This has given rise to the notions that God turned his back on Jesus, and the Father cannot look upon sin.[97] For example, Carson stretches the point when he comments, "The darkness covering the land must signal something like the loss of the light of the Father's presence" (Carson, 2010:647). The other side of the debate seems to argue that Jesus is declaring victory. The two options, then, are something like a cry of desolation or a shout of triumph. Although Morris thinks that this two-option

---

[97] One must grant that on the surface Hab 1:13 seems to affirm this idea when the prophet writes, "You are of purer eyes than to behold evil, and cannot look on wickedness." Morris even cites this verse in support of his interpretation of godforsakenness (Morris, 1992:721). However, one must interpret the passage in its own context before developing a grand theology of divine abandonment. Bruce comments on the passage from Habakkuk, "The Chaldean invaders have indeed been raised up by [God] for the punishment of the ungodly—this the prophet accepts without question. But here is his question: Should not Yahweh's instrument for the accomplishment of his purpose reflect something of his own purity and righteousness?" (Bruce, 1993:853). The point is to question God, not to teach that he cannot look upon sin. The prophet, and probably many other believers, were attempting to resolve a seeming contradiction between God's holiness and his allowance for evil. Thus, the verse really has nothing to do with Jesus' death on the cross and the Cry of Desolation.

interpretive framework is "inadequate," it does seem that commentators fall on one side or the other (Morris, 1992:721). Most Evangelical scholars do appear to side with some sort of divine abandonment, a severance in the godhead. Historically, though, interpreters have hesitated to attribute some kind of godforsakedness to the saying (Brown, 1994:1047).

One certainly must be willing to talk about the Father giving the Son over to be put to death. That was the prediction of Isaiah 53. One must also be willing to talk about the horrors of that death for Jesus both physically and in his soul as he took upon himself the sins of the world. Think of the gruesomeness of crucifixion plus the agony of soul already begun in Matt 26:36-46. However, one should be careful in advocating for some sort of divine abandonment. In the original context of Psalm 22, David may have *felt* abandoned, but he was *not actually* abandoned by God. Jesus' cry was one of physical torture and agony of the soul. He definitely felt the weight of taking the sins of the world upon himself. He knew the agony of being given over to the curse of sin and death. He did that in the place of sinners. That was his mission. But it may be problematic for the orthodox Christian who believes in the doctrine of the Trinity to claim some sort of severance in the godhead. An alternative view is perhaps necessary.

The figure of speech called *epizeuxis* (or duplication) is obvious in this verse. The feature is one of repetition and specifically "of the same word in the same sense" (Bullinger, 1898:189). Used ten times with names in the Scriptures, Matt 27:46 is the tenth and final use of the feature in the Bible, this time when Jesus speaks to God the Father (Bullinger, 1898:190). When Jesus says "Eloi, Eloi" the cry is emphatic and "calls special attention to the occasion" and to the "solemn moment of importance in the action, or of significance in the words" (Bullinger, 1898:190).

While duplication is easy to detect, few scholars interject the notion of what one might call *metalepsis* when interpreting Matt 27:46. The book has already underscored the literary brilliance of the Matthean Gospel. The possibility of literary metalepsis on Matthew's part is not farfetched. Moreover, Jesus may have very well have used metalepsis rhetorically. This literary and rhetorical feature needs to be clearly labeled and carefully defined. There are various definitions and debates about the meaning of the term. What is being called here "metalepsis" is defined specifically this way for the current chapter: "Metalepsis is a rhetorical or literary device in which a familiar phrase or citation is presented in a new setting in order to evoke remembrance of the entire text in which the reference is originally found." Again, only a sample of a text may be cited but is meant to cause the hearer or reader to think of the whole context. This is often done with the first line of a literary unit or the most famous line of a section may be referenced. In this case, the partial quotation is meant to bring to mind the whole. The claim here is that Jesus is possibly quoting the first line of the Psalm 22 but wants the bystanders (and thus, all future readers) to recollect the whole psalm. Even Carson affirms,

"OT texts are frequently cited with their full contexts in mind" (Carson, 2010:647).[98] In his Jewish New Testament Commentary, Stern affirms, "In Judaism, when a Bible verse is cited its entire context is implied, if appropriate" (Stern, 1992:84).

Metalepsis functions similarly to the figure of speech called synecdoche, although synecdoche is used for one-word metaphors. Various definitions of synecdoche would consist of: "A figure of speech whereby a more inclusive term is used for a less inclusive term, or vice versa. . . . Synecdoche may often be called either "part for the whole" . . . or "whole for a part" (DeMoss, 2001:119). The figure employs a "substitution of a part for a whole" (Quinn, 1993:58, 103). Synecdoche (or transfer) is "The exchange of one idea for another associated idea," and "Synecdoche of the Part is where a part is put for the whole" (Bullinger, 1898:613). Practical examples include phrases such as, "The nation has many boots on the ground" where boots, only part of the uniform, refers to the whole soldier and even the whole army. Another example would be a saying such as, "I like to drive a stick" where stick, only part of a vehicle, refers to a whole car with a manual transmission.

Approaching a more directly relevant example of metalepsis in contemporary usage, like the case of Matt 27:46, might be something such as a speaker quoting part of Shakespeare but intending the hearer to think of the whole story. Another more modern literary example is the beginning of the *Magician's Nephew* in C. S. Lewis' *Chronicles of Narnia* series. To set the scene, Lewis writes, "In those days Mr Sherlock Holmes was still living in Baker Street. . ." (Lewis, 2001:11). The author's intent seems to be to make reference to one literary character, Sherlock Holmes, but by doing so to cause the reader to think of the whole story and setting surrounding said character. The reader thinks of London in the mid nineteenth and early twentieth centuries, that is, Victorian era England. To supply one more example, in America, it is commonly known that if someone says the phrase, "I have a dream," the hearers immediately think of Martin Luther King Jr.'s famous 1963 speech delivered in Washington D.C.[99] Hearers may think of other parts of the speech, but they will likely also think of the person who delivered the speech, the historical context, and the historical movement for civil rights. The phrase "I have a dream" has come to be known as the title for the speech, although it was first said in the middle of the oration. The phrase, it should be noted, is the most famous saying from the speech and was repeated several times.,

---

[98] Carson is quick to say that OT texts "are never cited in such a way that the OT context effectively annuls what the text itself affirms" (Carson, 2010:647). This concern will be dealt with below.

[99] A transcript of the speech can be read at this link from the Marshall University website: https://www.marshall.edu/onemarshallu/i-have-a-dream/.

This practice of quoting a part in reference to the whole is also a common practice in biblical literature. For example, consider 2 Cor 3:15 where "Moses" represents the whole of the Old Testament Law and Matt 27:3 where "innocent blood" represents the whole person (and possibly even whole narrative). Bullinger gives an abundance of examples on page after page in his tome on biblical figures of speech (Bullinger, 1898:640-656).

What is left out of these biblical surveys for the figure of speech referred to here as metalepsis is the quotation of part of a scriptural passage in reference to the whole of the text. Synecdoche is used of one-word metaphors. However, metalepsis is a rhetorical or literary device in which a familiar phrase or citation is presented in a new setting in order to evoke remembrance of the entire text in which the reference is originally found. This works much the same way a simple allusion does but with specific quotations of phrases.[100] When one hears part of the lyrics, one is to think of the whole song. When one hears part of the poem, one is to think of the whole composition. When one hears part of a Scripture, one is to think of the whole context. Matthew 1:23 is likely an instance of this feature. Granted, the author directly references the prophet. However, he likely intends that the reader think beyond just the short quotation of "Behold, the virgin shall be with child, and bear a Son, and they shall call His name Immanuel." He likely intends that the reader think of the context of Isaiah 7, including the "sign" from God. He may even expect the reader to think of Isaiah 7-9 and Isa 9:6-7, in particular. This gives a much fuller picture than just the quotation itself. The same is true of Matt 2:15 and the quotation of "Out of Egypt I called my Son." These words alone, on a surface level, are surely not all that the author intended the reader to grasp. The reader likely thinks of Hos 11:1, but Matthew probably means even more than that. He probably wants the reader to think of the whole of the salvation of God in Israel's history, especially in the events at the time of the Exodus. The message is that God is intervening to do something great. This is a pivotal moment in salvation-history.

In Matt 27:46 Jesus appears to refer all of Psalm 22 to himself (Stern, 1992:84). The claim is not to know exactly what Jesus meant by the quotation from Psalm 22 or to even know exactly what Matthew was thinking by including the saying. The proposal is not to prove one interpretation over another but to give another possibility over against a prevalent notion of divine severance. Psalm 22:1 appears to be the title of the psalm. Jesus, then, quotes the title. In doing so, Jesus is saying by metalepsis that if you would understand his crucifixion you need to reflect upon that psalm.

Morris raises a couple of arguments against an interpretation that includes the whole context of Psalm 22. First, his objection, "But in any case it is perilous to argue from the use of one verse that Jesus was quoting the

---

[100] One definition of allusion is, "An indirect, imprecise or passing reference in which a verbal correspondence to the source text is relatively remote" (DeMoss, 2001:17).

whole psalm" has already been answered in the preceding paragraphs showing the prevalence and usefulness of metalepsis in literature, even the biblical literature (Morris, 1992:721). Secondly, Morris thinks that if Jesus wanted to refer to the more positive aspects of the psalm, then he could have chosen a better part to recite (Morris, 1992:721). However, to this claim one might respond that metalepsis often works with a famous line from a text. Psalm 22:1 may have been the most prominent line of the psalm, serving as its title. After all, it is the opening line. When bystanders who were immersed in the Old Testament Scriptures heard Jesus quote the first line of a Davidic psalm, it seems reasonable to believe that many of them likely knew the entirety of the psalm. The same is true of Matthew's original audience who likely knew the Old Testament Scriptures and contexts much better than the average contemporary reader. Even today, if a Christian teacher were to say in an assembly, "The Lord is my shepherd," it is probable that most in the group would think of Psalm 23, and it is not fantastic to believe that several in the group could recite the entirety of the psalm, only after hearing the first few words.

The question of taking one side or another should be answered. Were Jesus' words a cry of dereliction or a shout of triumph? To this question another question may be offered in reply: Could it not be that Jesus' cry of the first line of Psalm 22 from the cross was the result of both great spiritual and physical agony and also trust in God for triumph in the end? The context of the psalm, although ending on a high note of victory, does not deny the excruciating pain and spiritual sense of beleaguerment of the speaker (Nolland, 2005:1207). Why can this not be the case without building an entirely unbiblical argument about severance in the godhead? The Christian scholar should not be quick to construct a theology from silence. France wants to warn against reading between the lines. Yet, he goes on to convey ideas such as the fact that Jesus uses the title God and not Father, his customary reference to God, must mean that the "relationship appears to be broken" (France, 2007:1076). This way of interpreting the saying also seems to be forced and to go too far. Truthfully, there are interpreters on all sides of the debate who "read between the lines" (France, 2007:1076). However, this should be guarded against by all parties.

So, to learn what Jesus thought about his own death, and what Matthew thinks about the cross, one can gather much from Jesus' reference in Matt 27:46 to Psalm 22. Jesus was in great bodily pain and spiritual agony, and yet he also had confidence in God the Father. Notice that the phrase begins, "My God, my God." His making it so personal ("my") shows that he is still close with and confident in God. Moreover, is it purely an accident that Jesus quotes exactly the opening line of Psalm 22? Certainly not. Jesus is God in the flesh, the author of all Scripture, and the fulfillment of all the prophecies. He is in agony but also in his right mind, and he points the onlookers to this psalm which he relates to in the suffering he was enduring (of course, much more so than David, the original psalmist) but also his resilient trust in the Father and the mission. He knew that his Father would not abandon him to Sheol (Ps 16:10). Jesus was despised by the people (Ps 22:6), but he was not despised by God (Ps 22:24). Jesus cried out to God (Ps 22:2), and God answered (Ps 22:21).

Carson makes several connections from Matt 27:46 back to Matt 1:21 (Carson, 2010:647). He says that the purpose of the divine division (though one might disagree with this conclusion) is tied into the episode in the Garden of Gethsemane, the Last Supper in the Upper Room, and passions passages such as 1:21; 20:28; and 26:28 (Carson, 2010:647). Another connection to Matt 1:21 is the several references to salvation in the context of Matt 27:46. This causes the reader to think back to Jesus' mission to save his people from their sins. Even those who claim some kind of divine severance tend to soften their position, just as Carson concludes his discussion by writing, "Trusting God and being abandoned are not mutually exclusive—not in David's experience, and not in Jesus' experience" (Carson, 2010:648). Jesus' words, then, are simultaneously a shout of anguish and accomplishment.

5.7 Matthew 27:50-54 Immediate events at time of Christ's death

Several commentators see the immediate events at the time of Christ's death as the answer to Jesus' prayer to God in Matt 27:46. God the Father gives a perspective from heaven on the meaning of the cross. So, France writes, "The events of vv. 51-54 then follow as God's response to this call for vindication [that is, the Cry of Dereliction]" (France, 2007:1077). Additionally, Carson comments, "God's answer to this cry of desolation, then, is in the utter vindication of vv.51-54" (Carson, 2010:648).

This pericope is the third included in the chapter that does not fall within the brackets of the macro inclusio outlined in the book. However, the passage does speak to the subject of Matthean Christology. The reader ascertains a fuller understanding of what Matthew thinks about the cross by the details he includes and the way in which he relays the material.

What is interesting to the reader of the First Gospel is that Matthew does not dwell on the details of the crucifixion but only refers to it in the "briefest way" (Hagner, 1995:750). This can only be the case literarily speaking and even theologically because the inspired author has already presented an explanation of the mission of Christ and the meaning of the cross. This is seen most evidently in the macro inclusio and all of the related passages to those brackets, Matt 1:21 and 26:28. Jesus saves his people from their sins by shedding his blood on the cross for their forgiveness.

Since the author has made his theology of the death of Christ known throughout the narrative of his Gospel, he is able to share other historical and theological details to help heighten that Matthean Christology. Once the large inclusio was formed by Matt 1:21 and 26:28, and the key passages within the envelope structure were formed, the remaining details become accentuations.

The paragraph of Matt 27:50-54 relays the immediate events at the time of Christ's death. God the Father in heaven powerfully asserts what he thinks about the death of on his Son, Jesus Christ, as he brings about marvelous signs in the natural world that have supernatural implications. "[L]ittle of anything in the events surrounding Jesus' crucifixion and resurrection make sense on the normal historical level. These are all unique events that uniformly testified to the most unique acts of God in human history—Jesus' vicarious death on the cross and his vindicating resurrection" (Wilkins, 183).

5.7.1 Jesus Yielded Up His Spirit

Jesus cried out again with a loud voice and yielded up his spirit. Matt 27:50 begins with an adversative conjunction. Jesus is contrasted with the mistaken and mocking bystanders (Morris, 1992:723). Jesus was still strong at death, drastically different than the experience of most crucified individuals (Morris, 1992:723; France, 2007:1075; Nolland, 2005:1207). Matthew frames Christ's death as a voluntary event (Morris, 1992:723). Jesus yielded his spirit. Chrysostom is said to have commented that Jesus cried out with a loud voice and voluntarily yielded his spirit to show "that the act was done by power" (Morris, 1992:723). The "act" is taken to mean his death. "The verb is ἀφίημι, which is used 142 times in the New Testament but only here in the sense 'die'" (Morris, 1992:723). What is more, "None of the Evangelists uses any of the usual ways of saying that Jesus died, and this may be part of the way they bring out the truth that there was something in his death that set it apart from all other deaths" (Morris, 1992:723). While many crucified victims would simply collapse weakly into death, Jesus strongly gives himself over to it.

5.7.2 The Veil of the Temple was Torn

The veil (or curtain) referenced here is the one that separated the Holy Place from the Most Holy Place, sometimes called the Holy of Holies (Morris, 1992:724; Stern, 1992:84). This was the innermost sanctuary where God had promised to dwell in a special sense and to meet with the High Priest. The background information can be found in Exod 26:31-35.

Most likely, God means to state in a dramatic way that he has left the Temple, like the vision of Ezekiel 10-11 (see especially Ezek 10:18, "Then the glory of the Lord departed from the threshold of the temple and stood over the cherubim"). Of course, this also means that mankind no longer has to meet God specifically in Jerusalem at the Temple and through particular rituals of Temple sacrifices. Now, at any time and in any place believers can commune with God because of Christ's achievements on the cross. So, God apparently means to communicate to all people his judgment on the Jewish nation and the Jerusalem temple (Morris, 1992:724; Hagner, 1995:853). He also means ostensibly to convey the new covenant which allows believers to receive the forgiveness of sins through Jesus Christ.

Turner is right to say that "Matthew teaches vicarious redemption. . . . The tearing at the temple veil when Jesus died probably signifies the completion of this redemption" (Turner, 2008:488). France thinks the same, "But the tearing of the temple curtain does not belong to the conventional language of theophany, and it is apparently a more specific symbol of what Jesus' death signifies or accomplishes" (France, 1079).[101] So then, "[T]he meaning is surely that by the death of Jesus the way into the holiest has been opened" (Morris, 1992:724). All are welcomed into God's presence by way of Jesus Christ.

5.7.3 The Earth Quaked and Rocks were Split

Earthquakes are a somewhat common experience in this region (Hagner, 1995:852). The timing of the earthquakes reported in Matthew 27 is what is amazing and speaks to God's actions. In fact, God's intervention is often marked by the report of earthquakes in the biblical corpus (see Jdg 5:4; Ps 114:4-7; Jer 10:10; Joel 3:16; Nah 1:5-6). Matthew reports earthquakes at two crucial points in the development of his Gospel: Matt 27:51 and 28:2.[102]

A more direct parallel with Matthew's scene of darkness (Matt 27:45) and earthquakes (Matt 27:51) is found in Amos 8:8-10. In that prophetic passage, God is seen as bringing about the earthshattering events. The language there from God is, "I will make;" "I will turn;" and "I will bring." The Lord was at work what the darkness settled in midday and the earth began to tremble.

The tearing of the Temple curtain as well as the breaking forth of the tombs is often closely associated with and even attributed to the earthquake that Matthew reports (Hagner, 1995:849). In any case, the earthquake itself is, for Matthean theology, a message from on high about what has happened. God is making his point of view known.

---

[101] France also interestingly footnotes at this point: "There is no independent record of this damage to the curtain" (France, 1079). Matthew was apparently more concerned with the theological point than the historical evidence for the event. This does not mean that it was not a historical occurrence only that Matthew was not as concerned to provide the evidence.

[102] For some hints at what might be evidence of these earthquakes, consult Morris' commentary on page 724, footnote 99 (Morris, 1992).

5.7.4 The Graves were Opened; and Many Bodies of Saints were Raised

The information in Matt 27:52-53 is not found in the other Gospels or anywhere else, for that matter (Morris, 1992:725; Wright, 2003:632; Davies and Allison, 1997:629). The claim that tombs were opened at the time of Jesus' death on the cross is not all that surprising considering that there were earthquakes (Morris, 1992:724). What is surprising is that Matthew tells his readers that the bodies of dead ("sleeping") saints were raised. Morris is probably correct to think that "Matthew is telling his readers something about salvation" (Morris, 1992:725). What was first foretold in Matt 1:21 is now coming to fruition. Christ's death is opening up a whole new world.

There is no archaeological evidence behind the appearances of the resurrected saints in Jerusalem. Likewise, there are no other historical accounts of these events. Thus, one cannot say anything much about the historical evidence (Morris, 1992:725). However, one can and should speak to the theology of the passage.

The pericope, of course, is one that attracts many questions. Wright lists several of this passage and then answers himself by saying, "I do not think we can find certain answers to any of these questions—which may of course mean that they are, as we say, the wrong questions to be asking" (Wright, 2003:633).[103] This is a perceptive statement. Often contemporary readers demand of a text what the original author never intended to answer.

One may acknowledge the uniqueness of Matt 27:52-53 by echoing various commentators who describe the passage by using phrases such as "weird residual fragment" (Borg and Crossan, 2006:181); "strange report" (Licona, 2010:530); "strange little text" (Licona, 2010:548); one with "many puzzling features" and "strange happenings" (Wright, 2003:603, 633); and that the story has a good bit of "awkwardness" (Perkins, 1984:125). The report is certainly odd, to admit the least, but it is not that surprising when one considers that Matthew represents in his Gospel the belief that the Creator of the universe is personally at work; he has sent his Son into the world to save his people from their sins; and the mission-fulfilling, sin-saving, forgiveness-ensuring death of that divine being has just occurred.

Scholars from various interpretive perspectives and denominational traditions end up concluding much the same way: Matthew means to convey the theological significance of Jesus' death by including extraordinary details portraying the event as salvific and transitionary to a new age (Perkins, 1984:125; Senior, 1976:326-328; Wright, 2003:634; Hagner, 1995:853; Quarles,

---

[103] Davies and Allison similarly remark, "The text ignores a question so many have asked: what happened to the saints?" (Davies and Allison, 1997:634). It does seem that several questions of contemporary readers simply are not considered, much less answered, by Matthew.

2017:343; Blomberg, 1992:421). How the various interpreters get to their conclusions is typically altogether different.

Michael Licona published his tome some years ago entitled, "The Resurrection of Jesus: A New Historiographical Approach" (Licona, 2010). The book became notorious for the scholar's discussion of Matthew's record of the resurrected bodies of the saints (Licona, 2010:527, 548-553). Again, Matthew is the only one who includes this episode. For that reason alone, doubt is cast on the whole pericope for some. For those historians and interpreters who reject miraculous events by default, there is no surprise that the account of the resurrected saints is explained away or outright denied as being historical. What is unanticipated in Licona's treatment of the passage is his explaining the miraculous details away in favor of some kind of legendary or poetic literary description used by Matthew as a way of accentuating the narrative of the death and resurrection of Jesus Christ. He is not the first theologian to treat the passage this way, but his was the first in a long time to garner so much attention. This is most unexpected because Licona writes from an Evangelical perspective. He is open to the miraculous. In fact, he counts much of the phenomena throughout the Gospel up to this point as miraculous, divine intervention. Moreover, he argues for the historicity of the resurrection of Jesus Christ, the main motivation for the book, which by all accounts is the most miraculous event in all of human history. So, why does Licona diverge from his typical interpretive pattern when approaching Matt 27:52-53? One cannot speak to the psychology, so only the published arguments themselves can be reviewed and discussed.

Licona's published views on Matt 27:52-53 became hotly debated at the time of the book's release (Quarles, 2016:271). Among those who argued against his views were the late Norman Geisler (Geisler, 2011-2016) and Albert Mohler (Mohler, 2011).[104] Both theologians made solid points in their disagreements with Licona.[105] Mohler asserts that some of Licona's opening statements on the biblical material are "deeply troubling," and his argument for Matt 27:52-53 as legend or poetic is "shocking and disastrous" (Mohler, 2011).[106] Geisler alleges that Licona's view is a denial of "the complete

---

[104] Geisler links several articles on the webpage *Licona Articles*. Internet. http://normangeisler.com/licona-articles/.

[105] Unfortunately, the public back-and-forth became less than pleasant at times. The references here are to the actual exegetical and theological points that were made. For a summary of Geisler's arguments, see this article: *Ten Reasons for the Historicity of the Resurrection of the Saints in Matthew 27.* Internet. http://normangeisler.com/ten-reasons-for-the-historicity-of-the-resurrection-of-the-saints-in-matthew-27/.

[106] Internet. https://albertmohler.com/2011/09/14/the-devil-is-in-the-details-biblical-inerrancy-and-the-licona-controversy.

historicity and full inerrancy of the Bible" and has "seriously undermined" the Gospel truth (Geisler, 2012).[107]

Licona claims that given similar descriptions in other Jewish and Roman writings, the language of Matt 27:52-53 should be understood as "special effects" and "a poetic device;" the text should be read with Jewish eschatological notions in mind (Licona, 2010:552-553). This interpretation, determined after surveying a few non-canonical writings, seems to be a strained attempt to propose a historical interpretation of the events that is more palatable to secular thinkers rather than an explanation that would include both historical and theological dimensions (Licona, 2010:548). A better context to consult for Matthew's thinking would be the entirety of the Matthean Gospel rather than outside Jewish and Roman sources. As Geisler exclaims, "So what if other Roman or Jewish legends are similar? The context of biblical text and other biblical texts are the best way to understand what a given passage is teaching" (Geisler, 2011).[108] When one considers the reports of supernatural or miraculous phenomena in Matthew, one does not conclude that all of the other events reported throughout the Gospel are poetic or special effects. On the contrary, from the very first chapter which reports that Mary was found with child of the Holy Spirit, through healings of all sorts of sicknesses, casting out demons, calming a storm, raising the dead, and more, all the way down to the climactic event of the Gospel in the resurrection of Jesus Christ, the events are presented as historical and characteristic of God's intervention in the life and ministry of his Son, Jesus Christ. Even Licona acknowledges that it would be a problem to understand some events in Matthew as poetic and others as historical (Licona, 2010:553). And yet, he still proposes that Matt 27:52-53 is a poetic device! Licona must go to great lengths after this proposal to then argue for the historicity of the resurrection of Christ.

The point here is not to attempt to disrespect, much less discredit, Mike Licona. Several scholars have taken his arguments to task, and Licona has had the opportunity to defend himself. Licona is an important Christian scholar on several fronts. He has done good work on quite a few different projects. However, this one interpretation of this one passage is a flaw in his work. Licona writes as a historian and not a theologian, but the Christian tradition has a hard time distinguishing the two. The entirety of the Matthean Gospel presents numerous reports of supernatural activity including angelic interventions and miraculous occurrences. These episodes are presented as historic. One cannot disregard one or a few of them and accept others. For the

---

[107] Internet. http://normangeisler.com/a-response-to-mike-liconas-defense-of-dehistoricizing-the-resurrection-of-the-saints-in-matthew-27/.

[108] *An Open Letter to Mike Licona on his View of the Resurrected Saints in Matthew 27:52-53.* Internet. http://normangeisler.com/an-open-letter-to-mike-licona-on-his-view-of-the-resurrected-saints-in-matthew-27/.

consistent scholar, the extraordinary passages must all be either accepted or rejected as historical. Again, Matthew seems to present all of the events as historical. There are people, places, and situations all nestled in historical contexts when these extraordinary events occur. Thus, Matt 27:52-53 concerning the raising of the bodies of the saints at the time of Jesus' death must be taken as historical, even while conveying a theological message.

Rather than using non-canonical sources for a framework for interpretation as Licona does, N. T. Wright surveys the "biblical echoes" in Ezek 37:12-13; Isa 26:19; and Dan 12:2 for an "obvious starting point" (Wright, 2003:633). After doing so, he proposes four interpretive options for Matthew's intent before concluding that his first option is the best: "Matthew knows a story of strange goings-on around the time of the crucifixion, and is struggling to tell it so that (1) it includes the desired biblical allusions, (2) it makes at least some minimal historical sense . . . and (3) it at least points towards, even if it does not express, the theological meaning Matthew is working towards: that with the combined events of Jesus' death and resurrection the new age, for which Israel had been longing, has begun" (Wright, 2003:633-635). Wright seems to still leave the interpretation vague but also makes much better sense of the passage than Licona does. A different wording may be better suited for the book, but Wright's main points seem to be agreeable. He would rather leave the interpretation to mystery than to say too much, but he leans toward a historical raising of the saints. He concludes his comments on the passage by writing, "Some stories are so off that they may just have happened. This may be one of them, but in historical terms there is no way of finding out" (Wright, 2003:636).

Opposing Licona and even folks like Hagner and going beyond Wright, the current writer is willing to commit to an interpretation that affirms both the historicity of the events relayed in the passages as well as a theological message. There are several commentators who affirm the same (including Quarles, 2016; Carson, 2010; Blomberg, 1992).

When trying to discern Matthew's seemingly complex timeline, Wilkins is helpful. He summarizes well what many have come to conclude: "Perhaps the best . . . explanation is that a full stop should be placed after the phrase 'The tombs were also opened' (27:52a) with a new sentence beginning with the next phrase. In this approach, the text would read: 'The tombs were also opened. And many bodies of the saints who it fallen asleep were raised, and they came out of the tombs after His resurrection, entered the holy city, and appeared to many' (cf. Wenham 1981, 150-52). With this rendering, Matthew indicates the following sequence: (1) the tombs were opened at Jesus' crucifixion; (2) Jesus was raised three days later; (3) the bodies of the saints were raised following Jesus' resurrection rather than immediately following His death" (Wilkins, 2013:182; cf. Morris, 1992:725; Carson, 2010:650). To put it simply: The breaking of the tombs was on Good Friday, and the raising of the saints was on Easter Sunday (Morris, 1992:725). This is not their final resurrection, they will die again, but it is a prelude of God's resurrection power which he will use to raise up all the faithful on the Last Day to never die again.

Osborne is not alone in thinking that this is likely an allusion to Ezekiel's vision of the valley of dry bones (Osborne, 1992:678; Wright, 2003:633). Interestingly, he also thinks that "[T]he enigmatic raising of the saints in Matthew 27:51-53 provides a theological bridge from the cross to the empty tomb" (Osborne, 1992:678), and "the brief story summarizes the effects of Jesus' death (judgment and the defeat of the powers of death. . .) and resurrection (the raising of the dead saints and their appearance in the holy city). Thus Jesus' passion and resurrection are inextricably linked as a single event in salvation-history, and the effect upon the raising and uniting of the true 'saints' of God, both past and future, is guaranteed by this supernatural deed" (Osborne, 1992:678). Osborne moves directly from the narrative of the resurrection of the saints to its application to all Christians for all time. In this way, the resurrection (or maybe better, resuscitation) of the saints becomes a foreshadowing of the resurrection of believers at the end of the age. The resurrection power of God is put on display. God did it then, and he can do it in the end.

How does this relate to the theme of sin and the cross? This albeit odd account seems to support the meaning of the cross in Matthew's Christological narrative. Something divine, powerful, and effective happened in the death of Jesus of Nazareth. The resuscitation of saints who had died supports this theological position. Thus, sin really had been dealt with in Christ's death. This miracle is God's affirmation of the event. Atonement has been accomplished. In support of the historicity of the narrative, Osborne simply states, "Miracles of raising the dead permeate all the traditions behind the Gospels (Mark, M, L, John, and possibly Q). . ." (Osborne, 1992:678). This narrative is yet another on the miracle of resurrection in a long tradition of such events. Matthew is apparently detailing things that happened surrounding Jesus' death and resurrection. These folks were not raised until after Jesus' resurrection.

5.7.5 The Centurion's Confession

The last part of the immediate events at time of Christ's death reported by Matthew is what might be called The Centurion's Confession. A centurion is a significant military person, overseeing one hundred soldiers in the Roman army (Quarles, 2017:343). Matthew passes on the following report: "So when the centurion and those with him, who were guarding Jesus, saw the earthquake and the things that had happened, they feared greatly, saying, 'Truly this was the Son of God!'" This confession reads as a climax. All of the occurrences reported by Matthew to accompany Jesus' death leading up to the confession of the centurion are meant to be confirmation of Jesus' identity as the Son of God (Quarles, 2017:344). The centurion becomes the mouthpiece for Matthean Christology. Matthew, the Matthean community, the apostles (Matt

14:33), and the Gentile witnesses at the cross (Matt 27:54) all make the great confession concerning Jesus Christ: "truly this was the Son of God" (Hanger, 1995:852).

The soldiers are now witnesses (validated by two or three) as to what the cross of Christ means (France, 2007:1083). This Gentile man may not have had a full messianic understanding of the term "Son of God," but he certainly realized that Jesus was more than a mere man. He knew something significant had taken place. The soldiers most likely did not see the temple veil torn asunder or the resuscitated saints walking the streets, at least not immediately, but they had experienced all of the events that took place at Calvary. As France notes, "The earthquake explains their terror, but it was the whole scenario of Jesus' crucifixion and death which triggered their 'confession of faith'" (France, 2007:1083). To debate what exactly the Roman soldiers meant by the confession that Jesus is Son of God may not be very fruitful. They may very well have meant that Jesus is *the* Son of God (Brown, 1994:1146-1151). Morris finds that "Their *Truly* points to certainty; they were not making a tentative suggestion" (Morris, 1992:726). This author tends to agree. Nevertheless, "Whatever the phrase may have meant to the soldiers, it is clear that for Matthew (as for Mark) it conveys nothing less than the full christological sense" (France, 2007:1084).

Therefore, the immediate events at the time of Christ's death relate closely to the theme of sin and the cross. They are God's affirmation of the efficacy of the cross. Matthean Christology, especially concerning the death of Christ, is rounded out in Matt 27:50-54. Thus, Hagner can summarize, "The cross and the spectacular events that immediately followed point together to the reality of Jesus as the Son of God" (Hagner, 1995:853).

Matthew shows his readers that Jesus speaks to the meaning of his own death, God the Father testifies to its efficaciousness, nature itself authenticates it, saints of old bear witness to it, and even Gentiles endorse the uniqueness of Jesus and his death on the cross. This was an emphatic conclusion (Hagner, 1995:852).

5.8 Chapter Five Conclusion

The Matthean Gospel account has been making clear throughout that Jesus has come to save his people from their sins. This started all the way back in the birth narratives, Matt 1:21 in particular: Give him the name Jesus because "he will save his people from their sins." This affirmation was bookended by the Lord's statement in Matt 26:28 that the cup of the Lord's Supper is his blood which is shed "for the forgiveness of sins." The cross is the culmination, the full picture of what that inclusio referenced.

Are passages related to sin and passages related to the cross of Christ linked in Matthew's Gospel to provide an explanation of Christ's mission and the meaning of the cross? The answer is yes. This has been seen from two different angles.

First, sin has been shown to be dealt with by the death of Christ throughout Matthew's Gospel, within the two brackets of the inclusio. The prediction passages of Matt 16:21-25; 17:22-23; 20:17-19; 26:1-2, 12 were all analyzed for connections to the inclusio and to the theme of the mission of Christ as his death in behalf of sinners. With each new prediction passage, the reality of Christ's death and the meaning of it became more obvious. Then, Matt 20:27-28 was revealed to fit smoothly within the envelope structure. The saying was said to build upon Matt 1:21, giving more information about the mission of Christ, but still did not say all that Matt 26:28 would about the meaning of the cross. The texts of Matt 26:24, 31, 54, 56 described the death of Christ as the fulfillment of Scripture. These Old Testament passages and Matthew's acknowledgment of them were important for the reader to learn that Christ's death was on purpose. His crucifixion was always the plan.

Second, sin has been demonstrated as remedied even outside of the envelope structure. The reader discovers several events that accentuate the meaning of the cross. The only saying of Jesus from the cross reported in the First Gospel is found in Matt 27:46. That quotation was argued to be a use of metalepsis, that is, a citation of part of a passage with the intention of calling to the hearers' remembrance the whole passage. The death of Christ was revealed there to be both agonizing and faithful. The cross becomes a symbol of anguish and accomplishment. The other passage from outside of the envelope structure created by the inclusio that was considered was Matt 27:50-54. This pericope relays the immediate events at time of Christ's death. There was, once again, unique material here found only in Matthew. The text was a culmination of witnesses to the efficacy of Christ's atoning death. Thus, Matthew has declared that sin was decisively dealt with in the death of Jesus Christ.

Chapter 6: Full and Final Construction of the Argument that the Matthean Gospel Presents a Unique Contribution to New Testament Theology with Regards to the Mission of Christ and the Meaning of the Cross

6.1 Synopsis of the Book

Carson and Moo do not think that Matthew makes much of an independent contribution to New Testament theology (Carson and Moo, 2005:162). France seems to agree with them (France, 1989:279). Luz even goes so far as to state that there is little in Matthew that provides answers to questions related to the meaning of Christ's atoning death (Luz, 2001:546). Davies and Allison make what seems to be an inflated claim when they write: "Even when 1.21 and 26.26-9 are taken into account it is impossible to construct a Matthean theory of the atonement. We have in the Gospel only an unexplained affirmation" (Davies and Allison,1997:100). These are all examples demonstrating the lack of interest in Matthew's Gospel on the theme of the forgiveness of sins by Christ's sacrifice on the cross.

When scholars take the perspective of those examples above—that Matthew contributes little to nothing to New Testament theology, especially concerning atonement—then they will not offer much space to the subject in Matthean studies. However, this work has sought to discover Matthew's unique theology of Christ's mission and the meaning of his cross. Turner's response to Davies and Allison (and, by extension, the others of that persuasion) is reflective of the sentiment of this book: that their view is "overly pessimistic;" and Turner goes on to affirm, "No doubt there are some unanswered questions, but the general thrust is clear" (Turner, 2008:488-489).

The preceding chapters of the book have aimed to demonstrate a counterpoint—that Matthew does have a unique contribution to make. Instead of turning immediately to the other Gospels or to Pauline writings, the New Testament reader can possibly now see the value in Matthew's Christology, independent of the other New Testament documents.

The analogy used in Chapter Four serves well as a recapitulation of the book: the mission of Christ and the meaning of the cross begin to germinate in the opening bracket of the macro inclusio, Matt 1:21. Throughout Matthew's διήγησις, then, the theme sprouts and grows. By the time the reader makes it to Matt 26:28, the closing bracket of the macro inclusio, the theme has fully developed and then is able to produce its fruit in the epilogue, chapters 27-28 (Nel, 2015:4).

The book has aspired to establish the Christology of the Gospel of Matthew firmly within the discussion of the atonement by showing the book's message through its own distinctive content and design. Matthew has a robust theological understanding of Christ's mission and the meaning of the cross that is put on display with the literary feature of macro inclusio (Matt 1:21 and 26:28). The macro inclusio, and the content of the Gospel working within the brackets, emphasizes Matthew's theology of salvation from sins through the shed blood of Jesus Christ.

The motif explored in this book has not been presented in order to ignore, undermine, or overshadow other themes in the Matthean Gospel. On the contrary, the intention has been to demonstrate that the forgiveness of sins is another of Matthew's primary themes. In fact, it has been argued that the theme is highlighted by the macro inclusio of Matt 1:21 and 26:28. In other words, and to give an example, the macro inclusio concerning the forgiveness of sins of Matt 1:21 and 26:28 is not highlighted in such a way as to overshadow the macro inclusio concerning Immanuel of Matt 1:23 and 28:20.[109] The idea is that the forgiveness motif is yet another important one that Matthew has set alongside the Immanuel theme. However, the book at hand has sought to make a bold claim along the lines of: *If Matt 1:23 and 28:20 is a macro inclusio, then Matt 1:21 and 26:28 must be a macro inclusio as well.* Furthermore, *The mission of Christ is more than simply 'God with us' but 'God is with us to save us from our sins.'* Moreover, this work has sought to demonstrate that the inclusio of Matt 1:21 and 26:28 is even clearer than other commonly accepted inclusios. The theme of the forgiveness of sins by the death of Christ on the cross is just as prominent, if not more so, than any other theme in the First Gospel.

As noted in Chapter One, several outstanding writers have published quite a few important commentaries and studies on Matthean themes in recent decades. Still, no one has presented a full-developed argument and explanation of the large inclusio of Matt 1:21 and 26:28 and its supporting passages throughout the First Gospel. The present work has aspired to demonstrate that Matthean Christology maintains as one of the key themes of Christian doctrine the forgiveness of sins as central to the mission of Christ. Furthermore, forgiveness of sins is achieved by Christ's substitutionary death by crucifixion. The meaning of the cross is explained by the inclusio in Matthew's account.

---

[109] There are many scholars who identify Matt 1:23 and 28:20 as a large inclusio (Angel, 2009:527; Hagner, 1995:888-889; Gundry, 1994:597; Harrington, 1991:415; Carter, 1998:62; Kingsbury, 1998:33; Decaen, 2021:56-74).

6.2 Recapitulation of the Chapters

The five preceding chapters of the book were, in large measure, an analysis of the text of Matthew and current Matthean scholarship to ascertain whether the First Gospel makes a unique contribution to New Testament theology with regards to the mission of Christ and the meaning of the cross by forming a macro inclusio. Chapter One was an introduction. This opening chapter set the blueprint for the book. The background, research problem, and research questions were all set forth. The aims and objectives of the project were also described. The research methodology was also established in the first chapter. So then, the subsequent chapters have followed the design that was initially proposed for the book.

While a preliminary literature review was provided in Chapter One, the Second Chapter more fully overviewed the state of research on the subject. Peer-reviewed journal articles, special books, and major commentaries published in recent decades were all considered. No literature review could fully examine every publication ever written, but some of the most pertinent works were outlined, especially in reference to the major theme of the current project, that is, the forgiveness of sins in Matthew.

After the literature review in Chapter Two, the literary nature of the Matthean Gospel began to be investigated in Chapter Three. Before arguing that a large inclusio is likely present in the First Gospel, the various terms for the literary device were surveyed. Those terms included repetition, epanadiplosis, epanalepsis, anaphora, epanaphora, encircling, cyclus, bracketing, enclosing, envelope structure, bookending, sandwiching, and inclusio. As stated in Chapter Three, inclusio appears to be the most common term employed in biblical studies for the literary feature described in the research project (Longman, et al., 2008:323; Chapman, 2013:1). Thus, inclusio has been the default term used throughout the book.

After the survey of terms, a working definition for inclusio was offered. An inclusio is a literary and rhetorical device of repetition employed for several reasons including to give structure and to highlight main points and is recognizable because the same idea, even the same words at times, are repeated at the beginning and end of a sentence, section, or book. Another important aspect of the research has been to show the presence of large, or what might be called "macro," inclusios in the biblical literature. These macro inclusios would include the occurrence with large sections but even at the beginning and end of entire books. Examples were given of both small and large inclusios.

The Gospel of Matthew uses the literary device of inclusio in several places. Examples were provided. The device was even shown to be utilized in several books of both the Old and New Testaments. There are both micro and macro inclusios in these documents. Moreover, the various authors employ the literary feature for different reasons depending on their context and purposes.

Criteria were established in the third chapter for determining the presence of an inclusio in any given document or section of a document. After submitting those standards, the chapter then examined Matt 1:21 and 26:28 to see if it met the requirements. In the end, the chapter argued that the passages are deliberately linked together by the inspired author of the Gospel. Reading one without the other will not give the reader the fullest meaning of the mission of Christ and the meaning of the cross. In this way, Matthew is seen to make a unique contribution to New Testament theology.

Chapter Four answered the question of whether or not the forgiveness of sins is one of the primary Matthean themes. The chapter attempted to answer the question by showing that, throughout the Gospel, the author has sought to support the large inclusio. The premise is that a macro inclusio is a bracketing structure that envelops the material within the whole book. If Matt 1:21 and 26:28 bracket the entirety of the Gospel to reveal the major theme of the forgiveness of sins through the death of Christ, then the contents of the book should fall under that category as well. This is not to say that only material directly supporting that theme can be included but that supporting evidence for that theme must be incorporated. Sin and forgiveness are demonstrated by the macro inclusio as key concerns in Matthew's Christology (Nolland 2005:380). So then, the content of the Gospel should bear that fact out. The following passages of Matthew form key reinforcements of that theme: Matt 1:21 with the purpose statement that Jesus has come to save his people from their sins; Matt 6:12-15 from the Lord's Model Prayer in the Sermon on the Mount concerning forgiveness; Matt 9:2, 5-7, 12-13 relaying the narrative of Jesus claiming for himself the authority of God to forgive sins; Matt 18:11 containing the saying of Jesus that the Son of Man has come to save that which was lost; and Matt 26:28 regarding Christ's blood being shed for many for the forgiveness of sins.

Chapter Five also answered affirmatively the question of whether passages related to sin and passages related to the cross of Christ are linked in Matthew's Gospel to provide an explanation of Christ's mission and the meaning of the cross. This has been seen from two different angles. First, sin has been shown to be dealt with by the death of Christ throughout Matthew's Gospel. The prediction passages of Matt 16:21-25; 17:22-23; 20:17-19; 26:1-2, 12 were analyzed for connections to the inclusio and to the theme of the mission of Christ as his death in behalf of sinners. With each new prediction passage, the reality of Christ's death and the meaning of it became more obvious. Then, Matt 20:27-28 was revealed to fit smoothly within the envelope structure. The saying was said to build upon Matt 1:21, giving more information about the mission of Christ, but still did not say all that Matt 26:28 would about the meaning of the cross. Sin and the cross come properly together in the second bracket of the macro inclusio.

The texts of Matt 26:24, 31, 54, 56 were studied in Chapter Five as well. They were seen to describe the death of Christ as the fulfillment of prophetic Scripture. These Old Testament passages, and Matthew's acknowledgment of them, were important for the reader to learn that Christ's death was deliberate. The cross of Christ had a divine purpose to answer the problem of sin. Sin was explained as the remedy even outside of the envelope structure. The reader discovers several events that accentuate the meaning of the cross. The only saying of Jesus from the cross reported in the First Gospel is found in Matt 27:46, part of what this book has labeled the epilogue (or the fruit of the inclusio). That quotation was argued to be a use of metalepsis, that is, a citation of part of a passage with the intention of calling to the hearers' remembrance the whole passage.[110] The death of Christ was revealed there to be agonizing but also faithful. The cross becomes a symbol of both anguish and accomplishment.

The other passage from outside of the envelope structure created by the inclusio that was considered in the chapter was Matt 27:50-54. This pericope relays the immediate events at time of Christ's death. There was, once again, unique material here found only in Matthew. The text was a culmination of witnesses to the efficacy of Christ's atoning death, even witnesses from God in heaven. There were supernatural phenomena at that time that the Gospel writer attributes to the intervention of God the Father. Thus, through the recording of the narratives, Matthew declared that sin was decisively dealt with in the death of Jesus Christ. The mission of Christ is fulfilled in the events surrounding the cross.

6.3 The Main Research Question

When the researcher set out to do work in Matthean studies, the main research question was whether or not the Matthean Gospel makes a unique contribution to New Testament theology with regards to the mission of Christ and the meaning of the cross by forming a large inclusio with references to "sins" at the beginning and end of his Gospel account. The research presented has answered that initial research question in the affirmative. Chapter Three explored the question most completely and concluded that it is reasonable to suppose that Matt 1:21 and 26:28 form a macro inclusio, specially designed by Matthew to demonstrate his Christological understanding of the mission of Christ and the meaning of the cross. Scholars like Nolland have affirmed, "The bracketing effect of 1:21 and 26.28 establishes sin and its forgiveness as key concerns for Matthew. That the forgiveness of God is vital is assumed in 6:12, 14-15 and worked out in the parable in 18:23-35" (Nolland, 2005:380). The following section will reiterate the line of argumentation to show how the research question has been addressed in the previous chapters.

---

[110] The chapter provided a specific definition of the term metalepsis for use in the book. This definition may differ from other uses of the term.

The opening bracket of the inclusio, Matt 1:21, anticipates and even dictates what the mission of Christ will be. The name given to the Christ was "Jesus." What would he do? "Save." Who would he save? "His people." What would he save them from? "Their sins." The closing bracket of the inclusio binds the whole Matthean Gospel together as Matt 26:28 culminates the theme of the mission of Christ by foretelling and explaining the meaning of the cross. The reader knows by the time he gets to the end of the Gospel that the salvation of sins will come through the sacrificial death of Jesus Christ on the cross to procure forgive of sins through his blood. As Matt 1:21 determined that the mission of Christ would be salvation from sins, so Matt 26:28 divulges the means by which salvation from sins is attained, that is, the shed blood of Christ for the forgiveness of sins. Salvation comes through forgiveness. Forgiveness is procured by the blood of Christ. This is the meaning of the cross. Matthew's Christology, then, focuses on salvation. The saving work of Jesus Christ is the summit to which all of the other parts of the Gospel are reaching.

Once the inclusio is bracketed, the stage is set for the reader to fully understand the epilogue of the Gospel of Matthew. In chapters 27-28, Matthew relays the historical facts surrounding the crucifixion of Christ, but the reader already knows the mission of Christ and the meaning of the cross before he or she gets to that historical narrative (Nel, 2015:4). The theological interpretation of the person and work of Jesus Christ are already in mind.

Joseph surely had very little understanding of what was meant by the saying, "For he will save his people from their sins." The same was likely true and still is true for initial readers of the Matthean Gospel. The full comprehension of the statement from Matt 1:21 does not come for the reader until Christ is quoted as saying, "My blood shed for the forgiveness of sins" in Matt 26:28. Kingsbury notes the culmination of the inclusio and also the irony of the events when he writes, "As Matthew's story draws to a close, therefore, Jesus' cross becomes the symbol, not of his destruction at the hands of his enemies, but of the salvation God accomplishes in him on behalf of all humankind, whether Jew or Gentile (1:21; 20:28; 26:28)" (Kingsbury, 1988:124). The Gospel author was bringing the reader to the climax of Matt 26:28, and the remaining sections of the narrative simply bring to fruition what was already explained through the inclusio and its supporting passages.

6.4 Chapter Six Conclusion

Any inquisitor into the historical facts concerning Jesus Christ has the same set of details as any other. Anyone can look at the cross and see the man beaten, mocked, crucified, and dying. The question is the meaning of it all. Matthew provides the meaning of the mission and cross of Christ. He provides the theological understanding. The mission of Christ was to save his people from their sins. The meaning of the cross is understood in Matthew's Gospel as the fulfillment of that mission, that is, the forgiveness of sins through Christ's sacrificial death.

The most important findings of this study demonstrate that (1) Matthew forms a macro inclusio with Matt 1:21 and 26:28, (2) the content of Matthew's Gospel supports the macro inclusio by accentuating the major theme of the forgiveness of sins by Jesus' death, and (3) Matthew's Gospel provides a unique contribution to the Christology of the New Testament.

The thesis is that Matthew has a unique Christological perspective which is primarily conveyed in a large inclusio formed at the beginning and end of his Gospel account. The rest of his Gospel "connects the dots" with various supporting verses according to this theme. The macro inclusio of Matt 1:21 and Matt 26:28 has been shown to buttress Matthew's overall Christology. The mission of Christ has been shown to be the salvation of people from their sins. The meaning of the cross fits into that mission and is the climax thereof as the forgiveness of sins is secured in the death of Jesus Christ on the cross. Antwi summarizes the point well when he speaks concerning the Synoptic Gospels, "The Evangelists show that forgiveness of sins belongs essentially to the very mission of Jesus" (Antwi, 1991:26). This, of course, applies to Matthew as well.

An inquiring reader might also question what new knowledge this research project has contributed to the field of New Testament studies, and Matthean studies, in particular. The current work makes a valuable contribution to the field in several ways. For example, there seemed to be no standard consensus within contemporary scholarship by which to discern an inclusio and the relevant texts that connect to the brackets. Thus, the project has formed its own system of detecting and investigating a macro inclusio. Most of this work was organized in Chapter Three where a definition of inclusio was recommended: "An inclusio is a literary and rhetorical device of repetition employed for several reasons including to give structure and to highlight main points and is recognizable because the same idea, even the same words at times, are repeated at the beginning and end of a sentence, section, or book." The chapter surveyed various terms used for inclusio, several definitions, the uses of inclusio generally, the use of inclusio in Old Testament literature and then in New Testament literature, the use of inclusio within the Gospel of Matthew, the purpose of inclusio, the criteria for determining the presence of an inclusio, and the chapter also discussed the idea of macro inclusios.

Moreover, the book at hand provides a well-developed contribution to the field of Matthean studies by addressing Matthean Christology from a unique perspective. Few to no studies have explored the subject by arguing for a macro inclusio in Matt 1:21 and 26:28. While some have discussed the theme of the forgiveness of sins, very few have developed the theme from the inclusio and then found the support throughout the Gospel. This book provides a much-needed study of the connections between the macro inclusio brackets and the significant passages within the envelope structure.

Now that the work has been put forth in Chapters One through Five and recapitulated in Chapter Six, a conclusion may be given in Chapter Seven. The question for the next and final chapter of the book is: What relevance does Matthew's Christology, especially with regards to the mission of Christ and the meaning of the cross, have for the contemporary church and the broader society? This question will be thoroughly addressed in the following chapter.

Chapter 7: Conclusion and Application of the Study to the Contemporary Church and the Broader Society

Scholarship has argued at times that the Gospel of Matthew is intended as a guide for true discipleship in order to distinguish true disciples from false ones or that the point of the First Gospel is to proclaim Jesus for the precise reason of shaping a particular community (Gundry, 1994; Carter, 1996, Luz, 1993). Some would suggest that Matthew is simply telling a story so that the narrative itself allows the readers or hearers to place themselves into the story and thus find their applications (Schreiner, 2019; Westerholm, 2006). Others have proposed that the key feature of the book is to show exactly who Jesus is (Quarles, 2013; France, 1989; Kingsbury, 1998).

The book at hand has argued along the lines of the latter—that Christology is at the core of what Matthew is doing. While many scholars think that an attempt to discern Matthean theology or Christology is almost pointless, the work has argued for a fairly robust Matthean Christology, especially concerning his mission and the meaning of his cross (see Chapter Six; France, 1989:279; Luz, 2001:546).

Themes of divine presence, messiahship, the Son of Man title, Davidic Kingship, fulfilment of prophetic Scripture, the Exodus, discipleship, evangelism, ecclesiology, and more are all present in Matthew's presentation of the Gospel narrative. These are all themes worthy of study and often have been addressed by the scholarly community. What has been proposed in the book is that Jesus coming to "save his people from their sins" by shedding his blood "for the forgiveness of sins" is another major theme. This book can echo Repschinski when he writes, "In the present study I have taken one aspect of Matthew's Christology and followed traces throughout the Gospel. Obviously, the focus is very narrow, yet it has shown that there is a viable possibility of viewing Matthew's Jesus in terms of [in the case of this book, forgiveness of sins displayed by the inclusio]. Matthew unfolds this theme in the course of the Gospel. . . . Obviously, this is not a complete picture of Matthew's Christology, but it fits in neatly with other aspects of Matthew's Jesus. . . . (Repschinski, 2006:266). Again, the macro inclusio highlights the theme of salvation by the forgiveness of sins, which is an important theme alongside several others.

Now then, all of the research questions have been addressed in chapters three through six. However, one question remains outstanding: What relevance does Matthew's Christology, especially with regards to the mission of Christ and the meaning of the cross, have for the contemporary church and the broader society? To ask the question another way: What conclusions may be drawn from the book that can potentially benefit the academic guild, the contemporary church, and the broader society?

Starting with Matthew and his community and throughout the Common Era, the Church has proclaimed a message to the world concerning Jesus of Nazareth (Schreiner, 2019:241). At the heart of that message has been the proclamation of the forgiveness of sins by the sacrificial and atoning death of Jesus Christ and his subsequent resurrection from the dead (Gibbs, 2008:211, 224; Nel, 2015:8). Matthew's Gospel fits within that historical tradition. The intention of the book has been to reinforce that historic claim of the Christian Church by displaying Matthean Christology which is believed to be distinctive in its content and design. This has especially been seen in the macro inclusio bracketing the entire book.

7.1 Conclusion of the Study

As stated in the previous chapter, any inquisitor into the historical facts concerning Jesus Christ has the same set of details as any other. Anyone can look at the cross and see the man beaten, mocked, crucified, and dying. The question is the meaning of the cross. The Matthean Gospel provides an historic Christian understanding of the meaning of the cross that may be just as helpful as Johannine or Pauline theology. Matthew, John, and Paul all agree that Christ died. They even agree on the interpretation. What differs is their various *presentations* of that event. Matthew also has a unique contribution to make when it comes to his presentation, which has been displayed throughout the book.

As one considers the cross, the event must be interpreted. All examiners are exposed to the same details, but the *meaning* of the details is what is at stake. One could look at the event through the lens of history, or psychology, or sociology, or some other means. Even as one looks at the crucifixion of Jesus Christ theologically, there are various views. Among Christian denominations and traditions, there are various interpretations. Was Christ triumphing over Satan, or dying as an example to influence the world with God's love, or was he a penal substitute?

The symbol of a cross is one of the most common representations in Christendom. The symbol is found in church buildings, Christian universities, libraries, homes, or around the neck as a piece of jewelry. *What* is meant to be conveyed by that symbol? To say the word "cross" in the context of religion or philosophy conjures up certain thoughts.

Islam has a view of the crucifixion over against Christians. Did Jesus even die on the cross? The Jehovah's Witnesses have a similar view of the death of Jesus to orthodox Christians, but are the views exactly the same? The Latter-Day Saints have their own interpretation of the event. Skeptical writers, including progressive Christians, understand the crucifixion a certain way. Was Jesus simply a martyr? Critical writers, including atheists, see something completely different happening at Golgotha. Was Jesus an overzealous man who found a quick end?

Critical writers look at the cross and see only a man dying (Lüdemann, 1996, 1999, 2001). Some are even confident to attest their belief that the narratives concerning Jesus are legendary, a work of literary invention (Miller, 2017).[111] At best, the atheistic claim is that Jesus was an innocent man who was condemned to death in an unfortunate turn of events, "the victim of a criminal conspiracy" (Lüdemann, 2006:14). At worst, atheists believe that Jesus was an overzealous man who rose up in rebellion against the government and was put to death for it (Garber, 2005; Buchanan, 1984:247-248). Critical writers have no reason to give thought to the theme of the forgiveness of sins.

Some within skeptical scholarship operate from a naturalistic worldview that claims nothing supernatural can occur. Skeptical scholars tend to see the crucifixion as a tragic end to the life of a moralistic teacher (Ehrman, 2014; Crossan, 1991; Borg, 2007). Skeptical writers typically dismiss this theme of forgiveness of sins through the death of Christ. For instance, Seeley explains away the significance of salvation through Jesus' atoning death by claiming "that the Gospel of Matthew contains several distinct perspectives on salvation" (Seeley, 1994:98). There are writers who claim, on the basis that crucified criminals were held in contempt, that Jesus' body was not buried but simply decomposed and was eaten by scavengers (Casey, 2010:446; Crossan, 1991). Others deny the authenticity of the passion predictions and thus a favorable interpretation of the events (Bultmann, 1968:151). So, again, skeptical writers understand something different happening at the cross than a divine plan.

The Latter-Day Saints (also historically known as Mormons) consider the cross of Christ to be atoning in some sense. Much of the same language that historic, Reformed Christians will use for the cross of Christ, language informed by the Christian Scriptures, is also used by Mormons (Millet and McDermott, 2007:95-100). However, the definitions of those terms is of vital importance for the discussion. Of course, the heart of the differences between Mormons and Evangelicals is the very nature of the person of Jesus Christ (Millet and McDermott, 2007:107). The *person* of Jesus explains much of the *work* of Jesus, especially in the atonement. For example, the LDS movement teaches, "From latter-day revelation we learn that the Father and the Son have tangible bodies of flesh and bone. . . . All mankind are [Jesus'] brothers and sisters, for He is the eldest of the spirit children of Elohim. . . . The Holy Ghost

---

[111] This claim seems incongruous with scholarship and historically unsustainable. However, in practice, this is what many scholars seem to conclude. For example, Borg distinguishes between "the historical Jesus" and "the canonical Jesus" (Borg, 2001:190). While he does not reject historical Jesus studies as a valid pursuit, the fact that he distinguishes between the two reveals that he believes in "metaphorical meanings of the gospel texts" (Borg, 2001:191).

is also a God" (churchofjesuschrist.org).[112] Historically, the Christian Church has never taught that the Father has a tangible body or that Jesus is the spirit child of God or that the Holy Spirit is "a" God (britannica.com).[113] Therefore, while some sort of atonement is maintained in Mormonism, that work is articulated much differently and is based upon a different notion of the person of Jesus Christ than the historic Christian Church would understand.

Jehovah's Witnesses, much like the Latter-Day Saints, articulate their views of the death of Christ using much of the language of historic Christianity (jw.org).[114] However, their views also diverge from the historical norm. For example, the Jehovah's Witnesses stress that Jesus died on a stake that was a single post rather than a cross as if this minor, material point matters to the theology of the event (jw.org).[115] They also affirm things such as, "God rewarded his Son's perfect obedience, granting Jesus immortal life in heaven" (jw.org).[116] A statement like this one is out of step with the historic Faith since Jesus has immortal life and does not need it granted to him.[117] Again, the essence of who Jesus is becomes the crucial difference between the view of the atonement in the Jehovah's Witnesses organization over against the historical, orthodox Christian position.

Islam claims that Jesus did not actually die on the cross (Surah 4:157-158; see Ali, 1989:235-236). This is a crucial distinction between Christians and Muslims. One scholar has boldly emphasized, "There can be no Christianity without the event of the cross. There can be no Islam with it" (George, 2002:99). The idea that seems to be prevalent amongst Muslims is that the situation unfolded in such a way that people thought that Jesus had died but that he really did not; instead, he was taken up to Allah and now lives in heaven in the body (Ali, 1989:236). Many Muslims believe that Judas was substituted for Jesus on the cross (Lodahl, 2010:158). Many scholars, especially Christians, think that Muhammad was influenced by heretical teachers of the early Church to believe that the narratives concerning Christ's death in the canonical Gospels is to be rejected (George, 2002:97-98). So, Jesus, according to Islam,

---

[112] https://www.churchofjesuschrist.org/study/scriptures/gs/god-godhead?lang=eng#title4

[113] https://www.britannica.com/topic/Nicene-Creed

[114] https://www.jw.org/en/library/magazines/watchtower-no2-2016-march/why-did-jesus-suffer-and-die/

[115] https://www.jw.org/en/bible-teachings/questions/did-jesus-die-on-cross/

[116] https://www.jw.org/en/library/magazines/watchtower-no2-2016-march/why-did-jesus-suffer-and-die/

[117] Matt 9:25; John 1:1-4; 5:24; 10:27-28; 11:25; 14:6; 1 John 5:11.

did not vicariously die to atone for the sins of the world (Ali, 1989:236). In Islam, the cross is altogether something else. However, Christian scholars have responded, point-by-point, to these claims and attempted to show how they are historically untenable assertions (Geisler and Saleeb, 2002:278-293).

Christians do believe that the cross should be interpreted and that the event ought to be elucidated theologically. Even a word like "atonement" is a term coined in the English language to label and even interpret the meaning of the death of Jesus Christ. Christ is understood as having made a state of atonement—at-one-ment. Reconciliation with God is conveyed in the term. People can now be "at one" with the Creator based on the achievements of Christ which are imputed to those who repent of their sins and put their faith in the Savior.

Evangelical Christians, while maintaining the doctrine itself, tend to neglect the theme of forgiveness of sins in the Gospel of Matthew, especially in what they perceive to be the meaning of the cross in Matthew's presentation.[118] As noted previously, even highly regarded Evangelical scholars believe that Matthew does not have much to contribute that cannot be found elsewhere in the New Testament (Carson and Moo, 2005:162; France, 1989:279). These writers do not reject the doctrine of atonement through the death of Jesus, but they do neglect Matthew's presentation of the meaning of the cross. To state the point simply, the writers referenced before and others in the camp of historic Christianity believe in salvation by the forgiveness of sins, but they would prefer to explain the point from other New Testament books.

The historic Christian tradition, including what might be called the Evangelical heritage flowing out of the Reformation, takes Matthew's Gospel as God-breathed Scripture and receives his theological understanding as its own. Therefore, the angelic message of Matt 1:21 is respected as historically reliable and theologically true of the mission of Christ. Moreover, the passion prediction passages spoken by Christ, the didactic passages concerning forgiveness of sins, and the narratival recordings of Christ's actions in relation to forgiveness are all taken to be trustworthy. Furthermore, the words of Christ in Matt 26:28 are received as a truthful judgment of the meaning of the cross. Thus, the macro inclusio and the contents within the envelope structure come together to present a full and robust Matthean Christology.

7.2 Application of the Study to the Contemporary Church

A perceptive application is given by Bruner is his commentary on Matthew. He writes, "Our deepest single need is the forgiveness of sins. Our

---

[118] As noted in the first chapter, the lack of material on the theology of Matthew and, to give a more precise example, the doctrine of the atonement in Matthew's Gospel, in particular, demonstrate the neglect of the subject in New Testament studies.

main block in fellowship with God, others, and ourselves is our sin and our consciousness of sin. We feel certain that God must surely hate our evil proclivities, thoughts, acts, and words as much as we do and more, and that, consequently, God must have a profound aversion to us. The Lord's supper continually reminds us 'on the contrary!'" (Bruner, 1990:967). This quotation brings together so many of the points in the book. Likewise, Matt 26:28—in the context of the Lord's last Passover when the Lord's Supper was instituted—also brings to fruition what Matthew wanted to teach about the cross of Christ. This is the message of the Christian Gospel. Moreover, this message is what reconciles people to God and also people to one another. The Lord's Supper, an important aspect of worship in Christian Churches of every denomination, is a reminder of what Christ did on the cross to bring about salvation. Furthermore, if the forgiveness of sins was the mission of Christ and is the meaning of the cross, then the forgiveness of sins is what the Church of Christ should be about. As one scholar has put it, "Matthew seems to intimate that ecclesial readmission and divine forgiveness are concomitant [18.19-20]. That the commission to the 'loose' is practically equivalent to a commission to forgive sins is also implied by Matthew's insistence that God has given the authority to forgive sins to human beings (9.6, 8)" (Hägerland, 2012:125). All of Matthew's readers, from the first century down to the twenty-first century, learn that God expects of his people—the Church—to be not only those who proclaim forgiveness but also those who extend it and live it.

Luz underscores a similar point when he affirms: "The statement, however, that he will save the people 'from their sins' is unusual as a Jewish hope. This reflects the Christian experiences with Jesus. Matthew in particular has a special interest in the forgiveness of sins that happens through Jesus and continues to be effective in the church" (Luz, 2007:95). What was predicted from the very conception of the child had lasting ramifications in the experiences of the early Christians down to current days. What was difficult to see in the Jewish experience of the first century was brought to light through the revelation of Jesus Christ. This point has been a reminder to Christians throughout the centuries to allow the revelation of Jesus, primarily through the New Testament documents like Matthew's Gospel, to shape and even dictate how the church is to understand and proclaim the message of reconciliation with God. The Christian community—the beliefs of the Church—are to be informed by the teaching of the apostles. Thus, if the Church takes the book of Matthew seriously, as this research project has sought to do, then the Church will have a special interest in the forgiveness of sins. The Church must let the Scriptures shape the believing community.

Furthermore, the contemporary Church needs to maintain and safeguard the historic Christology which has been preserved, for example, in the Matthean Gospel. How can the Church maintain that Christology? In the first place, faithfulness to a high view of Scripture is absolutely necessary. Secondly, and flowing from the first point, devotion to the reading of Scripture, robust preaching, and expositional teaching are all essential activities for congregations that want to safeguard and maintain historic Christology.

Like the content of the bulk of this concluding chapter, the contemporary church must engage in Christian apologetics. Evidence and arguments must be made from the text, from history, and from philosophical reasoning. Scripture must be actively and rigorously studied by believing scholarship and also in the broader Christian community. Appeals to the historic Christian tradition should also be made. Thus, a continuous study must be made of Church history and all those theologians of the past, from the Church Fathers and the Reformers to trusted commentators today. Additionally, philosophical inquiries can be helpful and then reasonable concepts may be communicated to the broader society.

The contemporary church, if it truly embraces and maintains Matthean Christology as it has for all of church history, must be about evangelism. The declaration of the mission of Christ and the meaning of the cross has been the business of the church since the earliest Christians. In the Gospel of Matthew itself, the Lord Jesus is quoted in the end as saying, "All authority has been given to me in heaven and on earth. Therefore, go, and make disciples of all the nations, baptizing them in the name of the Father and of the Son and of the Holy Spirit, teaching them to obey all things that I have commanded you; and behold, I am with you always, even to the end of the age" (Matt 28:18-20). The macro inclusio and the major theme thereof detailed throughout this work comes with a substantial application within the pages of the Gospel itself. Matthew, by quoting the Lord Jesus and by showing his person and works throughout the Gospel, is not only telling his readers that Jesus' mission concerned the salvation of people and that his cross means forgiveness of sins, but the divinely inspired author is likewise telling his readers that the achievements of the mission result in an ongoing mission for the Church. That mission of the church is now to evangelize the world with the Gospel of Jesus Christ. That Gospel is a message of the forgiveness of sins, secured on the cross of Christ. Followers of Christ are to now take that message to all the nations and teach it to them.

7.3 Application of the Study to the Broader Society

The previous section sought to demonstrate that the present study has application to the contemporary Church. Now, the chapter may turn to a new section to consider the application of the study to the broader society. While the study has more direct application to the Church, the book may also have application to the society by way of the Church.

To begin with, one may say that the forgiveness of sins is a distinctive doctrine of Christianity. No other major belief-system offers atonement for sin the way the Gospel does. The Christian Faith explains why things are the way that they are—people have sinned against a holy God—and Christianity offers atonement for those sins. Jesus Christ, the Son of God, has come into the world and taken sin upon himself so that people may be saved and welcomed into everlasting life with God. In the Christian Gospel, people are told exactly how to be saved from this present wicked age and from the wrath to come: put their faith in the one whom the Father has sent, Jesus Christ, and they will be saved. To put the case in Matthean language, the nations are to be baptized into the name of the Father, Son, and Holy Spirit and learn to obey everything that the risen Jesus has commanded (Matt 28:18-20).

What could the broader society know about Matthew's Christology that could be helpful to them in understanding the Christian Faith? The broader society seems to not understand the mission of Christ and the meaning of the cross. This problem may primarily be due to the Church not clearly communicating these matters or either the Church not understanding herself. Therefore, the Christian Church has an opportunity to learn more definitively the message of the New Testament and then proclaim more clearly the actual mission of Christ and meaning of his cross. The macro inclusio of Matthew's Gospel can help to gain a richer theology for the Church and a clearer presentation of the Gospel of the forgiveness of sins.

The content of this book is the Gospel of Jesus Christ. While the book itself is technical and elaborates upon some of the finer details of Matthew's presentation, the Christian message of salvation in Christ alone is the point of the research project. Christian scholarship should be rigorous and thorough, but the heart of such scholarship should always remain the Good News of Jesus Christ. Forgiveness, as seen in Matt 6:12-15, for example, and the discussion in Chapter Four, is something that people need to share with one another. The broader society may have a difficult time with this instruction, but the culture suffers when there is a lack of forgiveness. Christianity affirms that people need to be forgiven by God, and people need to forgive one another. This makes for a healthier society at large.

7.4 Suggestions for Future Research

This study was limited to the Gospel of Matthew and primarily English and Evangelical sources. This was by design but is an acknowledged restraint, nonetheless. Despite this limitation, the book makes an important contribution to the field as stated previously in Chapter Six, section four. Future research building off of this work and seeking to move beyond its self-imposed limitations could compare and contrast Matthean Christology with the other canonical Gospels. The language of the inclusio could also be juxtaposed with the other three Gospel accounts in the New Testament.

Another area for future research comes from Chapter Three. One may consider whether or not the two macro inclusios in Matthew's Gospel (Matt 1:21 and 26:28 concerning salvation by the forgiveness of sins as well as Matt 1:23 and 28:20 concerning Jesus as Immanuel with his people until the end of the age) are meant to combine to express one main idea (Kunjanayil, 2021; Carter, 1998:62). While some highlight the Emmanuel/Great Commission passages as an inclusio to demonstrate that God has come near in the person of Jesus, what may be of more significance is the large inclusio of Matt 1:21 and 26:28.[119] This inclusio emphasizes the significance of Jesus' mission and the meaning of his cross. The bracketing that Matthew generates explains the meaning of Christ's mission and his cross, that is, the forgiveness of sins. Important to note in support of this view is that both passages refer to sins. Furthermore, the strength of this book lies in the fact that both passages are unique to Matthew's Gospel. The Matthean literary feature could be called a panoramic inclusio because of the all-encompassing nature of the literary device. This idea of whether the two inclusios could be combined would be an idea to pursue in further research. The proposition would go something like this: The two macro inclusios in Matthew's Gospel combine to communicate the main idea that God is with us to save us from our sins.

The identity of Christ as divine may be proven in the relevant passages about his virginal conception of the Holy Spirit and his role in the forgiveness of sins (Gibbs, 2006:108). This notion, briefly touched upon in Chapter Four, is one worth pursuing. This research in the Matthean Gospel could be pursued to see what connections, if any, are actually verifiable.

Another thought for future research plans also springs from Chapter Four. One could pursue a fuller exploration of the idea that by calling those whom Jesus would save "his people" the Gospel author was placing Jesus Christ in the position of God himself (Gibbs, 2006:107). This is another line of thinking that argues for the divinity of Christ but also from the unique passage of Matt 1:21 which is connected to the large inclusio.

Concepts from both Chapters Four and Five provide a couple more opportunities for further research. The Old Testament background of themes highlighted in the book could be explored (forgiveness of sins, the mission of Christ, the death of the Messiah, etc.). These backgrounds could be investigated in connection to the inclusio. Additionally, one could ask and attempt to answer the question: Are there other related passages to explore in connection to the large inclusio that have not already been identified or discussed in full?

Considering the content of Chapter Five, one could elaborate more fully upon the link between the Last Supper passage and the death of Christ in Matthew's Gospel. This may bring forth an even clearer presentation of Matthew's theology of atonement. The passages are obviously significant for Matthew and surely could use more consideration.

One last proposition for a future research project is similar to one that has already been suggested. One could compare and contrast Matthew's presentation of the mission of Christ and the meaning of the cross with the

---

[119] This inclusio has been noted and discussed previously in the book.

other Gospel writers, but one could also compare and contrast the Matthean presentation with that of the Pauline tradition.

7.5 A Final Word

The New Testament research herein conducted on a specific aspect of Matthean Christology has proven to be fruitful for the researcher. The hope is that the study is also fruitful for any future readers. The mission of Christ and the meaning of the cross are crucial subjects to consider for any thinking person. This thesis is a humble attempt to add insight to the ongoing conversation surrounding potentially eternity-forming questions. S. D. G.

Bibliography

Aland, Barbara, and Kurt Aland, Matthew Black, Johannes Karavidopoulos, Carlo Martini, Bruce Metzger. 2012. *Novum Testamentum Graece*. 28th edition. Stuttgart, Germany: Deutsche Bibelgesellschaft.

Ali, Abdullah Yusuf. 1989. *The Holy Qur'an: Text Translation & Commentary*. Brentwood, MD: Amana.

Allison, D. C. 1994. Anticipating the Passion: The Literary Reach of Matthew 26:47-27:56. *The Catholic Biblical Quarterly*, 56(4): 701-714.

Allison, D. C. 2005. Matthew's First Two Words. In *Studies in Matthew: Interpretation. Past and Present*. Grand Rapids, MI, Baker.

Anderson, J. C. 1994. *Matthew's Narrative Web: Over, and Over, and Over Again*. Sheffield, UK: Sheffield Academic Press.

Angel, Andrew. 2009. Inquiring into an Inclusio—On Judgement and Love in Matthew. *Journal of Theological Studies*, 60(2): 527-530.

Antwi, Daniel. 1991. "Did Jesus Consider His Death to be an Atoning Sacrifice?" *Interpretation*, 45(1): 17-28.

Appiah, John. 2018. The Dream Cultures of Matthew's Gospel and Africa: A Comparative Study. *Valley View University Journal of Theology*, 5:15-27.

Archer, Joel. 2022. The Saints of Matthew 27: Why Do they Linger in their Tombs? *Journal for the Study of the New Testament*, 44(4):477-495.

Baker, Mark and Joel Green. 2011. *Recovering the Scandal of the Cross: Atonement in New Testament and Contemporary Contexts*. 2nd ed. Downer's Grove, IL: IVP.

Bal, Mieke. 2017. *Narratology: Introduction to the Theory of Narrative*. Toronto, ON: University of Toronto.

Bauer, W.; Danker, F. W.; Arndt, W. F.; Gingrich, F. W., eds. 2000. *A Greek-English Lexicon of the New Testament and other early Christian Literature*. Chicago, IL: University of Chicago (BDAG).

Barr, J. 1961. *The Semantics of Biblical Language*. Oxford, UK: Oxford University.

Beare, Francis. 1982. *The Gospel According to Matthew: Translation, Introduction, and Commentary*. New York: Harper and Row.

Bird, Michael. 2017. *Jesus the Eternal Son: Answering Adoptionist Christology*. Grand Rapids, MI: Eerdmans.

Bird, Michael. 2020. *Evangelical Theology: A Biblical and Systematic Introduction*. 2nd edition. Grand Rapids, MI: Zondervan.

Bird, Michael. 2022. *Jesus Among the Gods: Early Christology in the Greco-Roman World*. Waco, TX: Baylor.

Beilby, James, and Paul Eddy, eds. 2006. *The Nature of the Atonement: Four Views*. Spectrum Multiview Books. Downer's Grove, IL: IVP.

Blanton, Thomas. 2013. Saved by Obedience: Matthew 1:21 in Light of Jesus Teaching on the Torah. *Journal of Biblical Literature*, 132(2): 393-413.

Blomberg, Craig. 1992. *Matthew*. New American Commentary. Nashville, TN: Broadman.

Blomberg, Craig. 1997. *Jesus and the Gospels*. Nashville, TN: B&H.

Blomberg, Craig. 2007. *Matthew*. In Commentary on the New Testament Use of
the Old Testament. Grand Rapids, MI: Baker.

Blomberg, Craig, and Jennifer Markley. 2010. *A Handbook of New Testament Exegesis*. Grand Rapids, MI: Baker.

Bohorquez, Davinson. 2022. The Cross and the Throne: The Son of Man of Matthew 25:31-46 in light of the Passion Narrative. *Crux*, 58(1):20-29.

Borg, Marcus. 2001. *Reading the Bible Again for the First Time: Taking the Bible Seriously But Not Literally*. New York: NY: HarperOne.

Borg, Marcus, and N. T. Wright. 2007. *The Meaning of Jesus: Two Visions*. New York, NY: HarperCollins.

Borgman, Paul, and Kelly Clark. 2019. *Written to be Heard: Recovering the Messages of the Gospels*. Grand Rapids, MI: Eerdmans.

Boring, M. E. 2010. Matthew's Narrative Christology: Three Stories. *Interpretation*, 64(4): 356-367.

Boxall, Ian. 2019. *Matthew through the Centuries*. Blackwell Commentaries. Wiley Blackwell.

Brooks, Stephenson. 1987. *Matthew's Community: The Evidence of His Special Sayings Material*. JSNTS, 16. Sheffield, UK: JSOT.

Brown, Colin. 1986. *The New International Dictionary of New Testament Theology*. 4 vols. Grand Rapids, MI: Zondervan.

Brown, Jeannine. 2015. *Matthew*. Teach the Text Commentary Series. Grand Rapids, MI: Baker.

Brown, Jeannine, and Kyle Roberts. 2018. *Matthew*. Two Horizons New Testament Commentary. Grand Rapids, MI: Eerdmans.

Brown, Raymond. 1993. *The Birth of the Messiah*. New York: Doubleday.

Brown, Raymond. 1994. *The Death of the Messiah*. 2 Vols. New York: Doubleday.

Bruner, F. Dale. 1990. *Matthew, A Commentary*. 2 Vols. Grand Rapids, MI: Eerdmans.

Buchanan, G. W. 1984. The King and His Kingdom. Macon, GA: Mercer University.

Bullinger, E. W. *Figures of Speech Used in the Bible Explained and Illustrated*, 1898. Grand Rapids: Baker, 1968 reprint.

Bultmann, Rudolph. 1968. *The History of the Synoptic Tradition*. New York, NT: Harper & Row.

Burge, Gary, Lynn Cohick, and Gene Green. 2009. *The New Testament in Antiquity: A Survey of the New Testament within its Cultural Context*. Grand Rapids, MI: Zondervan.

Burridge, Richard. 2014. Four Gospels, One Jesus?: A Symbolic Reading, 3rd ed. Grand Rapids, MI: Eerdmans.

Bruce, F. F. 1993. *The Minor Prophets: An Exegetical and Expository Commentary*. Vol. 2. Ed. T. E. McComiskey. Grand Rapids, MI: Baker.

Campbell, C. R. 2007. *Verbal Aspect, the Indicative Mood, and Narrative: Soundings in the Greek of the New Testament*. New York, NY: Peter Lang.

Capes, David. 2019. New Testament Christology. In *The State of New Testament Studies: A Survey of Recent Research*. Ed. Scot McKnight and Nijay Gupta. Grand Rapids, MI: Baker.

Carson, D.A. 1982. *The Sermon the Mount: An Evangelical Exposition of Matthew 5-7*. Grand Rapids, MI: Baker.

Carson, D. A. 1995. *God with Us: Themes from Matthew*. Eugene, OR: Wipf & Stock.

Carson, D. A. 2010. *Matthew*. The Expositor's Bible Commentary. Revised ed. Grand Rapids, MI: Zondervan.

Carson, D. A. and Douglas Moo. 2005. *An Introduction to the New Testament*. 2nd ed. Grand Rapids, MI: Zondervan.

Carter, Warren. 1998. "Jesus' 'I have come' Statements in Matthew's Gospel." *The Catholic Biblical Quarterly*, 60(1): 44-62.

Carter, Warren. 2001. *Matthew and Empire: Initial Explorations*. Harrisburg, PA: Trinity Press.

Carter, Warren. 2001. *Matthew and the Margins: A Sociopolitical And Religious Reading*. Maryknoll, NT: Orbis.

Carter, Warren. 2004. *Matthew: Storyteller, Interpreter, Evangelist*. 2nd ed. Peabody, MA: Hendrickson.

Casey, Maurice. 2010. *Jesus of Nazareth: An Independent Historian's Account of His Life and Teaching*. New York, NY: T&T Clark.

Chamblin, Knox. 2010. *Matthew: A Mentor Commentary*. 2 vols. Scotland, UK: Mentor.

Chapman, Anthony. 2013. *Inclusio in the Hebrew Bible: A Historical-Developmental Approach*. Thesis. Beer-Sheva, Israel: Ben Gurion University of the Negev.

Church of Jesus Christ of Latter-Day Saints, The. Internet. www.churchofjesuschrist.org.

Corley, Bruce and F. B. Huey. 1983. *A Student's Dictionary for Biblical and Theological Studies*. Grand Rapids, MI: Zondervan.

Craig, William Lane. 2018. *The Atonement*. Elements in the Philosophy of Religion. New York: Cambridge.

Craig, William Lane. 2020. *Atonement and the Death of Christ: An Exegetical, Historical, and Philosophical Exploration*. Waco, TX: Baylor University.

Crossan, J. D. 1991. *The Historical Jesus: The Life of a Mediterranean Jewish Peasant*. New York, NY: HarperCollins.

Crossan, J. D. 1995. *Who Killed Jesus?: Exposing the Roots of Anti-Semitism in the Gospel Story of the Death of Jesus*. New York, NY: HarperCollins.

Crossan, J. D. 2007. *God and Empire: Jesus Against Rome, Then and Now*. New York, NY: HarperCollins.

Culpepper, R. A. 2021. *Matthew*. New Testament Library. Louisville, KY: Westminster.

Davids, Peter. 1982. *The Epistle of James: A Commentary on the Greek Text*. The New International Greek Testament Commentary. Grand Rapids, MI: Eerdmans.

Davies, W. D., and Allison, D. C. 1988. *A Critical and Exegetical Commentary on the Gospel According to Saint Matthew*. Vol. 1. International Critical Commentary. New York, NY: T & T Clark.

Davies, W. D., and Allison, D. C. 1991. *A Critical and Exegetical Commentary on the Gospel According to Saint Matthew*. Vol. 2. International Critical Commentary. New York, NY: T & T Clark.

Davies, W. D., and Allison, D. C. 1997. *A Critical and Exegetical Commentary on the Gospel According to Saint Matthew*. Vol. 3. International Critical Commentary. New York, NY: T & T Clark.

Davis, Casey. 1999. *Oral Biblical Criticism: The Influence of the Principles of Orality on the Literary Structure of Paul's Epistle to the Philippians*. Journal for the Study of the New Testament: Supplement Series 172. Sheffield, UK: Sheffield Academic.

Davis, Casey. 2000. "Oral Composition." In Eerdmans Dictionary of the Bible. Ed. David Freedman. Grand Rapids, MI: Eerdmans. Digital: Olive Tree Bible Software.

Decaen, Christopher. 2021. "An Embedded Chiastic Order in Matthew?" *The Catholic Biblical Quarterly*, 83(1): 56-74.

DeMoss, Matthew. 2001. *Pocket Dictionary for the Study of New Testament Greek.* Downer's Grove, IL: IVP.

Dunn, J. D. G. 1996. *The Epistles to the Colossians and to Philemon.* The New International Greek Testament Commentary. Grand Rapids, MI: Eerdmans.

Du Toit, Andrie, ed. 2009. *Focusing on the Message: New Testament Hermeneutics, Exegesis, and Methods.* Pretoria, South Africa: Protea.

Edwards, Richard. 1985. *Matthew's Story of Jesus.* Philadelphia, PA: Fortress.

Edwards, James. 1989. "Markan Sandwiches: The Significance of Interpolations in Markan Narratives." In Novum Testamentum 31(3):193-216.

Ehrman, Bart. 2014. *How Jesus Became God: The Exaltation of a Jewish Preacher from Galilee.* New York, NY: HarperOne.

_____. 2016. *Jesus Before the Gospels: How the Earliest Christians Remembered, Changed, and Invented Their Stories of the Savior.* New York, NY: HarperOne.

Erickson, Millard. 2013. *Christian Theology.* 3rd edition. Grand Rapids, MI: Baker.

Evans, Craig. 2012. *Matthew.* New Cambridge Bible Commentary. New York: Cambridge University.

Fee, Gordon. 2002. *New Testament Exegesis.* Louisville, KY: Westminster.

Fee, Gordon, and Douglas Stuart. 2014. *How to Read the Bible for All Its Worth: A Guide to Understanding the Bible.* Grand Rapids, MI: Zondervan.

Foley, John. 2019. "Oral Traditions." In Encyclopaedia Britannica. Internet. Accessed July 3, 2022. https://www.britannica.com/topic/oral-tradition.

Forster, Dion. 2017. *The (Im)possibility of Forgiveness: An Empirical Intercultural Bible Reading of Matthew 18.15-35*. Eugene, OR: Wipf & Stock.

France, R. T. 1985. *The Gospel According to Matthew: An Introduction and Commentary*. Tyndale New Testament Commentaries. Grand Rapids, MI: Eerdmans.

France, R. T. 1998. *Matthew: Evangelist & Teacher*. New Testament Profiles. Downer's Grove, IL: IVP.

France, R. T. 2007. *The Gospel According to Matthew*. New International Commentary on the New Testament. Grand Rapids, MI: Eerdmans.

Furnam, Adrian. 1986. "The Robustness of the Recency Effect: Studies Using Legal Evidence." *The Journal of General Psychology*, 113(4), 351-357.

Garber, Zev. 2005. "The Jewish Jesus: A Partisan's Imagination." *Shofar: An Interdisciplinary Journal of Jewish Studies*, 23(3):137-143. West Lafayette, IN: Purdue University.

Garland, David. 1996. *NIV Application Commentary: Mark*. Grand Rapids, MI: Zondervan.

Garland, David. 2001. *Reading Matthew: A Literary and Theological Commentary on the First Gospel*. Macon, GA: Smyth & Helwys.

Gavett, Sandra. 2000. "Old Testament as Literature." In Eerdmans Dictionary of the Bible. Ed. David Freedman. Grand Rapids, MI: Eerdmans. Digital: Olive Tree Bible Software.

Geisler, Norman, and Abdul Saleeb. 2002. *Answering Islam: The Crescent in Light of the Cross*. Second ed. Grand Rapids, MI: Baker.

Geisler, Norman. 2011-2016. *Licona Articles*. Internet. Accessed June 22, 2023. http://normangeisler.com/licona-articles/.

George, Timothy. 2002. *Is the Father of Jesus the God of Muhammad?: Understanding the Differences between Christianity and Islam*. Grand Rapids, MI: Zondervan.

Gibbs, Jeffrey. 2006-2018. *Matthew*. 3 Vols. Concordia Commentary. St. Louis, MO: Concordia.

Gibbs, Jeffrey. 2008. The Son of God and the Father's Wrath: Atonement and
Salvation in Matthew's Gospel. *Concordia Theological Quarterly*, 72: 211-22.

Gorman, Michael. 2014. *The Death of the Messiah and the Birth of the New Covenant: A (Not So) New Model of the Atonement.* Eugene, OR: Cascade.

Green, Joel. 1992. "Death of Jesus." In *Dictionary of Jesus and the Gospels*. Ed. Joel Green, Scot McKnight, and I. Howard Marshall. Downer's Grove, IL: IVP.

Grudem, Wayne. 1994. *Systematic Theology: An Introduction to Biblical Doctrine.* Grand Rapids, MI: Zondervan.

Gundry, Robert. 1994. *Matthew: A Commentary on His Handbook for a Mixed Church Under Persecution.* 2nd ed. Grand Rapids, MI: Eerdmans.

Gurtner, D. M., and Joel Willitts, Richard Burridge, eds. 2011. *Jesus, Matthew's Gospel and Early Christianity: Studies in Memory of Graham Stanton.* New York: T&T Clark.

Gurtner, D. M. 2012. "Interpreting Apocalyptic Symbolism in the Gospel of Matthew." *Bulletin for Biblical Research*, 22(4):525-545.

Hägerland, Tobias. 2012. Jesus and the Forgiveness of Sins: An Aspect of His Prophetic Mission. *Society for New Testament Studies Monograph Series 150*. New York, NY: Cambridge University.

Hägerland, Tobias. 2019. Βίβλος γενέσεως: The Opening of Matthew's Gospel and Ethnic Ambiguity. *Svensk exegetisk årsbok*, 84:101-124.

Hagner, Donald. 1993. *Matthew 1-13*. Word Biblical Commentary. Volume 33A.
Dallas, TX: Word.

Hagner, Donald. 1995. *Matthew 14-28*. Word Biblical Commentary. Volume 33B. Dallas, TX: Word.

Ham, Clay. 2000. "The Last Supper in Matthew." *Bulletin for Biblical Research*, 10(1): 53-69.

Hanna, R. 1983. *A Grammatical Aid to the Greek New Testament.* Grand Rapids, MI: Baker.

Harrington, Daniel. 1991. *The Gospel of Matthew*. Sacra Pagina. Collegeville, MN: Liturgical Press.

Harris, Murray. 2016. *The Seven Sayings of Jesus on the Cross: Their Circumstances and Meaning*. Eugene, OR: Cascade.

Hauwerwas, Stanley. 2006. *Matthew*. Brazos Theological Commentary on the Bible. Grand Rapids, MI: Brazos.

Heider, George. 2008. *Atonement and the Gospels*. Journal of Theological Interpretation. 2.2 (2008) 259-27

Horton, Michael. 2011. *The Christian Faith: A Systematic Theology for Pilgrims on the Way*. Grand Rapids, MI: Zondervan.

Huizenga, L. A. 2005. The incarnation of the servant: the 'suffering servant' and Matthean Christology. *Horizons in Biblical Theology*, 27(1): 25-58.

Huizenga, L. A. 2008. Matt 1:1: 'Son of Abraham' as a christological category. *Horizons in Biblical Theology*, 30(2): 103-113.

Hurtado, Larry. 2015. *One God, One Lord: Early Christian Devotion and Ancient Jewish Monotheism*. New York, NY: Bloomsbury T&T Clark.

Jensen, Paul. 1993. "Forgiveness and Atonement." In Scottish Journal of Theology. 46(2), 141-160.

Jipp, J. W. 2024. *Reading the Gospels as Christian Scripture: A Literary, Canonical, and Theological Introduction*. Grand Rapids, MI: Baker.

Jongkind, D., P. J. Williams, P. M. Head, and P. James, eds. 2017. *The Greek New Testament*. Wheaton, IL: Crossway.

Keith, Chris, and Larry Hurtado, eds. 2011. *Jesus among Friends and Enemies: A Historical and Literary Introduction to Jesus in the Gospels*. Grand Rapids, MI: Baker.

Keener, Craig. 1993. *The IVP Bible Background Commentary: New Testament*. Downer's Grove, IL: IVP.

Keener, Craig. 2009. *The Gospel of Matthew: A Socio-Rhetorical Commentary*. Grand Rapids, MI: Eerdmans.

Kessler, Martin. 1978. "Inclusio in the Hebrew Bible." In *Semitics* 6: 44–49.

Kingsbury, Jack Dean. 1988. *Matthew as Story*. Minneapolis, MN: Fortress.

Kingsbury, Jack Dean. 1991. *Matthew: Structure, Christology, Kingdom*. Minneapolis, MN: Fortress.

Kingsbury, Jack Dean. 1998. *Matthew*. Nairobi, KEN: Evangel.

Kittel, Gerhard. 1964-1976. *Theological Dictionary of the New Testament*. 10 vols. Grand Rapids, MI: Eerdmans.

Klein, William, et al. 2004. *Introduction to Biblical Interpretation*. Nashville, TN: Thomas Nelson.

Kreider, G. R. 2019. Jesus the Messiah as Prophet, Priest, and King. *Bibliotheca Sacra*, 176(Apr-June): 174-187.

Kunjanayil, Paul. 2021. "The Interconnection between the Emmanuel Theme and the Forgiveness of Sins." In *Studia Biblica Slovaca*, 13(1):20-48.

Lefkowitz, Mary, and James Romm, eds. 2017. *The Greek Plays*. New York, NY: Modern Library.

Lewis, C. S. 2001. *The Chronicles of Narnia*. New York, NY: HarperCollins.

Licona, Michael. 2010. *The Resurrection of Jesus: A New Historiographical Approach*. Downer's Grove, IL: IVP.

Lightner, R. P. 1998. *The Death Christ Died: A Biblical Case for Unlimited Atonement*. Grand Rapids, MI: Kregel.

Lodahl, Michael. 2010. *Claiming Abraham: Reading the Bible and The Qur'an Side by Side*. Grand Rapids, MI: Brazos.

Longman, Tremper. 2008. "Inclusio." In *Dictionary of the Old Testament: Wisdom, Poetry & Writings*. Downer's Grove, IL: IVP.

Louw, Johannes, and Eugene Nida. 1988. *Greek-English Lexicon of the New Testament: Based on Semantic Domains*. 2 vols. New York, NY: United Bible Societies.

Lüdemann, Gerd. 1996. *What Really Happened to Jesus: A Historical Approach to the Resurrection*. Louisville, KY: Westminster John Knox.

Lüdemann, Gerd. 1999. *The Great Deception: And What Jesus Really Said and Did*. Amherst, NY: Prometheus.

Lüdemann, Gerd. 2001. *Jesus After 2000 Years: What He Really Said and Did*. Amherst, NY: Prometheus.

Lüdemann, Gerd. 2006. "The Life of Jesus: A Brief Assessment." In *CSER Review*, 1:1.

Luz, Ulrich. 1992. "The Son of Man in Matthew: Heavenly Judge or Human Christ." In *Journal for the Study of the New Testament*, 48:3-21.

Luz, Ulrich. 1995. *The Theology of the Gospel of Matthew*. New Testament Theology. Cambridge: Cambridge University.

Luz, Ulrich. 2005. *Studies in Matthew*. Grand Rapids, MI: Eerdmans.

Luz, Ulrich. 2001. *Matthew 8–20*. Hermeneia: A Critical & Historical Commentary on the Bible. Translated by Crouch, J. E. Edited by H. Koester. Minneapolis, MN: Fortress.

Luz, Ulrich. 2005. *Matthew 21–28*. Hermeneia: A Critical & Historical Commentary on the Bible. Translated by Crouch, J. E. Edited by H. Koester. Minneapolis, MN: Fortress.

Luz, Ulrich. 2007. *Matthew 1–7*. Hermeneia: A Critical & Historical Commentary on the Bible. Translated by Crouch, J. E. Edited by H. Koester. Minneapolis, MN: Fortress.

Luz, Ulrich. 2007. *Matthew in History: Interpretation, Influence, and Effects*. Minneapolis, MN: Fortress.

Marshall, I. H. 2007. *Aspects of the Atonement: Cross & Resurrection in the Reconciling of God and Humanity*. London, UK: Paternoster.

Mbabazi, I. K. 2013. *The Significance of Interpersonal Forgiveness in the Gospel of Matthew*. Eugene, OR: Wipf & Stock.

McGregor, W. B. 2015. *Linguistics: An Introduction*. 2nd edition. New York, NY: Bloomsbury.

Metzger, Bruce. 1994. *A Textual Commentary on the Greek New Testament*. 2nd ed. New York, NY: United Bible Society.

Miller, Richard. 2017. *Resurrection and Reception in Early Christianity*. Routledge Studies in Religion. New York, NY: Routledge.

Millet, Robert, and Gerald McDermott. 2007. *Claiming Christ: A Mormon-Evangelical Debate*. Grand Rapids, MI: Brazos.

Mohler, Albert. 2011. *The Devil is in the Details: Biblical Inerrancy and the Licona Controversy*. Internet. Accessed June 22, 2023. https://albertmohler.com/2011/09/14/the-devil-is-in-the-details-biblical-inerrancy-and-the-licona-controversy.

Moo, Douglas. 1983. *The Old Testament in the Gospel Passion Narratives*. Eugene, OR: Wipf & Stock.

Moo, Douglas. 2002. *Romans*. In Zondervan Illustrated Bible Backgrounds Commentary. Ed. Clinton Arnold. Grand Rapids, MI: Zondervan.

Morris, Leon. 1983. *The Atonement: Its Meaning and Significance*. Downer's Grove, IL: IVP.

Morris, Leon. 1992. *The Gospel According to Matthew*. The Pillar New Testament Commentary. Grand Rapids, MI: Eerdmans.

Mounce, Robert. 1998. *Matthew*. New International Biblical Commentary. Peabody, MA: Hendrickson.

Mowery, R. L. 1988. "God, Lord and Father: The Theology of the Gospel of Matthew." In *Biblical Research*, 33:24-36.

Jiri Mrazek, Jiri, and Jan Roskovec. 2004. *Testimony and Interpretation: Early Christology in its Judeo-Hellenistic Milieu: Studies in Honor of Petr Pokorný*. The Library of New Testament Studies. New York: T&T Clark.

Nel, Marius. 2013. "The Forgiveness of Debt in Matthew 6:12, 14-15." *Neotestimentica*, 47(1):87-106. https://journals.co.za/doi/epdf/10.10520/EJC141184.

Nel, Marius. 2015. "The Motive of Forgiveness in the Gospel According to Matthew." *In die Skriflig*, 49(1), a1917. http://dx.doi.org/10.4102/ids.v49i1.1917.

Nel, Marius. 2017. "Matthean Atonement Rituals." *Acta Theologica*, 37(2):104-124.

Nel, Marius. 2017. "The Conceptualisation of Sin in the Gospel of Matthew." *In die Skriflig*, 51(3), a2097. https://doi.org/10.4102/ids. v51i3.2097.

Newman, Barclay. 1988. *A Handbook on the Gospel of Matthew*. New York, NY: United Bible Society.

Niditch, Susan. 1996. *Oral World and Written Word: Ancient Israelite Literature*. Library of Ancient Israel. Louisville, KY: Westminster John Knox.

Nolland, John. 1996. No Son-of-God Christology in Matthew 1.18-25. *Journal for the Study of the New Testament*, 62:3-12.

Nolland, John. 2005. *The Gospel of Matthew*. The New International Greek Testament Commentary. Grand Rapids, MI: Eerdmans.

Nolland, John. 2008. *Built Upon the Rock: Studies in the Gospel of Matthew*. Grand Rapids, MI: Eerdmans.

Novakovic, Lidija. 2003. *Messiah, the Healer of the Sick: A Study of Jesus as the Son of David in the Gospel of Matthew*. Tübingen, GER: Mohr Siebeck.

O'Collins, Gerald. 2009. *Christology: A Biblical, Historical, and Systematic Study of Jesus*. Oxford, UK: Oxford University.

Olmstead, Wesley. 2019. *Matthew 1–14: A Handbook on the Greek Text*. Waco, TX: Baylor University.

Olmstead, Wesley. 2019. *Matthew 15-28: A Handbook on the Greek Text*. Waco, TX: Baylor University.

Ong, Walter, and John Hartley. 2012. *Orality and Literacy: The Technologizing of the Word*. 30th Anniversary Edition. London, UK: Routledge.

Osborne, G. R. 1992. "Resurrection." In *Dictionary of Jesus and the Gospels*. Ed. Joel Green, Scot McKnight, and I. Howard Marshall. Downer's Grove, IL: IVP.

Osborne, G. R. 2010. *Matthew*. Zondervan Exegetical Commentary on the New Testament. Grand Rapids, MI: Zondervan.

Overman, J. A. 1996. *Church and Community in Crisis: The Gospel according to Matthew*. Valley Forge, PA: Trinity.

Pao, David. 2012. *Colossians & Philemon*. Zondervan Exegetical Commentary on the New Testament. Grand Rapids, MI: Zondervan.

Perkins, P. 1984. *Resurrection: New Testament Witness and Contemporary Reflection*. Garden City, NY: Doubleday.

Perschbacher, W. J. 1990. *The New Analytical Greek Lexicon*. Peabody, MA: Hendrickson.

Piper, John. 1986. *The Beatitudes and the Gospel of the Kingdom*. Internet. Accessed July 5, 2022. https://www.desiringgod.org/messages/the-beatitudes-and-the-gospel-of-the-kingdom.

Pitre, Brant. 2015. *Jesus and the Last Supper*. Grand Rapids, MI: Eerdmans.

Pitrowski, Nicholas. 2013. 'I Will Save My People from their Sins': The Influence of Ezekiel 36:28B-29A; 37:23B on Matthew 1:21. *Tyndale Bulletin*, 64(1):33-54.

Pizzuto, V. A. 2012. The structural elegance of Matthew 1-2: a chiastic proposal. *The Catholic Biblical Quarterly*, 74(4): 712-737.

Porter, Stanley, and Bryan Dyer. 2023. *Origins of New Testament Christology: An Introduction to the Traditions and Titles Applied to Jesus*. Grand Rapids, MI: Baker.

Powell, Mark. 1990. *What is Narrative Criticism?* Minneapolis, MN: Fortress.

Powell, Mark. 1992. The Plot and Subplots of Matthew's Gospel. *New Testament Studies*, 38(2):187–204.

Powell, Mark, ed. 2009. *Methods for Matthew*. New York, NY: Cambridge.

Powers, B. Ward. 2010. *The Progressive Publication of Matthew*. Nashville, TN: B&H.

Prozesky, Martin. 1981. Christology and cultural relativity. *Journal of Theology for Southern Africa*, 35(Jun): 44-67.

Przybylski, Benno. 1980. *Righteousness in Matthew and His World of Thought*. New York, NY: Cambridge.

Quarles, Charles. 2013. *A Theology of Matthew: Jesus Revealed as Deliverer, King, and Incarnate Creator*. Explorations in Biblical Theology. Phillipsburg, NJ: P&R.

Quarles, Charles. 2016. Matthew 27:51-53: Meaning, Genre, Intertextuality, Theology, and Reception History. *Journal of the Evangelical Theological Society*, 59(2): 271-86.

Quarles, Charles. 2017. *Matthew*. Exegetical Guide to the Greek New Testament. Nashville, TN: B&H.

Quarles, Charles. 2022. *Matthew*. Evangelical Biblical Theology Commentary. Bellingham, WA: Lexham Academic.

Quinn, Arthur. 1993. *Figures of Speech: 60 Ways to Turn a Phrase*. Davis, CA: Hermagoras.

Repschinski, Boris. 2000. *The controversy stories in the Gospel of Matthew: Their redaction, form and relevance for the relationship between the Matthean community and formative Judaism*. Göttingen: Vandenhoeck & Ruprecht.

Repschinski, Boris. 2006. "For He will Save His People from their Sins" (Matthew 1:21): A Christology for Christian Jews. *The Catholic Biblical Quarterly*, 68(2): 248-267.

Ryken, Leland. 1984. *How to Read the Bible as Literature*. Grand Rapids, MI: Zondervan.

Ryken, Leland. 1987. *Words of Life: A Literary Introduction to the New Testament*. Grand Rapids, MI: Baker.

Sakenfeld, Katharine, ed. 2009. In New Interpreter's Dictionary of the Bible. Nashville, TN: Abingdon. Digital: Olive Tree Bible Software.

Schreiner, Patrick. 2019. *Matthew, Disciple and Scribe: The First Gospel and Its Portrait of Jesus*. Grand Rapids, MI: Baker.

Scott, John. 2014. "Primacy Effect." In A Dictionary of Sociology. 4th ed. Oxford, UK: Oxford University. Internet. Accessed Jun 21, 2022. https://www.oxfordreference.com/view/10.1093/acref/9780199683581.001.0001/acref-9780199683581-e-1888

Scott, John. 2014. "Recency Effect." In A Dictionary of Sociology. 4th ed. Oxford, UK: Oxford University. Internet. Accessed Jun 21, 2022. https://www.oxfordreference.com/view/10.1093/acref/9780199683581.001.0001/acref-9780199683581-e-1888

Seeley, David. 1994. *Deconstructing the New Testament*. New York, NY: Brill.

Senior, Donald. 1976. The Death of Jesus and the Resurrection of the Holy Ones (MT 27:51-53). *Catholic Biblical Quarterly*, 38(3):312-329.

Senior, Donald. 1992. The Death of Jesus and the Birth of a New World: Matthew's Theology of History in the Passion Narrative. *Currents in Theology and Mission*, 19(6): 416-423.

Senior, Donald. 1996. *What Are They Saying About Matthew?* Mahwah, NJ: Paulist.

Spencer, F. S. 2010. Scripture, Hermeneutics, and Matthew's Jesus. *Interpretation*, 64(4): 368-378.

Stagg, Frank. 1962. Christology of Matthew. *Review & Expositor*, 59(4): 457-468.

Stanton, Graham, ed. 1983. *Interpretation of Matthew*. Issues in Religion and Theology. Minneapolis, MN: Fortress.

Stanton, Graham. 1993. *A Gospel for a New People: Studies in Matthew*. Louisville: Westminster John Knox.

Stern, David. 1992. *Jewish New Testament Commentary*. Clarksville, MD: Jewish New Testament Publications.

Stinton, Diane. 2007. Jesus—Immanuel, Image of the Invisible God: Aspects of Popular Christology in Sub-Saharan Africa. *Journal of Reformed Theology*, 1(1): 6-40.

Swen, Blaine. 2012. *The Logic of Divine-Human Reconciliation: A Critical Analysis of Penal Substitution as an Explanatory Feature of Atonement*. Thesis. Chicago, IL: Loyola University.

Talbert, Charles. 2010. *Matthew*. Paideia Commentaries on the New Testament.
Grand Rapids, MI: Baker.

Tate, W. Randolph. 2006. *Interpreting the Bible: A Handbook of Terms and Methods*. Peabody, MA: Hendrickson.

The Holy Bible. 1982. *New King James Version*. Nashville, TN: Thomas Nelson (NKJV).

The Holy Bible. 2003. *New English Translation*. Second ed. USA: Biblical Studies Press (NET).

Thiemann, R. F. 1997. Matthew's christology: a resource for systematic theology *Currents in Theology and Mission*, 4(6):350-362.

Treier, Daniel, and Walter Elwell. 2017. *Evangelical Dictionary of Theology*. Grand Rapids, MI: Baker.

Treier, Daniel. 2023. *The Lord Jesus Christ*. New Studies in Dogmatics. Grand Rapids, MI: Zondervan Academic.

Tuckett, Christopher. 2001. *Christology and the New Testament: Jesus and His Earliest Followers*. Louisville, KY: Westminster.

Tucker, W. D. 2008. "Book of Psalms." In Dictionary of the Old Testament: Wisdom, Poetry & Writings. Downer's Grove, IL: IVP.

Turner, David. 2008. *Matthew*. Baker Exegetical Commentary on the New Testament. Grand Rapids, MI: Baker.

Viljoen, F. P. 2014. "Hosea 6:6 and Identity Formation in Matthew." *Acta Theologica*, 34(1):214-237. http://dx.doi.org/10.4314/actat.v34i1.12.

Viljoen, F. P. 2014. "Jesus Healing the Leper and the Purity Law in the Gospel of Matthew." *In die Skriflig*, 48(2), http://dx.doi.org/10.4102/ids.v48i2.1751.

Viljoen, F. P. 2014. "The Law and Purity in Matthew: Jesus Touching a Bleeding Woman and a Dead Girl (Mt 9:18-26)." *NGTT DEEL*, 55(1).

Viljoen, F. P. 2016. "The Matthean Community within a Jewish Religious Society." In *HTS Theological Studies*. 72(4), a3418. http://dx.doi.org/10.4102/hts.v72i4.3418.

Viljoen, F. P. 2016. "The Torah in Matthew: Still Valid, Yet to be Interpreted Alternatively." *In die Skriflig*. 50(3), a2036. http://dx.doi.org/10.4102/ids.v50i3.2036.

Viljoen, F. P. 2018. "Reading Matthew as a Historical Narrative." *In die Skriflig* 52(1), a2390. https://doi.org/10.4102/ids.v52i1.2390.

Viljoen, F. P. 2018. *The Torah in Matthew*. Münster, GER: LIT Verlag.

Viljoen, F. P. 2020. "The Matthean Characterisation of Jesus by Angels." In *HTS Theological Studies*. 76(4), a5859. https://doi.org/10.4102/hts.v76i4.5859.

Wallace, Daniel. 1996. *Greek Grammar Beyond the Basics: An Exegetical Syntax of the New Testament*. Grand Rapids, MI: Zondervan.

Wansink, C. S. 2000. "Roman Law." In *Dictionary of New Testament Background*. Ed. Joel Green, Scot McKnight, and I. Howard Marshall. Downer's Grove, IL: IVP.

Warrington, Keith. 2010. *Discovering Jesus in the New Testament*. Grand Rapids, MI: Baker.

Watch Tower Bible and Tract Society. Internet. JW.org.

Watson, Wilfred. 2013. "Epanalepsis." In Encyclopedia of Hebrew Language and Linguistics 1. Ed. G. Khan. (Leiden) 830-831.

Wells, David. 1993. *No Place for Truth: Or Whatever Happened to Evangelical Theology?*. Grand Rapids, MI: Eerdmans.

Wellum, Stephen. 2021. *The Person of Christ: An Introduction*. Short Studies in Systematic Theology. Wheaton, IL: Crossway.

Weren, W. 2014. *Studies in Matthew's Gospel, Literary Design, Intertextuality, and Social Setting*. Boston, MA: Brill.

Westerholm, Stephen. 2006. *Understanding Matthew: The Early Christian Worldview of the First Gospel*. Grand Rapids, MI: Baker.

Wilkins, Michael. 2003. *Matthew*. The NIV Application Commentary. Grand Rapids, MI: Zondervan.

Wilkins, Michael. 2013. *Matthew*. The Holman Apologetics Commentary on the Bible: The Gospels and Acts. Ed. Jeremy Howard. Nashville: Holman.

Wilkins, Michael. 2015. *Discipleship in the Ancient World and Matthew's Gospel*. 2nd ed. Eugene, OR: Wipf & Stock.

Wilson, W. T. 2022. *The Gospel of Matthew*. 2 vols. Eerdmans Critical Commentary. Grand Rapids, MI: Eerdmans.

Witherington, Ben, III. 2006. *Matthew*. Smyth & Helwys Bible Commentary. Macon: Smyth & Helwys.

Wright, N. T. 1997. *The Lord and His Prayer*. Grand Rapids, MI: Eerdmans.

Wright, N. T. 2003. *The Resurrection of the Son of God*. Minneapolis, MN: Fortress.

Wright, N. T. 2016. *The Day the Revolution Began: Reconsidering the Meaning of Jesus's Crucifixion*. San Francisco, CA: HarperOne.

Wyckoff, Chris. 2006. "Have we come full circle yet?: Closure, Psycholinguistics, and Problems of Recognition with the Inclusio." In Journal for the Study of the Old Testament. 30(4), 475-505.

Young, R. A. 1994. *Intermediate New Testament Greek: A Linguistic and Exegetical Approach*. Nashville, TN: B&H.

Zerwick, Maximilian, and Mary Grosvenor. 1996. *A Grammatical Analysis of the Greek New Testament*. Rome, Italy: Biblical Institute.

www.ingramcontent.com/pod-product-compliance
Lightning Source LLC
Chambersburg PA
CBHW071405120626
46546CB00002B/823